August 2012

# TOPGUN
## ON WALL STREET

# TOPGUN
## ON WALL STREET

### WHY THE UNITED STATES MILITARY
### SHOULD RUN CORPORATE AMERICA

*A Fighter Pilot's Unique Story—*
*From an F-14 Tomcat*
*to the Heart of American Business*

**Lieutenant Commander Jeffery Lay**
with **Patrick Robinson**

Vanguard Press
A Member of the Perseus Books Group

Copyright © 2012 by Lieutenant Commander Jeffery Lay

Published by Vanguard Press
A Member of the Perseus Books Group

Library of Congress Cataloging-in-Publication Data
Lay, Jeffery.
    TOPGUN on Wall Street : why the United States military should run corporate
America : a fighter pilot's unique story—from an F-14 Tomcat to the heart of American
business / Jeffery Lay with Patrick Robinson.
        p. cm.
ISBN 978-1-59315-717-3 (hardcover : alk. paper)—ISBN 978-1-59315-718-0 (e-book)
    1. Lay, Jeffery. 2. Capitalists and financiers—United States—Biography. 3. Fighter
pilots—United States—Biography. 4. Industrial management—United States.
5. Leadership—United States. 6. Wall Street (New York, N.Y.) I. Robinson, Patrick, 1939–
II. Title.

HG172.L395A3 2012
338.092—dc23
[B]

                                                                2011045983

Vanguard Press books are available at special discounts for bulk purchases in the U.S.
by corporations, institutions, and other organizations. For more information, please
contact the Special Markets Department at the Perseus Books Group, 2300 Chestnut
Street, Suite 200, Philadelphia, PA 19103, or call (800) 810-4145, ext. 5000, or e-mail
special.markets@perseusbooks.com.

10 9 8 7 6 5 4 3 2 1

*Most of us, most of the time, live in blissful ignorance of what a small, elite, heroic group of Americans are doing for us night and day. As we speak, all over the globe, American sailors and submariners and aviators are doing something very dangerous. People say, "Well, it can't be too dangerous because there are no wrecks." But the reason we don't have more accidents is that these are superb professionals; the fact that they master the dangers does not mean the dangers aren't real.*

*Right now, somewhere around the world, young men are landing high-performance jet aircraft on the pitching decks of aircraft carriers—at night! You can't pay people to do that; they do it out of love of country, of adventure, of the challenge. We all benefit from it, and the very fact that we don't have to think about it tells you how superbly they're doing their job—living on the edge of danger so the rest of us need not think about, let alone experience danger.*

—GEORGE F. WILL, Pulitzer Prize winner
and #1 *New York Times* bestselling author

*For Us*

# CONTENTS

# AUTHOR'S NOTE

*TOPGUN on Wall Street*, while loosely autobiographical, has one driving force behind its narrative: the demarcation line between military and civilian management philosophies. The majority of this story inevitably concentrates on the significant gulf between military beliefs, training, demands, and honor, and the diametrically opposed civilian dog-eat-dog ethos, breathtaking personal greed and susceptibility to convenient lies, frequently on a Wagnerian scale.

My first experience of this military-civilian clash involved my service as a Naval Aviator flying strike fighter combat missions from a giant US aircraft carrier parked in the middle of the Gulf of Iran at the turn of the twenty-first century. We were flanked to the east by the menacing shores of the Islamic Republic of Iran, while we in turn glared hard west toward the distant shores of the Republic of Iraq. Because there, the half-crazed Lion of Babylon, Saddam Hussein, swore by all that was holy to blow the US air patrols out of the sky.

We could, of course, have dealt with this quasi-Iraqi "warrior" in about twelve minutes, except for one thing. The White House had decided to assume command of America's front-line muscle, the 1,000 mph TOPGUN fighter pilots. For the first time, the guys at the Tip of the Spear were under their direct civilian "command" while operating in a war zone.

The result was a "phony war," right out there in the vaunted no-fly zone. It was a hideous situation, and it resulted in shocking mistakes, which had inevitably catastrophic and bloody consequences. Worse yet, it drove some of the finest United States Naval Aviators out of the service we all loved. I was personally tortured mentally by all this. How could these clever, accomplished presidential advisors possibly demonstrate such foolishness? A better question might have been, how could they ever be so uncompromisingly arrogant as to dismiss entirely the considered views of the best brains in the US military? I actually thought it might be some kind of aberration. But I spent the next dozen years finding out there was nothing unusual about these apparently eccentric civilian decisions. They make them all the time, in politics, in their dealings with the military, and in corporate life. They constantly repeat their mistakes; they operate in a way that is self-centered in the extreme. And there may be no way out for them or for the nation.

Unless, of course, the peerless US military was given leave to run corporate America. This may seem radical. Yet the selfless teamwork of America's men and women in uniform very likely holds the key to resurrection. So many times we have delivered this nation from the abyss, because America represents the greatest nation in history. Is it salvageable? Of course it is. If only we listen to that hidden voice that comes from the universe—a voice of fairness and reason that has always governed the United States.

I thus begin my story with a short factual account of Saddam Hussein's operations room, illustrating precisely what we were up against. And why *no* civilian committee member could possibly understand the depth of the problem—solvable, as it was, essentially, by high explosive alone.

LIEUTENANT COMMANDER JEFFERY LAY
*United States Navy (Retired)*

# PROLOGUE

**ABU GHURAYB PRESIDENTIAL SITE**
**WEST OF BAGHDAD, REPUBLIC OF IRAQ**
*August 2000*

The five-story sandstone palace sat shimmering under the desert sun—five stories downward, that is. Not upward. Sixty feet below ground level, in the vast and ornate Iraqi military command center, the twenty most trusted personnel in the country awaited the arrival of the Lion of Babylon.

Sipping hot, sweet tea beneath an enormous glittering chandelier and surrounded by walls edged in marble and gilded gold lettering, all twenty wore military uniform but no sidearms. Only the Lion himself exercised that privilege, presumably in readiness to shoot a wayward advisor between the eyes, a course of statesmanship not entirely new to him.

It was a vast and lavish room constructed beneath a domed steel-and-concrete ceiling, sixteen feet thick. The atom bomb that flattened Hiroshima would have bounced off this nuclear shelter. The air-conditioning system would have cooled off the corridors of hell. The fabulous deep red, hand-woven Persian carpet would have covered the south side of Times Square.

The Lion of Babylon was late, which surprised no one. They sipped their tea and chatted in their upside-down bombproof haven, unconcerned that the wrath of the United States of America must almost have been upon them—that the most awesome military power in the history of warfare must by now be on the brink of flaming retaliation.

The Republic of Iraq, smashed, humiliated, and bludgeoned into surrender by General Norman Schwarzkopf's Desert Storm, had, for the biggest part of nine long years, persistently defied sixteen different clauses in resolutions laid down by the United Nations Security Council. Not least the requirement to stay the hell out of the no-fly zones (Resolution 688) and to refrain from firing missiles at patrolling US aircraft (Resolution 949).

And now the most senior members of the Iraqi government and Revolutionary Command Council sat awaiting the entrance of the Lion, who would once more angrily reassure them, in his familiar guttural, half-educated tribal dialect, that there was no danger. That the Americans were a godless breed, led by a soft, cowardly, sex-crazed infidel who was frightened to death of the desert warriors of Iraq.

At precisely forty-two minutes after the appointed time for this weekly meeting of the Revolutionary Council, the Lion of Babylon, General Saddam Hussein Abd al-Majid al-Tikriti, president of Iraq, made his entrance, attired as always in the full dress uniform of a *mushir,* the highest rank in all Middle Eastern militaries.

That precision-stitched olive-green jacket displayed slip-on shoulder straps bearing the embroidered golden eagle over laurel branches and crossed swords. It denoted the equivalent rank of a five-star US Army general, or indeed a field marshal—not too bad for a camel driver's son who never served one day in the Iraqi army.

Saddam entered the room through enormous wooden doors, flanked by four armed members of his personal bodyguard. The doors were closed behind him, but the escort remained in the room, standing behind his chair, against the wall. From around a polished teak table the size of Washington's Reflecting Pool, the twenty chosen advisors rose and nodded deferentially.

The president gestured everyone to be seated. Then he pulled his 9mm Browning Hi-Power semiautomatic handgun from its holster and rested it on the table next to his right hand. A field marshal he may have been, but the habits and time-honored instincts of a nomadic tribesman fade slowly in the ancient lands of the Bedouin.

At his right hand sat his cruel and psychopathic son Qusay, at thirty-four, the chosen successor to the presidency, currently commander of the Special Republican Guard and the feared Iraqi Intelligence Service.

Beyond Qusay sat Saddam's cousin Ali Hassan Majid, the Southern Region commander, also known as "Chemical Ali," the man responsible for one of the twentieth century's most terrible acts of genocide, when he used poison-gas bombs to kill thousands of the northern Kurds.

On the president's left sat Taha Yassin Ramadan, the sixty-two-year-old vice president of Iraq and former commander of the Popular Army. Taha was Saddam's most brutal enforcer, probably complicit in the mass killings of the Kurds in Halabja in 1988.

Next to him sat the bald Mohammad Hamza al-Zubaidi, Central Euphrates commander, former deputy prime minister, and member of the Revolutionary Command Council. His closest colleague, Barzan Ibrahim Hasan al-Tikriti, was seated to his left. Barzan was a former director of the notorious intelligence service, the Mukhabharat. A known specialist in torture, he was probably as big a sadist as Qusay Hussein himself.

On the opposite side of the table, next to Ali Hassan Majid, sat another member of Saddam's fanatical tribal following, a man born in Tikrit, ninety miles from Baghdad, upstream along the Tigris. This was Izzat Ibrahim al-Dour, the sixty-one-year-old Revolutionary Command Council vice chairman and deputy commander of the armed forces, Saddam's day-to-day right-hand man. He was as ruthless a politician as he was a military commander. To him alone, Saddam offered a personal greeting, nodding his head and muttering one word: "Ibrahim."

To the other five senior men he said nothing, nor to the fourteen various ministers and commanders who made up the Council's quorum.

But when he finally spoke, having arranged his papers and notations before him, Saddam rose to his feet and addressed them as the anointed representative of the Prophet.

"Great people," he said, "exalted men of our valiant armed forces, I stand among you in the name of Allah the most merciful and compassionate. You, whose hearts are filled with faith and who have sworn to please Allah in the destruction of our most evil enemy, the Great Satan. Peace be with you, and Allah's mercy and blessings."

He spread his arms wide, hesitated, and resumed the high-backed armchair of his supreme national office.

"Those who have made Satan their protector have chosen to fly their terrible death machines against us," he stated. "We, who defend right against falsehood, and seek only the sublime meanings, and jihad. We, whose hearts are humbled in prayer only to Allah, whose name we glory, and to whom we pledge faithful obedience.

"On this side of the encounter, we stand as the people of civilization, the cradle of prophet-hood, and the torch of Allah's messages. We alone represent the anvil on which all hammers break. Thus, through the power of our endurance and our fortitude to reject injustice and oppression, we must cause that evil from across the oceans to collapse, and for Allah to turn the sun away from the face of the Great Satan. And in that, my Arab brothers, we have but one path to greatness.

"And now I beseech you to make it come to pass—and it is within our grasp, because Allah will guide our mighty desert rockets and missiles toward our enemies in the skies. We fear not retribution, because Allah has smitten the American leaders with the curse of cowardice.

"But thousands of miles away, in those godforsaken Washington offices which are used not for glory but for perverted sex with young girls, they send killers on their daily mission to bomb and harm us, the children of Allah."

Saddam paused from his sermon. He first leaned forward, then held his head in his hands. But he rose up again to a straight-backed position, spread his arms wide, and once more implored his commanders to strike a blow for the devout, and to smash one of their Allah-guided missiles into the heart of one of the American F-14 Tomcats—the fastest, heaviest, most feared strike fighter in the world.

"I have asked this for so long," said the Lion of Babylon. "Guided by Allah, I have begged each of you to grant me that joy. I have pleaded with the Prophet, but until now that triumph has been denied me. Now I ask you again. Our missile officers have been deployed to stations in the southern desert, into the holy sands of the Al Muthanna.

"We have mobile launchers which cannot be seen or traced. We are hidden, ready to strike. I seek only your assurances that my most treasured wish will be granted."

*Tell you what, the son of a bitch could really lay it on when he needed something.*

And now Saddam Hussein gestured down the enormous table to two more close confidantes from Tikrit, Muzahim S'ab Hassan, commander, Iraqi Air Defense Forces, and Hamid Raja-Shalah Hassan, his overall air force commander. Both men bore the tribal last name, al-Tikriti, as did Saddam himself.

Muzahim Hassan spoke first, rising to his feet and remarking that the US F-14 was a formidable opponent capable of locating Iraqi launchers and destroying them with the touch of a button.

"But they don't fire at us!" rasped the Lion of Babylon. "They hardly ever launch a big rocket, and they never use their thousand-pound bombs."

"Nonetheless, I must be aware of the dangers into which I place our missile directors . . . " Hassan was on the defensive, in more ways than one.

"*Rubbish!*" bellowed Saddam. "Can't you ever understand? The Americans are cowards. They have the soft worthless character of the infidel. If *we* drove those Tomcats instead of them, we would have conquered them by now, driven them away forever and destroyed their disgusting friends, the Zionists. We also would have saved the Palestinians. Because Allah fights with us. And Allah is the greatest. Let the debased Americans be despised . . . *Long live Iraq!*"

The president's mood was there for all to see. He was virtually demanding his force commanders cast aside all else to knock a US F-14 out of the sky.

Softly, Saddam added, "We have vast supplies of battlefield anti-aircraft rockets. We have the superb Russian radar-guided heat-seekers. We have thousands of the old Soviet SA-7s, SA-2s, 3s, and 8s. All of them lethal to any aircraft operating below 10,000 feet. It must be possible."

"But, sir, they rarely fly that low . . . "

"Then force them down. Or tempt them down. Get up there and engage with them."

"That, sir," replied Hassan, "would be like committing suicide."

"*Then do it!*" yelled Saddam. "I don't care what you do, but get me one of those American Tomcats. Take your courage in both hands and go tackle an enemy who has not shown the slightest appetite for a battle for the bigger part of ten years—that's the pampered army of the White House, whose very name insults the glory of Allah."

General Hamid Shalah tried to come to the rescue of the air defense commander. "Sir," he said, his arms spread wide in front of him, appealing to Saddam's sense of loyalty, "our friend General Hassan has spent months at a time in the desert arranging our anti-aircraft attacks. No one could have worked harder. But the US pilots, when they come, are wise to our intentions. They fly over the zone with radars scanning. The slightest sign of a missile from us sees them slide away to the south or the east."

"*I know that!*" shouted Saddam. "But we know when they are coming. We have eyes and ears in their command centers. And we have sensors ever present in Washington. We know the Americans are petrified of being seen as a bully toward the Arab nations.

"Their pilots are under orders to get a second opinion before they open fire. Right now the danger to us is minimal. The Americans are like desert jackals with no teeth. I curse them all, and I want one for a trophy to hang on my wall!"

"Sir, if those are your orders, then so be it," replied the air defense commander from Tikrit. "You shall have your Tomcat's head on a stick. I will certainly ensure we hit one, and capture the pilots, the way you like it—for the television."

"Thank you, General Hamid," replied Saddam Hussein. "Just one, that's all I ask. One Tomcat to demonstrate to the world our skills, our courage, and our devotion to our cause in the name of glorious Allah. *Long live Iraq—may we be free and proud from our rivers to the sea.*"

And with that, the president arose from his chair and asked his guards to bring in more tea and the sweet pastries he loved. "For everyone," he said expansively, "for these are my special people, each one of them exalted among the Arab nations, and their hearts are filled with faith."

AS A SENIOR FRONT-LINE member of the US Navy's "cowardly" armed forces, I have much to say about Saddam Hussein's opinions. Left to me and my colleagues, both he and all of his war-fighting capability would have been extinguished long ago. I should also add formally that as a TOPGUN graduate and one of the most qualified fighter pilots in our carrier air wing, I was, of course, never invited personally to attend any meeting of the Revolutionary Council in its subterranean hideout.

However, we knew as much about them as they knew about us. We were well aware of their orders, well aware of their ambitions, and well aware of the dangers of flying across that benighted stretch of the Syro-Arabian Desert in the south of his country.

I have listened to a thousand conversations about who was in the council meeting, what was said, and who was tasked to carry out Saddam's missions. I have seen US military intelligence photographs of the room; I have studied his speeches, his papers, his strategies, and his mode of address to his commanders. There are phrases he always uses, declarations he loves, the endless praising of Allah, the massive assumption that his god detests Americans as much as he does.

And, of course, there is the ancient truth, that both he and the fabled twelfth-century Arab warrior leader, Saladin, were both born in Tikrit. Saddam believed in his soul that he alone in the modern world still wielded the Sword of Saladin.

I understand the deference with which he was treated and, more important, the level of fear he instilled in all who served him. Saddam was a man rarely interrupted, never mind argued with. His towering rages when challenged by his military leaders became public in the years after his death.

During the long months we flew our depleted air wing over Iraq in the year 2000, the Iraqis threw everything at us except the Sword of Saladin. I was personally fired upon by anti-aircraft guns, rockets, heat-seeking missiles, and mortars. They've launched them at me from trucks and fixed desert launchers. They've loosed them from hand-held devices, from behind bushes, sand hills, dunes, trenches, and God knows where else—every one of them in total defiance of United Nations Security Council Resolutions.

I am, I believe, uniquely placed to understand their orders, their intentions, and their utter disdain for us as an enemy. I have much to explain. But I trust you'll forgive me a little poetic license to demonstrate what those meetings were like. I'll give you a better overview of what was said than most people could.

That vast presidential site of Abu Ghurayb is set just to the east of Baghdad International Airport, due west of the great southern loop of the Tigris River as it flows out of the city. It contains possibly eight palaces, the main one built in the middle of a huge, artificial lake, turquoise in color, approached by two causeways.

Imagine them all trooping out, crossing the bridge to the mainland, raised up by the confidence and power of their leader. There may have been doubts, and there may have been fears. But the principal drive of their battle orders was cast in stone: *knock one of those US F-14s out of the sky, no matter what it takes.*

Of that, let there be no doubt.

## CHAPTER 1

# Ninety-Nine, Shut Down

Late September 2000: Another hot and cloudless morning on the wide, shallow waters of the Gulf of Iran. Not a cloud in the sky from the Shatt al-Arab six hundred miles south to the Strait of Hormuz.

Except, that is, for one: a jet-black and somber formation, precisely 1,094 feet long by 257 feet wide. It hung doggedly over USS *George Washington* (CVN-73) as the American carrier patrolled the northern reaches of the Gulf, trying to keep a semblance of order in the nearly lawless lands bordering this 97,000-square-mile inland sea. Especially the one on the narrow northwest corner shore: Iraq.

The black cloud cast a shadow of despondency over the entire ship's company as the flight-deck personnel performed that breathtaking naval ballet, placing the world's most lethal strike fighter aircraft into position for takeoff. The morning's chosen delta-winged stars moved with delicate precision, from out of the back line of the chorus to center stage, engines howling, pilots signaling, all choreographed to within inches by the men in bright yellow shirts.

Among these people, this should have been one of the day's highlights: the spectacular daily confirmation of the naval might of the United States of America, the culmination of a zillion hours of training, the final proof positive that here indeed was the front line of American muscle, flexing, rippling, ready to stare down any enemy. Carrier Air Wing SEVENTEEN (CVW-17) ready to roll.

What a moment it had once been—that rip-roaring overture when everyone showed what they had trained for. When the very best of Americans clenched their fists and right in front of them there played out the awe-inspiring pageant of battle, for which they had pledged their lives.

The slogans on the patches of the pilots were revealing: *Any time, baby . . . Go ahead, make my day.* The Naval Aviators—especially the TOPGUN fighter pilots—had a real swagger about them. The skull and crossbones painted on the vertical stabilizers of my F-14 Tomcat symbolized Fighter Squadron ONE ZERO THREE (VF-103), the Jolly Rogers. The other fighter squadrons—each flying the F/A-18 Hornet—were the Blue Blasters, the Sunliners, and the Rampagers.

Guiding this howling brute of a strike fighter carefully through the massed ranks of the *Washington*'s air armada was a daily test of nerve and skill, and not just mine. The flight deck of a carrier is populated by inordinately brave young men and women, all carrying out hugely dangerous jobs, every one of them vital. Every one of them is out there on the frontiers of life and death. One mistake. One moment of inattention. Jesus Christ! Don't remind me.

Everyone operates under his own colors: the yellow-shirts, the white-shirts, the green-shirts, the purples, the reds, and the browns. All of them are specialists, and all of them wear crash helmets with colored tape corresponding to their shirt.

Right now I'm done with the Grapes—that's the purples, responsible for gassing up the aircraft. The greens have checked the avionics; the reds have hauled up the bombs and missiles on the weapons elevators, fused them correctly under the wings, checked them over and over.

In the distance there are a couple of white-shirts, the supervisors, Navy chief petty officers, talking to a couple of kids, brown-shirts, both carrying chains, the ones they use to lash the strike fighters to the deck. Everyone starts out there. I'm done with them as well, and I'm moving out, watching the signals, my nerves on a hair trigger ready for the high crossed arms of the yellow-shirt directly in front of me—that's his signal to stop *right now!*—before we do a couple of million dollars' worth of damage and possibly kill several people.

The delicacy required to get this thirty-three-ton weapon of war into takeoff position is beyond comprehension to the layman: *Don't hit the throttle!* The blast from one of those F110-GE-400 turbofan jet engines could blow any one of those kids straight over the side, and it's always touch and go whether anyone sees it happen.

On either side there's often only inches to spare as I make my way to the stern of the ship. The yellow-shirt's signaling to his colleague . . . looks like I'm headed for the catapult. A new guy picks me up, signaling the starboard turn, walking backward in front of me. I'm headed over the four wires already stretched wide to grab the hook when the next strike fighter comes screaming home.

I cross the solid walls of the JBD (jet blast deflector), which will rise up hydraulically right behind me as I move the Tomcat into position. And already they're fixing the hydraulic catapult four (Cat 4), which will hurl me down port-side runway number four, into the air, zero to 180 mph in under two seconds (G-Force 3), surely the most thrilling sight in all the US military, the moment when several hundred hearts on the flight deck stop dead for fleeting seconds. Not just this time. Every time.

I glance to my right. The light on the island glows red: *four minutes to launch, visual checks completed.* Right behind me, my radar intercept officer (RIO) is, like me, strapped in. The red light flicks to amber—*two minutes*—and the yellow-shirt motions us slightly forward, positioning the Tomcat's launch bar on top of the shuttle attached to the catapult.

The light flashes green, and the "shooter," a young lieutenant in a yellow shirt, standing out in front of the aircraft, raises his right hand and points straight at me. I'm ready, and I formally salute him, left hand on the throttle as he points two fingers: *Go to full power.*

I can see him muttering into his walkie-talkie as I lean slightly forward, tensing for the impact of the catapult shot. The shooter salutes me, bends his knees, and touches the deck, gesturing *forward!*

A second crewman, kneeling on the narrow catwalk next to the Tomcat, hits the button on Cat 4, ducking low as the stupendous force of the hydraulic mechanism flings the big strike fighter on its way.

Engines screaming, a massive blast of hot air in our wake, I feel like I've been kicked in the chest as we thunder toward the port-side bow. Out over the water, the aircraft sags downward, like always. I pull back on the stick and hit the afterburners, and we rocket skyward.

"Good shot," calls the RIO.

My eyes scan the sea of dials, checking the rpm's and the temperature.

"Good engines," I reply.

And once more we're on our way, headed northwest toward the Arabian Peninsula, toward the arid wasteland of Saddam Hussein's southern desert.

This is the full majesty of the launch of Uncle Sam's front-line fighting force. At least my part as carrier air wing strike leader, and one of the most qualified TOPGUN fighter pilots stationed on the *George Washington*.

For me it's pure poetry, the precision of the organization, the mass dedication of the personnel, the checks and balances, the *professionalism*—and in my game, that precise word has nothing to do with money. It means the total elimination of mistakes. We do, of course, very occasionally make them. Once.

Hence that black cloud, which hung so menacingly over CVN-73, the 100,000-ton Nimitz-class giant, and cast such an enormous shadow over the flight deck and all who worked on it, and indeed on those who worked above and below it.

In the nine years since General Norman Schwarzkopf bulldozed Saddam's army out of the way in 1991, the Navy had undergone a most terrible reorganization, masterminded principally by the National Security Council.

Front-line defense cuts were relentless, as the administration tried to be all things to all people, but nonetheless dismantled a military built by Ronald Reagan. They tried to appease liberal politicians who wanted mainly to offer the limp and facile hand of friendship to some of the most vicious killers on the planet.

I believe they call it "triangulation" politics, the fine art of seeming to support both left- and right-wing philosophies, trying to befriend both sides of the House, and steering a precarious course down the middle. The Brits have a phrase for it: to run with the fox, and hunt with the hounds.

The constraints on our budgets came in many forms. The one that affected us most was the ever-increasing shortages of gas, especially jet fuel. Our carrier strike group consisted of destroyers, several frigates, two nuclear submarines, and a cruiser. But we did not have a fleet oiler with us, and we always refueled in flight, from an airborne tanker.

This ought not to have been a great problem, since we were getting all of our fuel from the Saudi Arabians, free of charge, in return for our protection from the hotheaded and warlike Lion of Babylon. He had, after all, in 1991 marched his Iraqi troops straight across Kuwait to within a few miles of the very Saudi oil fields that keep much of the Western world on the move.

Nerve-wracked by Saddam's continuing presence as Iraq's leader, the men in Riyadh bargained easily for American protection, in return for all the fuel we needed. I guess it was like a free US military force for the Eskimos, in return for boatloads of snow.

I have no idea how much of that oil came specifically to us. But we never had enough. We were constantly flying with just enough fuel to reach the tanker, just enough to fly our mission, in "The Box" for seventy-five minutes, with barely enough gas to get home. This was a state of grace known colloquially among the pilots as skosh. That's as near as it gets to fresh out of gas, without hitting the deep blue waters of the Persian Gulf.

As the cuts bit deeply, we were instructed to fly slower, conserving gas, then even more slowly. By the fall of 2000, we were down to three hundred knots, substantially slower than a passenger jetliner.

And instead of lancing across those desert skies at six hundred knots, flying missions 24/7, which would have frightened the goddamned life out of that son of a bitch Saddam, we were flying out there just once a day. There were never more than six or eight of us, trundling along at half speed, dorking around, punching holes in the skies, same time every morning, giving them a target, taking photographs of the terrain, on what our senior command described as "mirror-image" strike missions. Whatever the hell that was supposed to mean.

We were virtually banned from opening fire. Each flight had an entire book on board, masterminded by civilians, detailing if and when we could shoot back if fired upon—which was, like, every day. We had rules for everything: Don't drop a thousand-pound bomb on this or that, only a five hundred–pound bomb. This is too big, that's too fast, because that's a village with a mosque and someone might be praying.

Don't unleash a missile on this or that because there's a mosque three streets away. If you see a missile coming toward you, take evasive action but then check in with mission control in Riyadh for permission to hit back. *Permission!* We're up here a few seconds from being burned alive or blown out of the sky by a Russian-made guided missile and are told to *stand by!* By a *civilian* who needed to check in with Washington! Not USS *George,* the Pentagon, or the White House, or whatever.

The fact was, the Iraqis could fire at will, hit us if they could. On the other hand, we fought with both hands tied behind our backs. We all felt we were some kind of bait, stuck up there waiting for the day when Saddam's missile men finally hit one of us.

Even senior flight commanders were given no insight into what the hell we were doing there—except to give Saddam's guys target practice and knock the hell out of our aircraft in one of the hottest climates on earth.

EVERY SIX MONTHS we transported an entire air force to the other side of the planet on one of these gigantic warships from the United States. We were just moving aircraft around, wasting millions and millions of dollars, flying recces across the Gulf, and over the desert, above the banned areas, up to the Thirty-Third Parallel, just to check whether this Hussein nutter had broken the rules—again.

The eight-year rule of that 1990s National Security Council was one of the rare occasions when a branch of the US military came under strict civilian control, under a president who wished to befriend our sworn enemies.

It was a disastrous time, a period totally alien to our own creeds and cultures. It was a perfect example of civilian incompetence, a group of them taking precedence over the military. It was also a heartbreaking example of what can happen when the men in suits can somehow outgun the guys in uniform. Especially when their sympathies lie on the left-hand side of Congress.

Imagine the effect all these multibillion-dollar exercises had on the guys in the aircraft carrier. Morale was at rock bottom, as it always is when a fighting force has no idea why it's doing whatever it's doing.

There was an overpowering sense of irritation, frustration, and ultimately demoralization. Every day thousands of America's finest played their role in massive preparations; the pilots took off, flew three hundred miles to the Southern No-Fly Zone, dodged Iraqi anti-aircraft fire for an hour, and then returned home, leaving the Lion of Babylon laughing his head off. End gain for the United States? Nothing.

You could see the pure frustration in the attitudes of the air crews, especially among the Navy staff, whenever we conducted our debriefings and heard how close one of our guys had come to being hit and probably dying out there above the Iraqi desert.

Remember one thing: It was hotter than hell. Temperatures on the flight deck often hovered around or above one hundred degrees. Remember also that we as a race, the Navy Air Wings, would gladly have walked through the fires of hell for our country. But by that late summer, the guys simply did not know what was going on. Are we supposed to kick this Iraqi devil in the head, or what?

Below the burning flight deck the heat was not much better, because on a US carrier the air conditioning can be only ten degrees below sea temperature, which was about one hundred degrees. It was uncomfortable, often boring, and packed with irritable people, sick of the sound of Saddam's name. All we wanted to be told was, "That's it, guys. Go get him."

At the time we were experiencing the rise of al-Qaeda, the constant stories of Osama bin Laden, the rumors of heavy connections between Osama and Saddam, the links between Afghanistan and Pakistan, the suspected involvement of the Yemeni, Sudanese, and other Muslim republics. Everyone could sense the growing menace of the jihadists.

All someone had to do was say the word, and CVW-17 would have taken the Iraqi air force, and its missile capability, clean off the map. That's what we were there for. At least that's what we used to think. But in 2000, it was just smoke and mirrors, the pretense of ferocity against an enemy who believed, with some reason, his US opponents were cowards, too scared to open fire, without a leader who "qualified" as a warrior.

Most of us had joined the US military in the Reagan era, attended the United States Naval Academy, with our courage high, our ambitions burning. For us, President Reagan was a god. No president was ever more beloved by the military, at least no president since Teddy Roosevelt, with his chilling mantra: "Speak softly and carry a big stick." Reagan understood that.

Week after week, people would arrive from Washington to tell us over and over what we could do and what we could not, lecturing us, sometimes berating us, going over which bomb was acceptable and which one wasn't.

They often pointed out the dangers we faced, of being sent to jail if we overstepped the boundaries. All of us had the impression they had made the long journey out to this aircraft carrier to ban us from doing what every last one of us wanted to do: flatten Saddam's military.

*Now, you can't use this type of bomb on this type of building . . . there may be civilians nearby . . . human rights . . . Geneva Conventions . . . self-defense . . . wait to be fired upon . . . lethal force . . . WMDs . . . innocent until proven guilty . . . US bullying . . . balance of power . . . yada yada yada.*

Sometimes they were mere representatives of the US administration, bureaucrats with rules. Sometimes they were US Navy Judge Advocate Generals officers (JAGs). And they kept right on arriving, by air, at God knows what cost, to tell us the strict guidelines.

We had to face it: this was a police force. These guys were coming out here, lecturing seasoned, decorated, professional battle commanders serving in the US Navy. On active duty. In a quasi–theater of war. In the biggest warship on earth, one that was constantly on high alert for terrorist attacks. Bureaucrats telling *us* how to conduct ourselves. We, who put our lives on the line every day. Who spent years and years preparing for situations such as this.

And that was not the worst of it. During the course of unwinding President Reagan's unstoppable American military, that administration not only slashed our budgets, they turned us into policemen, nothing more. But the most sinister thing they ever did was to take away our right to make command decisions.

This had been the solemn promise made to every young Naval Aviator: when he reached the appropriate rank and found himself in a hot-war scenario, the command decision to hit back, open fire, or attack in any way he considered correct was his alone to make.

That was the promise. That was the sacred covenant that caused young men such as myself to aspire to the highest level and risk of fighter pilot command. That was the pledge that made it worthwhile: that one day I might sit astride the battle charger of the United States of America, make the decision upon which my country may depend, and draw my sword. The way they taught me at Annapolis. That decision, I was promised, would never be questioned. Down the ages, America's commanders have lived with the responsibility of that binding trust.

That promise meant the whole world to me. And to dozens of naval officers like me. But it was taken away, stolen from us all, from every fighter pilot.

We were informed that all decisions made in combat would henceforth be made long-range from Washington.

Pilots who came under attack would report to Combined Air Operations Center in Riyadh, which would check in with Washington, for a decision to relay back to the high command in the mother ship, which would send the final message back to Riyadh.

From there an operator would let me know that another pilot had been selected to fire a small(ish) missile at the approximate area I had pinpointed, by now one hundred miles away. By which time Saddam's illegal missile men would probably be home for dinner, while I would be running out of gas, flying at half speed, wondering what in the name of Christ was going on.

It was nothing short of a circus—all these people, mostly civilians, trying to make military decisions. And of course, there was only one decision, and the military would have made it in about one-tenth of a second, roughly like this:

*Tomcat one-o-three . . . under attack . . . two Iraqi bruisers—Russian SA-8s . . . Okay, Jeff, go get 'em.*

At which point my buddies and I would have come screaming in at nearly seven hundred knots and vaporized the entire area from where the missile had been launched. And that would have been an end to it. *Saddam, old buddy, you want to fuck around? We'll show you how to REALLY fuck around.*

The removal of our command decision had the most shocking effect, as if we had been somehow castrated. It knocked the swagger out of us. We were somehow diminished, no longer held in the highest regard. Those White House committees had cut a little piece out of the heart of every combat member of the armed forces.

By that I do not include officers of high rank, men who are mostly fighting for political approval or promotion. I am talking about robbing the men who form the Tip of the Spear, the up-front warrior-class commanders, whose courage and skill not only have been hard earned, but also have a unique value: priceless.

Take, if you will, my own long journey toward stepping into the F-14 that morning, just by considering the following stats:

Fewer than one in ten who apply to the United States Naval Academy is accepted. One in ten of those Annapolis graduates will make it to flight school. And only one in ten of those will make it to advanced jet training. And just one in ten of those will be selected as a fighter pilot.

For the record, just one in ten of those fighter pilots will make it to TOPGUN. Which means you need to come out on top of 100,000 others to stand where I was that morning on the deck of the USS *George Washington*.

As a carrier air wing strike leader and forward air controller I was one of the most qualified TOPGUN pilots on the ship. I had better landing grades than my boss. I was the specialist coordinator between Navy SEAL teams on the ground waiting for an air-wing strike.

When I arrived at my aircraft, I was greeted by the plane captain, who saluted and snapped, "Morning, Commander Lay, aircraft one-o-three, preflight, fueled, and ready for combat."

And now I had to take combat orders from a civilian? Do we still have a commander-in-chief? It sure seemed like a very gray area out there on the Tip of the Spear. We all had the distinct feeling there were American civilians somewhere in Washington who were a bigger goddamned nuisance than Saddam.

I guess we were all brought up to believe in the US military, to respect the traditions and the culture, to accept the iron discipline and thoroughness, the proven correctness of the system, and the wisdom of our veteran commanders. The title of this book will confirm we have good reason to believe we can do almost anything better than civilians, simply because we are about ten times harder on ourselves and do not, cannot, deal in lies, half-truths, exaggerations, and evasions. Not if we intend to go on breathing.

Let me invite you once more into the cockpit of the Tomcat (call sign Victory 103), which was, in its way, a profound irony, given we were exclusively banned from any form of victory by our own commander-in-chief, sitting in his plush, carpeted White House office.

And here we are again, moseying along at three hundred knots across the Gulf of Iran, at the head of a small flight of US Navy strike fighter aircraft on the daily and utterly useless mirror-image strike mission. Generally speaking, we're the world's most overqualified photographers.

WE'RE CLIMBING to our cruising altitude of 28,000 feet. Our call sign is Bulldog 24. We're moderately well-armed, with our six-barrel Vulcan cannon, air-to-air, 6,000 rounds a minute, and AIM-54C Phoenix missiles. The F/A-18C Hornets are carrying their AIM-120C missiles. We all carried AIM-9Ms and AIM-7M Sparrow missiles.

The Hornets carried the GBU-31s, satellite-guided bombs. Which is great, except we're not allowed to drop them. Also we all have chaff and flares—small canisters loaded with tiny metal strips and pyrotechnics—to seduce Iraqi missiles away from the aircraft just as soon as we are fired upon. You need to react real quick, and we're pretty good at it. That's why they've never actually knocked one of us down.

The *George Washington*'s ops area straddles the Twenty-Ninth Parallel and it's a little over one hundred miles west-northwest to the coastline. We cross over the Kuwaiti town of Mina Saud and keep heading west to the tanker area for about another hundred miles, leaving Saddam's highly dangerous southern desert to our starboard side. The journey takes about an hour at this airspeed, but our tanker guys are swiftly on hand with a refill, which we conduct at around three hundred knots.

Then we head north, into the skies above the no-fly zone, from which the Iraqis are forbidden and into which they are plainly banned from shooting missiles at their erstwhile conquerors (that's us . . . Stormin' Norman 1991).

The resolutions, drawn up by the United Nations, were explicit. America and its allies would cease fire and refrain from completely destroying the Iraqi military, in return for a signed document in which the Iraqis, among other matters, agreed to pull out of Kuwait, not molest its neighbors further, and refrain from making war on anyone else.

Saddam gratefully signed the treaty, regrouped his fighter jets and missiles, and proceeded to break every last one of the sixteen principal surrender conditions over the next nine years.

In the considered opinion of Saddam and his commanders, the snarling US ground and air forces, which had all but reduced him to rubble in 1991, were no more. Instead there was a weak-willed left-wing administration in Washington, and a US strike force that had been robbed of its will to fight. Which more or less meant he could do what he liked, with no fear of reprisal. Not from us anyway.

So here we go again, heading north over the Saudi/Iraqi frontier, knowing full well the vast sandy wasteland below is bristling with Saddam's banned missiles, and we'd better stay real sharp if we want to make it home.

Thirty minutes into Iraqi airspace, we spot two missiles streaking straight up at us. The RIO unleashes chaff and automatically switches on the jammer to screw up incoming radar. I ram open the throttles and we wheel away left. Instantly I open the encrypted communications line to Combined Air Ops Center in Riyadh and report we've been fired on.

"This is Bulldog two-four . . . Confirm engaged MUD 6 . . . I'm Tropicana one-one-four, seventy-five. Angels twenty-eight."

That's the secret language of the combat pilots.

"Okay, Bulldog two-four, stand by."

Okay for who? Not for me. Jesus! Here comes another SAM. *Stand by!* I ought to go right down there and blast those assholes off the planet.

"Bulldog two-four, stand by . . . Calling Bobcat seven-two . . . confirm you have Walrus weapons. Bulldog two-four's been engaged MUD 6— need you to hit back—confirm weapons, GBU-12 laser guided."

Meantime I'm diving across the sky trying to stay out of the way of missiles, bullets, and flak fired by these villains on the ground. The control guys are going back and forth trying to get permission to do something. *Anything!* I'm now about fifty miles from the action, putzing around, awaiting instructions.

Here it comes: "Bulldog two-four . . . RTB MOTHER. And check out Gold Seven (Radio)" (that meant "go home—return to the carrier").

God knows what Bobcat 72 was up to—I guess another pansy retaliation, firing something not too dangerous at different Iraqis, who had not been firing the missiles in the first place. The usual. Lazy, passive 1990s response, guaranteed to make Saddam and his Iraqis laugh their heads off. At us. Wasn't that just great?

I set off easterly across the Gulf, heading back to the carrier, watching my rapidly diminishing fuel gauges, keeping my airspeed down, watching for the tiny postage stamp up ahead, upon which I am required to land this fully weapons-laden strike fighter, an always harrowing procedure.

It was again obvious to me that the Iraqis had been waiting for us, confident we would arrive precisely when they expected. Of course I had no idea whether they'd hit one of the US aircraft. But I doubted it. We're too sharp for them, too well-equipped and -trained.

It was nonetheless a gloomy procedure. None of us had the remotest idea why we had gone up to the no-fly zone or what our photographic mirror-image mission had been for.

And now I faced up to the most demanding aspect of any fighter pilot's day: slamming the old Tomcat hard into the flight deck. I'd done it literally hundreds of times before, but that never lessened the pure danger of the exercise. The operation was such an obvious life-and-death test of nerve and skill, we were required to make a *night* landing every seven days, just to make sure we stayed right up there with our A-game, every hour, every day. No bullshit.

By now the weather had made a turn for the worse, with a typical squall racing down the Gulf from the northwest and swirling toward the coast of Iran. These conditions are common in the autumn and occur very suddenly, the high rain clouds blown out to sea by the remnants of the desert's summer wind, the *shamal*.

The carrier is still visible, engulfed by the rain and very gray, but stark against the slate-colored ocean. I'm in touch with the tower, and I've reported my altitude, 8,000 feet. I'm circling ten miles out before heading in, at around 160 knots, aiming directly at the stern of the carrier. My fuel tank registers a tad above "empty."

An aircraft carrier landing bears absolutely no resemblance to a passenger aircraft touching down on a mile-long airport runway. We don't just glide in, "flaring out" gracefully, nose up, main landing wheels down, airspeed cut back, reverse thrust at the ready. We come in at around 180 miles an hour, a thirty-three-ton strike fighter with enough fused high explosive under the wings and in the bomb bay to knock down Grand Central Station.

I'm watching the landing lights, bucking along in this gusting hot wind trying to assess the rise and fall of the carrier's stern. I'm guessing around twenty feet in the long ocean swells, and I'm casting aside the fighter pilot's prayer, for the hook to grab the arresting wire. Because if it misses, I have about a twentieth of a second to ram open the throttles and charge for the carrier's bow with enough airspeed to get off again and have another try. If I don't have the airspeed as we hurtle over the bow, we'll just dive straight down and punch a hole in the ocean. In fact, I'll have the throttles open as we slam into the deck. This isn't an aircraft landing. It's a controlled crash.

I'm about two miles out now, and the landing signal officer, Lieutenant Bill Frado from Massachusetts, a good buddy of mine, is in contact, staring through the rain, focusing his binoculars, tracking my flight path. Above the howl of the engines I can hear him talking me in, glide slope, center line, and airspeed.

"Okay one-o-three . . . wind gusting three-five . . . check your approach line . . . gotcha visual . . . looking good from here . . . gear down . . . flaps down . . . hook down . . . you're all set, Jeff . . . c'mon in."

The arresting gear officer, a petty officer, is shouting down the phone to the hydraulics team below. I know he's looking out for me, scanning the deck to make sure there's not a single speck of litter, and he's checking the arresting wire for the fourth or fifth time, making certain nothing's broken or uncoupled.

Because when these things go awry, we're looking at carnage. That wire, whipping around against the full force of an incoming Tomcat, can lash back and kill a half dozen people, chop their legs off, at minimum. Not to mention the complete certainty of sending me clean over the side into the ocean, wrecking the aircraft.

"Stand by for Victory one-o-three . . . two minutes!"

I'm fighting to hold her steady in the unpredictable wind, three degrees above the horizontal. The carrier's pitching through one-and-a-half degrees to either side of the horizontal, the stern rising through twenty-five feet every thirty seconds.

We're screaming through the rain now, and I can hear them yelling, over the radio, "Groove!" That's code for *She's close—stand by!*

Twenty seconds later he yells, "Short!"—the final order, *everyone away from the machinery.* And as the massive stern of the carrier rushes up to meet me, I make infinitesimal adjustments, most of them subconscious. I'm only one hundred yards out now, hurtling toward the deck, and the ensign bellows at the top of his lungs, "Ramp!"

The satanic shape of the Tomcat comes thundering out of the skies, lights flashing like some kind of a monster riding the devil's swept-back wings. In a deafening dark apparition, she's through the rain and across the stern, and now she's hit the landing surface, engines howling, the wheels catching, then bouncing.

And then, thank God, I feel the hook grab, and that mighty hydraulic piston down below hauls us to a standstill, a stupendous change of speed, from 180 mph to a dead stop in two seconds, lurching me forward, tight against the harness.

Astern, the arresting wire is in a taut V shape but hardly anyone can see it through the thick swirling cloud of rain, wind, and jet blast. For the record, my heart's going about 4,000 beats per minute—a sharp contrast to all the other hearts on the flight deck, which have stopped altogether, like they always do.

Doesn't matter how many times you've done it, or how many times you've played any kind of a role in landing a strike fighter returning home, hell, it really has a way of concentrating the mind. Everyone breathes again as the deck crews come racing out to haul Victory 103 back to her allotted spot, to chain her down for the night.

I climb out of the cockpit, and I can see the petty officer already back on the stern of the ship, binoculars raised in the driving rain. Bill's made contact with the next pilot: "Okay, one-o-five . . . wind's gusting three-five . . . check your approach line . . . looking good . . ."

It's a strange thing. But when danger threatens, no one cares what the cost might be to extinguish that danger. But in the fall of 2000, the vast costs of running our mirror-image operations preyed on our minds in a way I had never before experienced.

I suppose any educated American could not possibly stand blind to the gigantic waste of public money expended on these pointless sorties up in the no-fly zone. The politicians plainly had not the slightest intention of raising a finger to discourage the Iraqi dictator from breaking every rule in the book, turning the United Nations into a laughingstock and embarrassing every combat member of the United States Armed Forces.

The trouble was, it seemed to us as if it might somehow be our fault, the millions of dollars, the frustration. And every day: nothing. I have no doubt the Pentagon was fed up with blowing a large part of its budget and being told at the same time to ensure no one actually attacked the Iraqis, whatever they did. Also the Saudis were fed up with us and wanted us out of there. Everyone was fed up with us. *We* were fed up with us.

However, we were more aware, perhaps, than anyone else that within the Arab nations, a wide brotherhood was becoming united in their loathing of the West. As military intelligence probed ever deeper into Iraqi intentions, everyone suspected there was a major link between Saddam and al-Qaeda. Saudi nationals were strongly rumored to be financing bin Laden's terrorist operation. As ever, the more sinister side of the Yemeni was in the thick of it. Iran, glowering along the not-too-distant shore to our starboard side, was known to be financing the ferocious terrorist operation Hezbollah, not to mention Hamas. In a sense, I suppose, we were there as a show of American muscle, to be on station if anything major blew up anywhere in the Middle East.

There was nothing firm, no strategy. This 100,000-ton carrier, home to the most powerful air strike force on earth, was there at the behest of the Pentagon, in response to a subliminal thought process emanating from the White House. This involved a multi-motivational strategy: (1) to prevent the United States from being seen as a bully toward the Middle East, (2) to nurture friends in various countries on the Arabian Peninsula, and (3) to keep both sides of the House happy.

The problem was, from our point of view Saddam's missiles were not subliminal. They were Russian steel, fire, and high explosive, and every last one of them was directed at us.

This general unease among the carrier's middle management (battle commanders) was sufficiently obvious to the high command that regular briefings were instituted, in which we were informed that one day, probably in the not-too-distant future, Saddam would overstep the mark. He would pull something so diabolical we would finally be unleashed to vent nine years of American fury straight at the fraud field marshal in his underground palace.

In a way, that did sustain us, keeping us on top of our game all through those long, hot Arabian days when we achieved precisely nothing. Worse yet, we were not allowed even to try. But there was hope. One day we would be permitted to operate in the way we'd been trained and, finally, attack our enemy. As the September days grew shorter, Saddam finally fulfilled our dreams. He pulled something so diabolical even the National Security Council realized something had to be done.

I was on my way back from a conference in Turkey, flying in the Carrier On-board Delivery (COD) aircraft. Right after we arrived back on the flight deck of the *George Washington,* it was clear something was seriously wrong. There were no aircraft on the deck. Every one of them was missing—they must have all gone charging up into the no-fly zone.

"Where the hell is everyone?" I demanded. The reply was swift and very military-sounding.

"They've saturated The Box, sir."

"They've done *what?*"

"Er . . . saturated The Box, sir."

"What's that?"

The ensign finally explained that every aircraft had been dispatched to the no-fly zone, in what looked like a hard-core attack, but had been canceled by Washington and turned into a large-scale mirror-image operation.

Since we'd just spent nine years logging every missile launcher, every target, darn nearly every grain of sand, I was at a loss to understand what good more photographs were going to prove.

In a rapid-fire series of conferences, however, the pieces swiftly fell into place. Saddam apparently had been tipped off that today was the one day we had no plans to fly; that's why they'd chosen it for my conference in Turkey.

Shortly before noon he'd sent a flight of former Russian fighter aircraft, two MiG-23s and a MiG-25, into the four spots in all the Middle East he was supposed to avoid under threat of death: the skies over Kuwait, the marshes, the no-fly zone down to the Saudi frontier, and of course the frontier itself, which guarded not only the Kingdom of Saudi Arabia but also our huge refueling zone, above which were the sacred aerial tanker lanes where our fighters collected the gas to get them home.

Saddam launched two MiG-23MFs from Balad Southeast, his main air strike base situated thirty-three miles north of Baghdad, just south of the Tigris. These light, heavily armed strike fighters packed a major wallop with radar-guided AS-7s and two R-60 short-range infrared missiles.

From Balad they flew north of Baghdad and then low across the marshes, pulling hard right across al-Basrah, then making a wide sweep across the UN-forbidden lands of Kuwait, before returning to base straight up the middle of the no-fly zone.

From the same base he also launched a MiG-25 Foxbat, Russia's supersonic interceptor, with a top speed of Mach 2.8 and radar-guided missiles. This fast intruder came streaking high over the Euphrates River heading due south directly through the middle of The Box, over the Al Muthanna Desert before crossing the Saudi border.

From there the Foxbat made a hard right turn, flying high and fast, directly and deliberately through the US refueling tracks 28,000 feet above the desert—a crime judged to be so utterly egregious that at last Saddam had to be stopped.

Evidently the White House could put up with him trying to kill US pilots every day, but not to reach this level of arrogance, thumbing his nose and laughing at the US military, and finally demonstrating, beyond doubt, that he could, if he so wished, eliminate our precious lifeline of fuel, both on and over Saudi Arabian territory.

That was one step too far, because he was telling us he could kill off our entire operation, cut off our lifeline. At the same time he was terrifying the Saudi royal family, which had long given up on the Americans doing *anything* to discourage their highly unstable neighbor.

But now, by any standards, Saddam was so seriously in breach of the conditions of the UN surrender document, the might of the US Navy was about to be unleashed upon him. The supreme air combat force, embarked in the *George Washington,* bottled up for all these years and packed with hard-eyed TOPGUN pilots who'd come rushing out of the Reagan era, was ready to go. This moment was the only reason half of them had stayed around, acting as policemen in what we thought was just a schoolyard, with a daily photography class mostly for the RIOs.

Most of the guys had been away from home for nine of the past twelve months. And boy, had they ever been waiting for this day. The White House had called off the instant attack, but it was obvious the Navy intended to hit back at the earliest chance.

I was told to report to the strike cell, our planning room, situated one deck below the roof and one above the aircraft hangar. When the door finally closed, we were told, "This is it. They've really done it this time." And everyone agreed. We were going to take out both of Saddam's main air bases up around Baghdad, the previously mentioned MiG fighter headquarters at Balad Southeast, and the other specialist MiG base at Al Taqaddam, which lies on the northeast shores of Lake Habbaniyah, around forty-five miles west of the capital.

Both of these bases contained huge aircraft hangars, the doors of which had to be opened around noon because of the intense heat buildup inside the structures. Right after this, two US preemptive air strikes would come in and demolish the Iraqi air force on the ground before it had time to get airborne.

The US bombs and missiles would be targeted straight through the hangar doors. It would be a surprise attack similar to the one on June 5, 1967, when the Israeli air force, under Major General Mordechai Hod, practically wiped out the entire Egyptian air force on the opening day of the Six-Day War. Hard, fast, and ruthless, the way we like it.

The plan required us to fly the usual route up to the refueling tankers over Saudi Arabia, south of the border near a little town called Rafha, and then swerve north across the desert, crossing the Thirty-Second Parallel, where the Iraqi tracking system ceases.

From there we would fly a fast, low formation straight up the forty-mile Lake Ar Razzazah up to Majarrat and then cross Lake Habbaniyah itself, coming in off the water for the al-Taqaddum strike from the southwest.

The second wing of the mission would peel away here and head northeast over the desert directly to Balad Southeast. Within about five minutes the air forces of Iraq essentially would be history, while we flew back the way we came for the refuel, south of the border, once more over Saudi Arabia, through clear, empty skies—this time with the Lion of Babylon back in his cupboard, and a long-overdue mission complete.

There would be no more restrictions on our buildup. No more conserving weapons and aircraft. This was six hundred knots all the way, heavily armed, everyone on high alert. For the Iraqis, this was "Goodnight Vienna." And about time too.

For us, who would fight the action, there was a lot more to it than a mere heavy-handed bombing and missile raid. This would be a catharsis of our subconscious fears that the Muslim extremists were getting on top of the situation. There was a dread that they now regarded us entirely too lightly, and if we did not finally take action, they might just act on their definitive opinion that we were just too soft to worry about.

There was not one member of the front line, working in the *George Washington*'s air wing, who did not believe that Saddam needed a very sharp, harsh lesson, and one that would echo around the world of the terrorists: that the United States of America was not to be trifled with. And that when Uncle Sam decided to hit back, he would swing very hard, with an iron grip on Teddy Roosevelt's "big stick."

I guess you could say it was time. Time to slow these maniacs right down, with a high-explosive solution, delivered by us, ASAP. Our task was not just brutal destruction. It was to frighten the life out of the jihadists, to discourage them in all their activities, and in our opinion, that could not wait.

What followed was an enormous two-day buildup of weaponry, as every aircraft was prepared and every kind of missile was brought up and fitted to the undersides of the wings of the F/A-18 Hornets. They loaded the SLAMs—that's Navy speak for Standoff Land Attack Missile, an all-weather, over-the-horizon weapon with a five hundred–pound blast warhead. The F-14 Tomcats would carry the massive GBU-24, a 2,000-pound bunker-busting bomb. A few of those into the hangars would probably slow the Iraqi ground staff down some.

They loaded the Hornet with lethal Joint Direct Attack Munitions (JDAMs), twelve-foot-long, improved, fixed-target, precision weapons; a real smart bomb hooked up to a GPS system with a range of up to fifteen nautical miles—effectively "can't-miss," especially a target as big as an aircraft hangar.

They unpacked our huge supplies of Paveway IIs, the laser-guided bombs perfected by Raytheon with a warhead of up to 2,000 pounds of high explosive. If that wouldn't do it, there was an updated version of Paveway III, the GBU-24E/B, and we had a stock of those as well.

In these terrible temperatures, the kids were hauling this stuff up and loading the aircraft night and day. This was the first time, in my experience, that cost-cutting had been forgotten. There were no fuel restrictions, no airspeed restrictions, and definitely no weapons shortages. This mission was what we all had lived for. After nine years we were going.

The entire air wing was not so much elated as relieved. Kids who had thought their careers had just swerved away to nowhere were suddenly involved in the action, real action, preparing for a genuine US Navy strike against the enemy.

Every one of us answered a call to the flag, I guess me especially, because I had waited twenty-two years, since I was a kid in high school, for this precise moment, ever since I first saw a photograph of a US strike fighter. All of my ambitions had led inexorably to this moment, when I would be unleashed on a real, live enemy of the United States. Never had a Navy carrier strike group been prepared with such enthusiasm and excitement.

Our start-time was 1000 hours on the fourth morning after Saddam's "crime." The pilots were on board, gassed up, weapons fused. Shortly after 0900 we had the engines running. You could see the enthusiasm in the faces of every member of the deck crews, young guys, hugely intelligent, working in their designated teams. Nothing too much trouble. No mistakes. No sir.

But at 0930 there was a sudden announcement: "Delta 30!" That's a half-hour delay. God damn it. No reason given. Some of the guys cut an engine. The ten o'clock departure just became 1030. What the hell was that all about ? I can only say this was not a good sign. Not after nine years of passive acceptance of Saddam's antics.

Certainly there was *nothing* on the high-alert flight deck of the *George Washington* that could have caused even a four-second delay. The dread of those wishy-washy Washington bureaucrats and politicians hung heavily on my mind.

At ten a.m. there was a brand new announcement: "Delta 60!" Another delay, this time until 1040. You could have heard the groans of disappointment from twenty miles away. This was not looking good. Engines were left running, though more of us cut one, to save fuel. The world's most feared fighting carrier strike group was once more twiddling its thumbs.

And then, forty minutes after our original 1000 launch time, they finally called it off: "Ninety-nine, shut down." The mission was off. And you could tell the new somber mood of the ship by the utterly depressed tone of voice of the announcer. He stopped only just short of adding, "Can you believe this crap?"

Most of us climbed out of our cockpits and went downstairs. We kept our flight gear on in case there was a change of heart. But a lot of the guys were dejected, especially when we finally understood the mission had been called off direct from Washington, by order of the National Security Council.

Of course, none of us knew anything of the political ramifications involved, and to tell the truth none of us wanted to know. The US Navy is extremely good at keeping its eye on the ball. We're all taught what we call mental compartmentalization: separating thoughts, filing the bad stuff away until a more appropriate time, keeping right on with our most pressing critical path.

Whatever the politicians thought, and however smart they thought they were, they turned out to be a lot less smart than us.

Because we knew, out here on the front line, that these jihadist creeps needed to be stopped and brought into line. Because if Saddam could threaten our supply line with MiGs, he and every al-Qaeda nutter would stop at nothing. Maybe some presidential advisors did not agree with that, but they were wrong. More wrong than anyone would believe was humanly possible. More wrong possibly even than when the United States gave away the Panama Canal.

So there we sat, chewing the fat, waiting to be reinstated. But of course we weren't. There was a kind of halfhearted announcement that we would try to launch tomorrow same time. By now no one had any faith whatsoever in the guys who made these big decisions in the White House.

All I know is that the highest command in the US Navy darn near begged the National Security Council to allow the military to do what it considered to be prudent and correct, and hit this crazed Iraqi, wipe out his air force, whip those jihadists into line.

No one slept much. It was hotter than hell in the ship, and a lot hotter on deck. But we all got up at 0500 the following morning, and got ready for the second time, including a new three-hour brief. We headed for the cockpits in broiling heat, everyone revved up and raring to go. Everything was fueled and fused, launch time 1000 hours. The whole atmosphere was one of high alert. You could feel it everywhere. Now we really were on the move.

At 0930 we were moving out toward the catapults. Could this really be it? Were we finally going? There was a sudden "Delta 30!" A half-hour delay until 1030. So we stayed right where we were, in a kind of no-man's land, halfway to launch, apparently waiting for Washington to locate its courage, while the US Navy, from Cat 1 on the *Washington* flight deck all the way to the Pentagon quietly seethed.

The minutes ticked away toward the 1030 launch time and there were no further announcements. The sense of anticipation was everywhere. And then they called it: "Ninety-nine, shut down." This time the announcer sounded like those were the last words he would ever utter. He spoke them with melancholy and resignation, capturing the grim atmosphere on the ship. To tell you the truth, we all felt emasculated, no longer the front-line warriors. Just policemen.

The president and his team had funked it again. None of us ever got over it. It was as if our whole careers had been for nothing. It felt like we'd all been kicked in the groin. The strike on Saddam's air force was never mentioned again. And now the Lion of Babylon and the al-Qaeda network knew what they had always known: that the United States didn't have any guts worth a damn.

Twenty-eight days later Osama bin Laden's al-Qaeda launched a suicide attack and blew a forty-foot hole in the port-side hull of the US Navy destroyer USS *Cole,* killing seventeen sailors and injuring thirty-nine others while they were lining up for lunch—the deadliest attack on a US warship in thirteen years.

The *Cole* was parked and refueling in the Yemeni port of Aden. The blast was caused by a "shaped" charge, molded into explosives against the hull of the boat. Up to seven hundred pounds of dynamite may have been used.

The question stands up on its hind legs and begs to be asked: Would al-Qaeda have dared to pull something like that if the US Navy had just destroyed Iraq's air force less than four weeks before? Judging by the terrorists' traditional behavior, the answer is a resounding no.

When an exasperated President Reagan launched forty-five strike bombers against Tripoli and Benghazi on April 15, 1986, it virtually silenced Libyan dictator Muammar Gadhafi for years. The United States unleashed three hundred bombs with 227 hits, not including forty-five homing missiles, a couple of which flattened Gadhafi's house in Tripoli.

And after President George W. Bush unleashed the might of the US military on the Tora Bora Mountains in Afghanistan after the 9/11 attacks, it ended direct terrorism against the US mainland for the remaining seven-plus years of his presidency. Thousands died up there in the terrorist camps, including almost the entire bin Laden high command.

The history of these sneak-attack jihadist organizations is one of high courage in the face of a pansy or nonexistent response. When the United States comes slamming back into the fray, they are all apt to rush for cover. The US military, especially the Navy, has known that for a very long time.

It's an enormous pity that civilian politicians and advisors cannot grasp that we are at least as smart as they are. Often a lot smarter. If they had listened to us on that outrageous Saddam adventure over the forbidden lands in September 2000, the bombing of the USS *Cole* would certainly never have happened.

And probably not 9/11 either. In the Arab mind, there is nothing quite so nerve-wracking as a US president unafraid to slam back at his enemies with weapons so powerful they cannot be resisted. That's our privilege. And it's probably worth noting that if we had smashed the Iraqi air force on that fateful morning in September 2000, the second Iraq war probably would not have happened either.

Our Arab terrorist enemy has never shown any appetite to deal with US fire and steel. And it would have been a great deal better for all of us if the politicians had understood this better than they did. Because doing things their way could scarcely have been more catastrophic.

## CHAPTER 2

# The Tip of the Spear

The ferocious attack on the USS *Cole* in the Port of Aden that October was a terrible blow to all personnel in the *George Washington* carrier strike group. First of all, the suicide bombing never should have happened. Second, it most certainly would not have happened if we had eliminated Saddam's air force the previous month.

Al-Qaeda simply would not have dared if the US government had demonstrated even a shred of determination, or even outrage. Those, however, were not fashionable in those years. There were a thousand reasons in 2000 to zap Saddam, and our government never reacted correctly to one of them.

The civilians in Washington, fumbling around trying to run the military, had no idea that the *Cole* was a blood brother to all of us. The 9,000-ton guided-missile destroyer was a member of our carrier strike force—our heavily armed instant weapon that accompanied us all the way from Norfolk, Virginia, to the Gulf.

Every morning we could see her out there on the horizon, gun-gray and ready for anything, riding shotgun. She was our fast-response gunslinger, scanning those dangerous seas for the enemy, prepared to torpedo a submarine, blow an Iraqi fighter out of the sky, or slam an intruding foreign warship.

USS *Cole* was one of the carrier's principal bodyguards, patrolling the area, while we sat up here, high, wide, and handsome, operating the air wing. She was about one-third of our size and about five times more maneuverable. She was fast, twin-shafted, and ran hard on four GE gas turbines.

She was also capable of a serious bang against any enemy, with her deadly Tomahawk cruise missiles, vicious Harpoon surface missiles, and phalanx of six-barreled Vulcan Mark 15 guns.

The *Cole* was our tenacious little brother, built at the great Ingalls shipyard at the mouth of the Pascagoula River in Mississippi. She was DDG-67, a member of the proud and sturdy Arleigh Burke class—named for the hard-charging Admiral Burke, one of the towering heroes of the WWII Pacific campaign, and later commander-in-chief of the Navy Forces Far East during the Korean War.

I guess you have to have served in the Navy to understand fully our folklore and our history, and further, that ships like the *Cole* have souls. To the men and women who serve in her, she's a kind of steel-rimmed matriarch, their home, their life, and very probably their shelter and protector. Even the ship's company in the carrier felt a strong and emotive attachment to our pugnacious little bodyguard, scowling out there on the horizon, flexing its muscles.

A few of us were out on the flight deck on the September morning when she sailed away. Most of us felt that little tug on the heartstrings at the sight of a departing brother. *Cole* was the first of the group to begin the journey home to the United States, the idea being that she would steam down the Gulf of Iran, into the Arabian Sea, before pulling into the Port of Aden for a goodwill, show-the-flag visit.

There's a special vulnerability about an aircraft carrier, because everyone knows a bad fire, with all those tons of fuel on board, could actually finish her. Hit by a bomb, or a missile or even a suicide pilot, a big carrier would be in far more danger than any other warship. That's why the USS *Cole* meant so much to us.

And that's why, at noon on October 12, when we were told a small group of those sneaky little al-Qaeda bastards had virtually destroyed her while she was on a goodwill visit, every one of the 5,000 men and women on board the *George Washington* seethed with pent-up anger.

We, more than any other members of the US Navy, understood that we could and should have prevented it . . . by kicking the goddamned Lion of Babylon straight in the ass, showing the Arab world we could be pushed only so far.

I have not plumbed the very depths of Socrates to understand that somewhat elementary facet of human behavior. Al-Qaeda is a furtive, cunning little organization, specializing in secretive attacks, where instant retribution is unlikely.

Al-Qaeda has made an art form of the word "sneaky," attacking its perceived enemy from the sidelines, usually slaughtering innocent, defenseless civilians and rarely, if ever, confronting an armed foe.

The dictionary definition of the word "cowardly" includes the phrase, "showing fear of those who are equal or stronger." In all of its infamous history, Osama bin Laden's al-Qaeda has never shown the slightest inclination to tangle directly with a well-armed, aggressive enemy.

Any serving officer in the US military, any former student, cadet, or midshipman, from West Point or Annapolis, will tell you that victory or defeat, in any theater of war, is invariably in the commander's mind. That a nation in which the military is instantly prepared to hit back to vicious effect is innately safer and more secure than some quasi-pacifist behemoth the United States had become.

I say, without a shadow of a doubt, if we had up and slammed Saddam in September, al-Qaeda would not have hit the USS *Cole* four weeks later, though many of us have wondered whether some spy may have informed al-Qaeda's high command that *Cole*'s rules of engagement, as laid down by the White House, stated, "No shooting unless we're shot at."

A petty officer on board the destroyer stated they were forbidden to open fire at the small boat that bombed her, as it approached from across the harbor, loaded to the gunwales with high explosive.

He further confirmed he had been ordered to turn an M60 machine gun *away* from a second small boat approaching. "In the military," he said, "it's like we're trained to hesitate now. On that day, if anyone on board had seen something wrong and opened fire, they probably would have been court-martialed."

Which leaves an uncomfortable truth: that the trained professionals in the *Cole*'s ship's company would have been in more trouble for shooting two goddamned terrorists than they were for losing seventeen American sailors.

And so she perished, with that gaping hole blasted into her hull amidships on the port side, fifty-six young Americans blown to hell, either killed or maimed or badly injured, and all in that terrible aftermath of silence, broken only by the screams and the cries and the whispers of the wounded.

You wonder about the universal fury aboard the USS *George Washington*? I will never forget it. And exactly what did our great civilian leader in Washington do about it? *Nothing.* That's what. Precisely as the terrorist leaders knew he wouldn't. Which, of course, is why they attacked us in the first place.

In so many ways, it was all so much worse than that. The hearts of everyone serving in the carrier strike group went out to the *Cole*. We wanted her to go home with dignity. There was a huge amount of discussion, mostly about how badly she was crippled. But we wanted her patched up, and to return to the United States, possibly under tow, but by a US warship.

In the opinion of the Americans who form the Tip of the Spear, how we all *look* to our enemies is monumentally important. We all wanted the wounded *Cole* to be borne home to the United States like a chief, symbolizing the spirit of the warrior. There are times when symbolism has a place.

Imagine how those guys felt, how emasculated. Like us, they were trying to operate with their hands tied behind their backs. This was the ship's company of a fighting destroyer, smashed out of the game, but determined to get home, and to bring their battered ship with them. I guess the infamous US Navy battle cry comes to mind, the one roared in defiance by the captain of the *Chesapeake* in the War of 1812: "Don't give up the ship!"

All of our plans to sail down and escort her north along the Red Sea and through the Suez Canal—with our strike fighters flying a constant combat air patrol high above her—came to nothing. They floated the destroyer onto a semi-submersible Norwegian heavy-lift salvage ship, the *Blue Marlin,* and hauled her all the way back from Aden, via South Africa, to her birthplace on the Pascagoula River, Mississippi, where she was rebuilt.

There was something so ignominious about the *Cole*'s return. What kind of a Navy had we become? Our commander-in-chief did not even comprehend that essential requirement of every national military force: the infusion of pride into all of its actions.

The *Cole* was battered, but not beaten. And she would return to the fray. She did, however, need to get home publicly, flying her colors, the flag of the United States of America. She ought not to have been strapped to the deck of a Norwegian heavy lifter, like a stricken passenger ferry.

Even the most powerful Navy in the world needs to confirm its battle readiness and willingness to engage any enemy. The crew requires the sure and certain knowledge that they are of value, with a correct sense of real purpose.

Any US commander should be empowered to open fire on any enemy he perceives as a threat. That's why, after years and years of intensive training, they made him a commander. Otherwise military morale cannot be maintained. I can state categorically that some of the best men in the US Navy left the service during those terribly disheartening years. I was among them, and we saw ourselves only as the remnants of the Reagan Revolution, when the great president embarked on his dream of an amazing fighting force, a six hundred–ship Navy. In the time between the retirement of President Reagan and the inauguration of George W. Bush, too much went wrong, and I was an eyewitness, with a front-row seat.

When you see something going drastically wrong with the United States, you're watching a major problem at the biggest corporation in the world: the biggest corporation there has ever been. And by that I mean US citizens getting murdered by military pygmies.

When something that unacceptable happens, there's only one place to look, and that's right at the top. Because you're going to find two things: (1) you have the wrong management, and (2) inevitably a crisis of leadership. Political Washington and corporate America are both filled with people masquerading as leaders.

Leaders are either born or highly trained. You cannot simply announce yourself a leader. You cannot pretend to be a leader, because leaders need to be men of clear vision who can identify, clarify, and issue attainable goals. It's no good announcing unattainable goals that can never be reached. And it's even worse to keep changing your mind, announcing goals and then canceling them.

In much of my time as a naval commander, the White House contained a bunch of men trying to instruct the military without ever having been there. "Okay . . . let's smash Saddam Hussein's air force tomorrow. No, sorry, let's not do that. Let's wait until the next day. No, let's give it another half-hour . . . No, we'd better cancel the entire thing."

That's not leadership. That's a dithering committee totally out of its depth, with no right to be influencing high office, never mind the commander-in-chief. President Reagan and President George W. Bush were both leaders in that they could hear the voice of the people, and they gave them what they wanted. Reagan understood they wanted the United States to kick Gadhafi's ass, and President Bush understood he was required to slam al-Qaeda.

Both missions were planned and executed, because both presidents were leaders with clear, attainable objectives. A few months after the *Cole* was hit, a US judge found the Sudanese government responsible for helping al-Qaeda carry out an unprovoked act of terrorism against the United States. *A US judge?* How about a US president! Or is that asking too much?

Once you get the wrong guy in the Big Chair, the vacillation never stops. Soon after the Norwegians set off on their journey to carry home the *Cole,* we also set sail out of the Gulf of Iran bound for the Red Sea and then the Mediterranean, steaming along the southern reaches with our remaining escorts.

Before we went, without a word to our civilian masters, we made a significant decision of our own. We understood we were shortly to be replaced by our twenty-five-year-old sister carrier USS *Dwight D. Eisenhower* (CVN-69), "Ike" to her friends, and one of the most battle-efficient warships in the Atlantic fleet. She'd spent more time on patrol in the Gulf than any other US carrier, with a long deployment during the first Gulf War.

We would almost certainly rendezvous with her somewhere in the Mediterranean Sea, where there would be a substantial amount of cross-decking (transporting supplies, equipment, ordnance, and aircraft parts, from the homegoing ship to the incoming warship bound for the Gulf).

This was an exercise the Navy was becoming increasingly expert in xecuting. The operational cuts made in those years had turned a culture

of improvisation into an art form. The fact was, we were short of everything, especially jet fuel and spare parts.

As such, we had to cannibalize aircraft prior to takeoff on almost every
operation we undertook, even the mirror-image strike missions. It was, I
suppose, just a part of the slow wrecking of President Reagan's carrier air
wings. It began with a severe cutback to our maintenance budgets. The
parts we needed became less and less available, and the mechanics and
aircraft engineers had begun taking aircraft down to the hangar on a daily
basis and stripping them apart.

This often involved quite important components that had to be deli-
cately removed and then manhandled to a crippled aircraft and fitted as
a replacement. Without that component, the Tomcat or Hornet simply
could not fly. Toward the end of our deployment there was a line of aircraft that had been taken below, just to be cannibalized, big strike fighters,
whose purpose had been reduced to that of a box of engine spares.

At the end of the decade we were not sufficiently well equipped, so
we just used two battered aircraft to make one. Often we did not have
sufficient jammer pods, which were absolutely crucial to us, enabling
US pilots to completely screw up the radar-homing capability of Saddam's missiles. We had to borrow them from each other, waiting while
the mechanics removed them from one aircraft and then fitted them to
another.

We were even out of night vision goggles. I saw guys waiting in line
for the catapults, borrowing goggles from the pilots who had just landed.
America's finest, kept on a kind of operational breadline, by an administration that did not consult them or, apparently, care about them.

I am certain, then, that you can imagine the size of the cross-decking
operation that finally took place in the middle of the Mediterranean Sea
when *Ike* met *George*. We were there for hours, transferring anything they
might need, leaving only the bare essentials for us to return across the
Atlantic to Norfolk, Virginia.

But there was one welcome-home gift about which she may never
learn. In the dying days of our own deployment, in the utmost secrecy,
we elected to flatten a critical nerve center in Saddam Hussein's integrated
air defense system, a large building situated seven miles north of the 32.30
line of latitude, just south of Baghdad. It was in an area from which we
were essentially banned.

The building housed Saddam's entire southern command decision-making operation, and they'd deliberately built it there, since they believed we were a squadron of pure-bred pansies who would not dare fly anywhere near the thirty-third parallel because it was against the international agreement. They understood the character of our president. They did not, however, understand the precise psyche of an American warrior.

They had stepped up their ground-to-air missile attacks on us, after al-Qaeda's successful hit on the USS *Cole*. We were uncertain how prepared the *Eisenhower* air wing would be for the number of illegal Iraqi missiles likely to be hurled at them during the first of their daily flights up into The Box.

So, with only a few days left of our time in the Gulf, we assembled a hit squad of a dozen strike fighters, eight F/A-18C Hornets, and four F-14B Tomcats. Our principal weapon was a 2,000-pound air-to-surface bomb fitted with the sensational latest guided bomb unit (GBU-31) installed in its JDAM tail-guidance system.

This is a big, bad, nasty weapon that can be hurled in quick succession from an aircraft making just one pass, at high speed, high altitude or low. It can't miss, and we planned to unleash it so it would hit at a ninety-degree strike angle: that's straight down, vertical impact. No defense known to man can stop that baby.

It delivers a diabolical explosive double whammy—kind of a *bah-boooom!* And then, even louder, a *bah-bah-booom!* Quick succession. To be perfectly honest, we felt there was nothing else left for us. They were firing missiles at us every day. It was a matter of time before they hit someone. We could not get permission to slam the building, in case there was a mosque or something nearby.

But neither did we think it reasonable to let the *Eisenhower* fliers come hurtling into a potential death trap, so we made an executive decision, based on the theory that it was better to ask for forgiveness afterward than to request permission now.

Also we considered that the thirty-fourth president of the United States, General Dwight D. himself, would have loved it, right behind that lopsided grin of his. Of course, if he'd been in the Oval Office, Saddam's entire air force and missile capability would have been well extinguished a long, long time ago.

We set off in the morning, headed west across the Gulf straight for the shores of Kuwait, our normal route. From there we flew on west along the Saudi border toward our tanker lanes where all twelve aircraft were refueled. At this point we turned onto a north-northeast bearing and flew fast for almost 150 miles, high over the An-Najah Desert, aiming for a launch point just south of 32.30N.

Staying well west of the Euphrates River, we were now flying through a zone devoid of Iraqi tracking. The Iraqis had no idea we were there. At a given point our little strike force split, the Hornets swinging left in a wide arc to the drop zone, my four Tomcats headed north directly toward Saddam's command center.

Details of the actual strike are still classified, but I will not easily forget the massive impact as the 2,000-pound bombs fired straight down into the building. The earth shuddered and the skies thundered, and then we could see the gigantic rings of dust, cement, and sand across the entire area, forming a huge billowing circle about one mile in diameter.

No one thought we'd completely destroyed Saddam's missile strike capability, but we'd sure as hell slowed him down. It would surely take months to reinstate his air command system.

Among the pilots there was a palpable sense of relief. We were dealing with nine years of frustration, nine years while we all sat and dodged his rockets, evaded the flak, and gritted our teeth. Nine years during which Saddam Hussein on a daily basis ordered his missile men, illegally, to open fire on us. Nine years when we were expressly forbidden to fire back at will. Nine years of humiliation and fury, embarrassment and sinking morale.

We all understood our actions would be frowned upon in the highest possible places, if and when news of our air strike ever leaked out. And if it did, I was never told. But I do remember the feeling of elation, after we had at last slammed the Lion of Babylon, even if we did sense simultaneously that this was one action we would never discuss with anyone. Unless, of course, we were begging for forgiveness.

And remember the time of year. It was October 2000, and the world had *two* current arch-villains, both guilty of genocide, Saddam Hussein and Slobodan Milosevic, the Serbian who had caused four wars and the deaths of possibly 200,000 people.

As war criminals go, Slobodan was right up there; not yet charged with crimes against humanity, but forced to operate in some kind of limbo. He was reported to be somewhere southwest of Belgrade, on the Adriatic coast near Montenegro. In the past couple of weeks, he had resigned from his position of president of Yugoslavia, after a major revolution in which both the Parliament building and the national television building were burned by the infuriated crowd.

In the broadest terms, Slobodan was characterized as the world's most wanted man, and the ruling powers in the White House decided—somewhat rashly, we thought—to grab the son of a bitch and cart him off to the United States in irons, then make him stand trial.

Once more, Washington's civilian hierarchy came up with a plan of such astounding vagueness and woolly thinking, it was hard for a trained carrier strike group to work out where to start. USS *George Washington* was on her way through the Suez Canal and would very shortly be passing a point west of Malta, some 360 miles south of the Adriatic port of Montenegro, where commandoes ought to be able to go ashore and seize the ex-president of Yugoslavia.

The reasoning was clear—at least to civilians. The carrier was trundling along with a fully armed air wing on board, she was escorted by several warships and a nuclear submarine, and there was a US Navy SEAL team embarked. Therefore, the operation should be strictly routine . . . just get in there and snatch Slobbo, right?

Wrong. We would do it, but an operation like that requires the highest possible degree of planning, somewhere along the following lines.

1. An address for Milosevic with detailed charts showing entry routes and exit strategy.
2. Level of armed guards surrounding him, and the dangers of killing him if too much force is required (like high explosive to gain entry).
3. Strategy for the landing, since the carrier draws maybe thirty or forty feet of water and is the size of a Yugoslavian town (i.e., not unobtrusive).
4. Do the SEALs hit the beach from a helicopter drop, or paddle in, using inflatable boats?
5. Are the close coastal waters patrolled or swept by radar?

6. Land transport. If Milosevic is in residence far from the shore, how do the guys get to it?

7. Is his building equipped with anti-aircraft fire and might the SEALs need to land and then walk into the ops area?

8. Pinpoint the surface-to-air missile sites around the city, in case we need to (a) send in a few strike fighters to take them out, or (b) take out just one single site, to get a helo down for the getaway.

9. Faced with either killing Slobbo or just leaving him, because escape has been somehow rendered impossible, do we gun him down or just leave ? This must be clarified.

10. Is there any help or cooperation in the city, or are we on our own?

11. Is the SEAL team unit commander happy? He will not send his guys on a suicide mission.

It seemed like no one had even thought of consulting the SEALs. We just had this half-assed instruction, emanating from the National Security Council, to kidnap Milosevic. Our high command immediately convened a strategy meeting down in the strike cell.

I was included in the group because of the near-certain requirement for air cover to protect the SEALs. That was my specialty. For the next several days we tried to hammer out a plan, utilizing every possible form of intelligence, from CIA and military sources.

For us, this was an intensely serious operation. No one gets any credit if SEALs are killed. Coronado hates it, the Navy hates it, and worse, the public hates it. I personally worked with the special forces for a solid eighteen hours a day, trying to formulate a workable plan for kidnapping the world's most wanted man.

As the USS *George Washington* swung hard to starboard, up into the Ionian Sea headed for the "heel" of Italy and the Adriatic, we examined every possibility. But no one was certain where the bastard was stationed. We had leads, we had spies, we had information, guesses, tip-offs from the police, and God knows what else. And in the end we had it pretty well narrowed down. We knew where old Slobbo was. Nearly.

On roughly the ninth day of operational planning, everything jumped into perspective. *Here comes the ninety-nine, shut down.* They canceled it. We're not going. Someone in Washington had funked it yet again. So we just kept steaming west through the Med, toward the Atlantic, a gigantic US carrier strike force, whose achievements in six months added up to precisely zero.

That was the way our commander-in-chief apparently wanted it. There was little regret on board the carrier that there would shortly be a changing of the guard in the White House. So little had been done to assist the military, and a great deal that was detrimental. It did not much matter what happened now. The damage was done.

The message to us from Washington had been "Do more with less." In the end, we did *nothing* with less. Someone had an undeniable vision of cutting down the military, to turn the great Reagan military engine into a police force. While we always retained our traditional respect for the office of the presidency, it was hard to understand the current philosophy.

Because on board the big carriers, we went from twenty-four battle-ready Tomcats to ten. From two embarked F-14 fighter squadrons to one. President Reagan would not have liked that.

## STAND UP AND TAKE YOUR GRADE

I have concentrated my opening two chapters on the events surrounding my final tour of duty in the US Navy—my beloved alma mater that had thus far been my whole life, and for which I would have laid down that life, any hour of any day.

In fact, the day I finally understood I could not remain in dark blue was without doubt the saddest I had ever known. I'd been in the US Navy since I was eighteen, and in the year 2000 I was thirty-five years old. Desolate—that's the only word I can use to describe the feeling on that melancholy day. More than ten years later, it still is.

The Navy, to me, represented the way things ought to be done. Her past heroes were my gods, her traditions were forever my guiding light, the iron discipline, the teaching, the training, the moral and military standards, and the chain of command were all I knew.

But because I could not bear to watch the systematic dismantling of the greatest seagoing armed force the world has ever known, I had to go. I may as well record that in the final moments, alone with my thoughts, when I comprehended fully that my letter of resignation was going through, I retreated to my study. And very privately, very quietly, wept.

No naval officer in all the tumultuous and glittering history of that branch of the US military ever went with more reluctance. With more of a broken heart. I have never gotten over it.

I have examined microscopically the situation in my own naval air wing during that late summer and autumn, my final operational days in an aircraft carrier, and the events that were slowly engulfing us all, as the White House steadily took us down.

And I have applied two basic tests to the entire scenario: (1) What did *they,* the politicians, do? And *why?* (2) What would *we,* the military, have done, had the decisions been ours to make? And *why?* The results were very different, and decisive.


> ### *Leadership*

The US naval system of creating battle commanders is probably the most searching test of character and ability in all the world. In that, I tentatively exclude Great Britain's Royal Navy, although its traditional willingness to fight was badly undermined by the country's tragic thirteen-year socialist government from 1997 to 2010.

The American midshipman, from his very first moment at Annapolis, must prove himself every single day until he retires. No one is spared the endless necessity to not just say you can do something, but to get out there and prove yourself. I, of course, realize that applies to every branch of my service, be it aircraft carriers, surface warships, or submarines.

However, my acknowledged expertise is as a Naval Aviator, and I intend to illustrate my point that the Navy leadership system is absolutely superior to the civilian method. I will point out briefly what is required from any officer with determination to command, and I speak in particular of the elite battle flying corps of TOPGUN.

Aside from the obvious truth that only one applicant in 100,000 actually makes it through from Annapolis to Navy pilot, to strike fighter pilot, to TOPGUN, the position of TOPGUN graduate and strike fighter weapons and tactics instructor is a rarefied place.

The men who lead our air wing strike forces are subjected to a searching examination every time they bring that fighting Tomcat or Hornet out of the sky and hammer it down on the flight deck. Every time they come in to land they are personally assessed—marked with comments and awarded a grade. That's not once a week or once a month. That's every single time they ram that hook into the arresting wires.

There are no recognized ranks on the flight deck. It matters not whether you're a young lieutenant, a lieutenant commander, or even an admiral. A relentless assessment of your performance at the controls of that strike fighter will be made by the landing signal officer (LSO) who brings you in. An accomplished fighter pilot himself, he very definitely knows of what he speaks. He has already earned your gratitude and your profound respect, even if you do refer to him as "Paddles" on account of his operational signaling equipment.

In the debriefing room below, again no rank will make anything one iota easier for you than for anyone else. You're not only rankless, you're nameless. When the LSO comes through that door, I don't care if you're newly qualified or if you're Admiral Chester Nimitz, just come in from the great hangar above, you will stand up and take your grade.

And that's what you do. You stand to attention in a manner that conveys the utmost respect for the man with the clipboard. And the words trip off his tongue. And you might be thirty-seven years old and he might be twenty-four. It makes no difference.

*Victory one-o-three . . . High fast start, not enough power on the comedown in the middle . . . fly-through down in close, low at the ramp—for a no-grade one-wire landing.*

You probably guessed what he really meant to say was, "That really sucked." And he might easily have added, "And if you go on like that we're going to get rid of you." And this exercise in humiliation takes place in front of everyone.

There's no hiding place in my game. It's all about accountability. Nobody gets a pass, from the top to the bottom. Our unspoken creed, the one they start to teach us on the first day at Annapolis, is "I hold you accountable. And you hold me accountable in return."

The chilling words of the LSO after a moderate landing are just part of daily life. But we don't see them as embarrassing. We all want that feedback. If I'm screwing up I need to know. If that LSO doesn't tell me what I'm doing wrong, I might go out there and kill myself. Or worse yet, someone else.

The LSO understands I was doing about a thousand things as that aircraft came screaming in to land. He knows full well my eyes were darting everywhere: airspeed, altitude, watching the ball, nose up, nose down, wind speed, wave height, the rise and fall of the carrier deck, the lights, the center line, the churning white wake directly below, I'm just left, too far in the crosswind.

Above all I'm aiming at a landing area that is steaming away from me, especially if there's little wind and the ship has to make her own, accelerating forward. I'm eight hundred yards out and through the radio I can hear the LSO shout, "Foul deck! Foul deck!" Which probably means another aircraft is still in the landing area, right in my path. I need to make instant allowances for that. I may have to hit the afterburners and take a pass until the deck is clear.

This is no game for men in short pants. And the LSO understands that. He understands everything that is going on, and he probably knows perfectly well I've done this more than four hundred times and *never* received a no-grade. But the standards of Naval Aviators remain inviolate. The LSO will deliver his verdict without flinching, whoever the pilot, whatever his record and experience. For us there is no other way.

So if you ever see a film clip of a strike fighter making an aircraft-carrier landing, or you ever manage to stand on the flight deck of *Ike* or *George,* or *Big John* (USS *John F. Kennedy*) or *Connie* (USS *Constellation*), let the stark and pitiless words of the US Navy stand before you: *stand up and take your grade.* Because those words hold us together, in good times and in bad.

When the Navy appoints a commander or indeed issues any promotion, there are no mistakes. Every officer moving up the ladder has proven himself, over and over. Which makes a very interesting comparison with life in politics and in corporate America, where CEOs move from one massive job to another, apparently regardless of their success in their prior situation.

These days I expect everyone can think of a CEO, especially in the financial world, whose incompetence was little short of breathtaking, men who have caused catastrophic failure, and who, upon close examination, ought never to have been there in the first place.

Those characters, with their multimillion-dollar salaries, would have lasted in the US Navy for approximately seven minutes. Not for years and years of grotesque and self-serving shenanigans, hiding and evading, assisted by other men who were only half certain of their talents.

Someone should have marched into a few Wall Street boardrooms with a clipboard and demanded, "Stand up and take your grade!" Because if they had, the shattering financial collapse of 2008 most certainly would not have happened.

Between 1999 and 2008, Wall Street oligarchs moved through a period of bounteous greed and acquisitive lifestyles. It all ended in tears, in a succession of headlong crashes into bankruptcy, or near bankruptcy, and the losses of billions of other people's dollars.

It happened because of an obvious and acute lack of understanding by Wall Street CEOs of a financial system that was running so fast it ultimately disappeared up its own backside. Looking back to 2008, we were in some kind of acronym hell with the CDOs (collateralized debt obligation—subprime), the CDSs (credit default swaps), NINJA (no income, no job, and no assets) mortgages, SIVs, CMBSs, CLOs, Alt-A mortgages, LBOs (leveraged buyouts), and RMBSs.

It was all so suspect and so complicated, it was obvious that half of the men who should have been slamming on the brakes had no idea where the brakes were. Worse yet, they did not recognize the looming iceberg to which they were headed at high speed. As one brilliant Wall Street wag once observed, even the *Titanic* swerved.

I should perhaps issue a reminder right here that both Wall Street in the 2000s and the *Titanic* in 1912 were commanded by civilians. So far as I know there is no record of a US battle commander steering a warship straight into an iceberg.

The truth very quickly emerged that a whole raft of these CEOs simply did not understand the subject of the new investment world. They could not comprehend they were diving in front of an express locomotive to pick up a $50 bill.

Most of them were warned over and over of the dangers, but the culture of greed prevailed. And they all hit the iceberg together. This kind of acute dumbness could not possibly have happened in the US Navy, or any other branch of the American armed forces. We'd have found those guys out long, long ago. It would not, could not, have happened.

Which brings us back directly to the point of leadership. How in God's name did major Wall Street corporations end up with guys at the helm who did not fully comprehend the subject, the pitfalls, the dangers, and the possibility of financial ruin?

The answer is simple. Because these quasi-leaders somehow convinced their boards of directors that they were real leaders, men who could take the firm forward. They plainly managed to stay in their big chairs, in that soft civilian way, by coercing, bribing, glad-handing, and bullying.

They also had some kind of expertise in cozying up to the press, whose judgment generally is absurd—not because they are particularly dumb, but because their main interest is the value of the "story."

The media pretend to be fearless seekers of truth, but that's not so. They would rather make an argument that reads well, in an inflammatory way, than to concentrate on being right. And these two lines of expertise are very different. Reading the press about Lehman Brothers boss Dick Fuld in the early years of the new century, Christ, you would have thought he was some kind of Roman emperor, rather than a guy on course to cause the biggest bankruptcy in the history of finance.

Whatever corporate America was doing in those rather heady years, it was flat-out stupid. I state this as one who saw it coming and acted upon my own conclusions. Out of the service, my first position was with a Washington firm, owned by Lehman, and like any half-decent naval officer I spotted the iceberg a long way out. I walked out, long before the crash.

Meanwhile, I'll assert this one truth: the military way of selecting its leaders is about 1,000 percent more effective than the civilian way. We'd have made Richard S. Fuld get in that cockpit and land that strike fighter in front of a squad of LSOs.

There'd have been no hiding away behind a board of directors, no promoting people to places where they were, like him, out of their depth, and beholden to the boss. No, sir. *Fuld! Stand up and take your grade!* We'd have found out all about him, in short order.

The second critical point about naval leadership is that you cannot come in sideways. Civilians move from one industry to another, apparently effortlessly, entering a brand-new field of endeavor at the highest level, starting off as a vice president. If a civilian CEO applied to the Navy for a post as an admiral, they'd probably send for men in white coats (that's not, by the way, dress whites).

We do not entertain the idea of anyone taking any position of command without the most searching test of the applicant's ability. If a serving admiral decided he wanted to return to his old profession as a fighter pilot, he'd be required to start over, right over, at the bottom of the pile, along with everyone else.

And then he would have to work his way back up the ladder, every day forced to stand up in that debriefing room to take his grade. As required under US naval law. In our game no one gets away with anything. No one ever tries. We're not, after all, civilians, and our standards are not the same. We've been taught and brought up differently.

The situation in politics is even more acute. Men who are good at making speeches are suddenly thrust into situations of critical command, surrounded by men who depend on them for their own livelihoods and are reluctant to argue.

The White House of the 1990s is a case that begs to be aired. Because in the year 2000, it was given a thousand warnings by the military about the dangers of al-Qaeda, and their considered opinion that the United States was soft on terrorism. That administration, albeit unknowingly, was dealing with a chain of circumstances that would lead in the next few months to untold tragedy—the *Cole,* 9/11, and the war in Iraq.

Every high-ranking naval officer I have ever spoken to regards those events as utterly avoidable, if only we had slammed Saddam's air force and frightened the life out of the Islamic extremist organizations. Certainly the war never would have happened, because Saddam's defiance would have been cut off at the pass, and anyhow, he no longer would have possessed the capability of air warfare.

The truth was the United States at the time lacked real leadership. These politicians did not understand how to deal with these murderous terrorists. We did, however, understand, and they should have listened. Suffice to say none of them could possibly have charmed their way into the highest seat in the US Navy, because they all would have been required to stand up and take their grades. That's when we discover who's who.

### ➤ *Management*

I do not know precisely who assisted our commander-in-chief in allowing Saddam Hussein to go on doing anything he wanted. But I do know there were some highly intelligent people on the National Security Council: lawyers, financiers, and intellects. The question remains: Did anyone have the experience to understand the mind-set of those whose principal objective in this life was to smash into the United States and force the US military out of the Middle East? And to obliterate Israel while they were at it?

You can very easily convince people of your wisdom if you happen to sit in high political office. However, you may not be right, you may not have the firsthand experience to comprehend the warped, fanatical psyches of these terrorists. In fact, I don't think anyone can fully comprehend terrorists until they've faced their missiles and artillery being blasted at US forces on a daily basis.

The phrase "fired a missile" is a pretty facile description of what it's really like—watching a fiery steel projectile blasted out of a launcher anchored to the floor of a foreign desert by half-crazed tribal warriors, whose one objective is to smash it straight through the fuselage of your aircraft, explode the warhead, and probably incinerate you and your RIO.

To get it completely, you need to be at the controls, muttering the words "holy shit!" to yourself, yelling for the chaff, hurling your aircraft left or right, ramming home the throttles, knowing that if you screw it up, you'll almost certainly be dead in the next few seconds.

That's knowledge. That's real insight. That's when you have a serious handle on your enemy, and on what he is most certainly capable of. That's known as understanding the subject.

And when the entire air wing of one of your biggest aircraft carriers, and all of their senior commanders, are telling the administration their foe has to be stopped, and they are ready to do so immediately, it is probably unwise to ignore them.

If you truly believe they do not know what they are talking about, and you propose to do precisely the opposite, then you are almost certainly steaming into some kind of hell—the *Cole,* the Twin Towers, and ultimately the war with Saddam's Iraq. It should all be filed away in a big folder labeled "wrong management." Because, like it or not, that's what you have.

Consider for a few moments the personnel the US Navy would bring to the table if they had to decide whether to take out a particular enemy: probably three admirals, one of them a former carrier strike group commander, plus the commander of a nuclear submarine fleet.

There'd be a couple of captains of surface warships with experience of the waters surrounding the targets. There'd be fighter pilots, veterans with a record of action over the territory, and there'd be representatives of the special forces who may be required to go in first. SEALs, that is. There'd also be at least two senior officers from the Pentagon.

Their decision would be crisp, definite, and attainable. No unclear areas.

> ### Planning

Civilians do not know how to plan. They think they do. They go through some kind of a charade trying to convince one another that they know. But they do not understand how we do it. And that's what matters. You can take four civilians and ask them to submit a plan for any operation: financial, political, marketing, advertising, anything you like. And all four of them would come up with a different plan.

Give the same data to four of my commanders, and they'd all come up with the same one, because we have a huge database detailing mistakes from the past. Every commander knows what happened before: this didn't work, this went wrong three times, this is only good if you don't lose an aircraft, this is too risky, this has been used and cost too many lives, this takes too long, this is inaccurate, this is okay but too dependent on good weather, if it rains we're dead, this is hopeless in a bright moon, we'd have to postpone.

The military undertakes the most breathtaking operations, and the planning has to be seen to be appreciated. Its objective is always clear, measurable, and attainable. Especially those hatched and executed by the SEALs. The difference between us and normal citizens is that our databases are there for everyone. If there's been a foul-up anywhere in the comparable past, we will not make it again.

We do not have people trying to be more clever than anyone else. We only have people who want the mission to succeed, and for colleagues to do as well as they possibly can. That, again, is how we're taught. It's all we understand.

The checklists would frighten the life out of a NASA computer: the timing, the kit, the weapons, the bombs, and missiles required. Every aspect of our plan was learned, gleaned from someone else's mistake. Every last item was based on the past and things that went wrong. We ask every possible "What if?"

We even have meetings to plan how to present the plan, just so everyone knows precisely what's going on. No mistakes. And we never forget: our execution is better on time with a good plan than running late with a perfect plan.

IN CIVILIAN LIFE, especially in politics and commerce, there are too many people trying to show themselves to be superior, holding information too close to the chest, trying to be the most brilliant person at the table. That's a breed that is totally foreign to the US Navy. And quite obviously it is counterproductive in almost every case. In the US Navy we do not have agendas. We have objectives. We sometimes refer to them as E squared. That's E to the second power: Execution Excellence.

Our culture is perfectly simple. It's the relentless pursuit of perfection, built on four bedrocks: vision, leadership, communication, and teamwork. They're all important, but excellence lives at the intersection of those four principles. You need them all. By themselves, they are not enough.

I have been one of that rarefied breed of Naval Aviators who made it to TOPGUN. That's just about the pinnacle of my profession. I can swear on my most solemn honor that the most joyful and satisfying achievement of my many months in the job came when I succeeded in teaching one of my students to be better than I was.

That was the highlight of my career as an instructor—that one shining moment when a kid came along, and I taught him how to be the best there is. He knows who he is, and he'll make admiral one day. The Navy never misses talent like that. Not one of us begrudges him that talent.

He's joined a system geared to locate and then nurture men like him. And it all comes back to planning, learning from the past, and utilizing every aspect of our time in the Navy together.

The National Security Council did not have the right plans in place when Saddam began to step drastically over the foul line. No one had worked out precisely what to do, come the day the chief of naval operations or whoever in the Pentagon declared the Iraqi despot had finally gone too far.

It should, of course, have been right in front of their eyes—a solid document that laid out the exact moment when any US president says, "Okay, guys, that's it. The military on the ground out there are saying he's overstepped the mark, and they want to remove his air force forthwith. Our plan has always been to make that operation a go, when these circumstances arose."

But there was no plan. No one knew what the hell to do. No one even knew whether to listen to us. The result was, of course, chaos. And tragedy. And heartbreak, death, and sorrow, on a scale not seen for many years. And all because we had a leader in the White House who was not a leader at all. A guy without military vision, or a plan, or the ability to come up with the right one, fast. Just like all those Wall Street bankers who rode at the head of their troops, leading them blindly into total disaster.

No one knew better than us what should be done about Iraq. But the politicians in Washington did not want to know what we thought. This refusal to heed our warnings and advice was nothing short of pure arrogance, foisted upon us, the Tip of the American Spear, by men who scarcely knew how to salute correctly.

## ▶ Succession

Succession is constantly on the mind of the highest command of the US Navy: the handing over of the torch to a newly trained younger generation. And no one, in all the years of military history, has ever done it better than us.

Remember there are 5,000 personnel on board a Nimitz-class carrier as it steams back and forth to the Iranian Gulf. Every three years that ship's company, and the air wing, changes over: different pilots, flight-deck crews, and sailors driving us forward.

Is that not absolutely incredible? A 5,000-man turnover in thirty-six months, without missing a beat? You think that's some kind of a fluke? A bit of luck that just happens? Trust me, it's not. It's the culmination of years of intricate planning, promoting the best onward and upward, every man making certain his replacement is as good as himself.

In the US Navy, succession is a matter of life and death. I must make certain the man who succeeds me knows everything I know. I'm not envious of him, and he's not envious of me. I'm not trying to make certain everyone misses me when I'm gone. I'm trying to make certain there are no screwups when I'm not there to prevent them.

I realize that if this happens, no one is going to blame me. No one will know whether I taught my successor properly. But I will know that somehow I failed my buddies, that a disaster happened I should have foreseen long ago. And it would not make it any easier, just because I was not held publicly culpable.

I guess it's called esprit de corps, and it's badly lacking in corporations, where *no one* wants his successor to be as good as he was, in any given job. Departing personnel are far too busy keeping their knowledge to themselves, and that's a luxury no one in the US Navy could possibly afford.

If they could, I guess we'd have aircraft carriers running aground, up the beaches of Saudi Arabia, or colliding with each other, knocking down oil rigs, pilots bombing Istanbul, and God knows what else. But we don't, because we all make absolutely certain our replacements are as good as we ever were.

I realize there is a level of separateness involved in rival US corporations that is not present in the Navy, where we all play essentially on the same team. But I have witnessed a level of underhand behavior among people leaving corporations, which is just north of honest.

In a sense they cannot be entirely blamed, though I cannot speak for their consciences. However, corporate management should make it their business to ensure that no one reaches a position where they alone understand a critical aspect of the firm's business. Where they alone have the contacts and know-how to make that part of the operation work.

The US Navy would never in a million years allow that to happen. Everyone knows everything. That's how we slay the dragon of self-centered greed and opportunism. It does not exist in the Navy, because it cannot exist. For instance, navigating through the treacherous channels of the Strait of Hormuz, with the sullen shores of Iran to the north, is mind-blowingly tricky.

There are a myriad of tiny islands and rocky headlands all around the Musandam Peninsula, and a fine line of navigation straight down the middle of the channel, beyond which, to the north, foreign ships are forbidden by the ayatollahs who run Iran.

As we move north up the Gulf we are headed into fairly shallow waters, which are detailed on one of the most intricate charts in the world. There are pipelines, oil fields, gas fields, rights-of-way, loading terminals, restricted areas, sandbanks, and heaven knows what else.

Do you think Navy leadership would allow all this knowledge to be in the hands of one or two men? Of course not. The navigation officer in the *George Washington* would share this with at least three assistants, not to mention the boatswain, helmsman, and the executive officer, as well as the captain, and possibly three naval warfare officers. There'd be a half dozen other operational aircraft carriers with men on board of similar learning.

My point is that this is a basic strategy of excellent management: never allow too much power into the hands of one person. To illustrate the point, I know of a shipping corporation in New York that allowed one long-serving executive to handle its biggest annual contract with a huge public oil corporation. He did it for half of his working life and never was required to share his knowledge and contacts with a younger executive.

As a result, when he retired, the contract was lost. It was transferred to a friend of the oil company's president. Whose fault? The self-interested exec, who had no regard for his colleagues? Or the management of the corporation, who should have been grooming the successors for years, making the introductions, ensuring everyone knew one another as well as what the future held.

All over the United States corporations depend on a particular executive for their daily contact with major clients. The same applies to Wall Street, broker to broker, client to investment banker, billions of dollars' worth of business hanging by the most tenuous of threads. And every day someone walks off with a major account to a new corporation, bringing with him a personal gold mine, the rightful property of his former employers.

It's all in the technique of management, and the endless study of succession. Corporate America would be well advised to pay attention to the way the military operates, because it is very definitely superior.

As for the politicians, well, by the end of the year 2000, those men on the White House committees had proved what a natural-born catastrophe they were. For future reference, all politicians somehow inveigled into positions of power and influence over their own military should take one single leaf out of the playbooks of Ronald Reagan and George W. Bush: pay attention to all international threats and dangers; listen carefully to the experienced voices of your top commanders; heed the instincts of the men who operate at the Tip of the American Spear—and act accordingly.

## CHAPTER 3

# Hippity-Hop in
# the Garrison of the Immortals

Having spent two chapters in praise of the men who wear dark blue, I intend now to visit the stern and moral training that every future naval officer must undergo. Concurrently I shall highlight the very root of Wall Street's problems, the part that puts them on an extremely suspect course right from the start.

I refer to the area through which some of Wall Street's finest charged blindly, before the colossal crash of 2008—the part that deals with character and honesty or otherwise, greed and self-interest.

That's the part that allows men who should have known better deliberately to mislead the investing public. I point up the absence of real teamwork, particularly certain CEOs, whose teams consisted largely of men like themselves: slightly duplicitous and very far removed from the hardworking engine rooms of their ships.

It was, of course, all in the interest of self-aggrandizement, gigantic cash bonuses, helicopters, art collections, and multiple homes worth tens of millions of dollars.

Thereafter, I will establish the difference between men like that and the young men who begin a far more important career dedicated to defending our nation, at whatever cost that may demand. I intend to start at the bedrock of the American system, which locates and trains such men, and to point out the obvious chasm between becoming a US naval officer and becoming a Wall Street financier.

I have thrived in both arenas, and each is utterly dependent on mathematical skills. Do not for one split second even consider that the Wall Street types are in any way superior. Because I assure you, they're not. They're richer, and sometimes more cunning and ruthless. But not when the chips are really down. Not when it's life or death.

That's why we have these enormous recessions and stock-market crashes. We do not, however, in an endlessly dangerous world, habitually get conquered by some other nation because the Navy has somehow screwed it up. No, sir. And it's essentially a question of duty, not money. In our game, character has to be king.

Allow me to return to the formative years of my education, because there we will find the earliest point at which the US military parts company with those whose ambitions involve only acquiring money.

And I should perhaps confirm that I personally heard the wisdom of my tutors with only two-thirds of my academic grasp. The other third was mostly deafened by the vividly imagined roar of those mighty Pratt & Whitney TF30 engines of Grumman's supersonic two-seater F-14 Tomcat, the US Navy's own multi-role strike fighter.

IT BEGAN WHEN I was around fourteen, sitting at the back of the class at my small country school in rural Ohio. On a low bookshelf, with three glass panels, right next to me was a pile of magazines. Idly I picked one up and there on the jacket was a color photograph of the Tomcat, climbing steeply, afterburners glowing, six Phoenix missiles beneath the wings, and an aircraft carrier in the distance. There was just one word on the big jet's fuselage: Navy.

Right there I had a sudden intuitive leap of understanding that caused me, instantly, to shelve all plans to become an architect.

At that very moment I understood with absolute clarity that I needed to join the Navy, and also that I felt an unstoppable compulsion to become a Navy fighter pilot. Not just to fly any old jet, but to fly that jet, the F-14 Tomcat, the one in the picture.

Carefully I ripped the jacket off the magazine, folded it up, slipped it into my jacket pocket, and took it home. Thirty-four years later it's still in my study, a bit worse for wear, but framed and hung over my desk.

That picture inspired me throughout my teenage years. I hardly ever went anywhere without it. In my mind, it set me apart. I was operating in a class full of kids in Little Miami High School who in every other respect were just like me: from average parents, and everyone walked to school, past endless midwestern cornfields. I actually lived right next to one.

There was nothing very different about any of us. We were just country kids trying to make it through with halfway decent grades. Except for me. That Tomcat photograph signified to me that I was already in the Navy. No one else knew a strike fighter from a lawnmower. I was an expert, a future pilot just waiting in line for my first command.

Did any of the others know that this was the largest, heaviest fighter ever to leave the flight deck of a US aircraft carrier? Who else knew the function of its variable-sweep wings? Were they aware of its opening role in the Vietnam War? And how about its air-to-air missiles, the Phoenix, the AIM-7 Sparrow, radar homing, or the AIM-9 heat-seeking Sidewinder?

Had any of them ever sat in the 360-degree all-around-vision cockpit, opened fire with the Vulcan M61 20mm gun, knowing that if we got hit, both I and my RIO would be blasted out of the cockpit in our Martin-Baker GRU-7A rocket-propelled ejection seats?

The hell they did. None of them even understood that the chaff dispensers were situated way down in the belly, at the tip of the tail. Fat lot of good they'd have been in the face of incoming missiles.

This was an aircraft designed to act effectively in every possible area of air combat, and I awakened most mornings in its two-seater cockpit, sometimes a bit tired after the nightly dogfights. The bombing raids were less draining. How could my knowledge of this stupendous aircraft not make me different from the rest?

I heard those engines howl in every aspect of my student life. Especially when I was bored. I even heard them in the middle of school basketball games. I'd come in to land with one engine on fire in the middle of a poetry class. Occasionally I'd shoot one of my air-to-air missiles while someone was attempting to teach me English literature or even grammar.

It's a miracle that I can spell. My full-time occupation as a fourteen-year-old jet fighter pilot kept me otherwise extremely busy.

All the time, right until I reached sixteen, there was only one word in my mind: Annapolis, which stood five hundred miles to the east on the shores of Chesapeake Bay. Annapolis, home of the United States Naval Academy. I had to get in there.

Fortunately, I had no idea of the gigantic step it would be to burst out of a cornfield in Maineville, Ohio, way out there in Warren County, and make it to the greatest naval academy on earth, alma mater of the legends, Nimitz and Halsey and Rickover; Admiral Raymond Spruance, one of the heroes of the Battle of Midway, commander-in-chief Pacific Fleet. All of the old Spruance-class destroyers were commissioned in his honor.

The legendary WWII Pacific commander Admiral Arleigh "31-Knot" Burke is buried in the Academy cemetery. Most of the modern guided missile destroyers in the US Navy were placed in a single class named in his honor. Admiral Burke's nickname was the result of his propensity to steam toward the battle with boiler-bursting ferocity.

The sacred bond between the midshipmen of Annapolis represented a lifelong trust. Chester Nimitz and Raymond Spruance, in company with the aircraft carrier commander, Admiral Richmond K. Turner, and the commander-in-chief submarines Pacific Admiral Charles A. Lockwood, ultimately were buried in adjacent graves at the Golden Gate National Cemetery in San Bruno, California—the result of a four-way pact forged in the darkest days of WWII in the Pacific.

I understood back in the late '70s, with my thoughts fixated on gaining entry to that holy place in Maryland, that I must somehow make the leap into this fabled garrison of the immortals, all the way from my tiny Ohio village, whose hitherto most revered resident was the chairman of a tractor corporation.

Unsurprisingly, I became an enthusiastic participant in my school's Naval Junior Reserve Officers Training Corps (NJROTC). In class I knuckled down to its excellent national courses in naval history, sharp in my dark blue uniform, though profoundly disinterested in the battle strategy of Ray Spruance's destroyers. If it didn't fly sensationally fast, I considered it someone else's problem.

In my junior year they made me senior cadet. And the next year I graduated in the top ten with honors out of 250 students. Unsurprisingly,

I applied immediately for admission to the United States Naval Academy and was frankly appalled when they wrote back and informed me I had been selected to undergo a one-year course at the official Naval Academy Preparatory School in Newport, Rhode Island.

*Preparatory school! What's that all about? I'm trying to get into Annapolis.* However, I was swiftly informed this was a hugely important accolade, a near guarantee for a young future officer to march straight into the Academy one year hence, with a head start on many other applicants.

Placated, I packed my bags and headed east to the shores of Narragansett Bay. They were right. This was a really big deal, located, as part of the vast naval educational complex around Naval Station Newport. Instantly into uniform, we marched everywhere laden with books, to class at six thirty in the morning, and from there we marched everywhere else. I was Seaman Jeff Lay, and I worked hard all year, before being awarded a place at the United States Naval Academy in Annapolis.

It was early July 1983, and my parents drove me out of the long, flat plains of the Midwest. I crossed the Ohio River for the first time in my life. The journey took us over the Allegheny Mountains and into northwest Virginia, where we ran onto the main highway toward Baltimore, an almost straight shot into the old coastal town of Annapolis on the shores of the Severn River, my Holy Grail for as long as I could recall.

We drove through the main gates, and I asked my parents to leave me and return home to Ohio. This was such an intensely private moment for me, the realization of a thousand dreams, that I somehow could bear no intrusion into these most profound moments.

I just stood there for a while, right outside Bancroft Hall, the largest college dormitory in the world. I wondered whether I might just be swallowed up entirely by this majestic and grandiose campus, a place so indoctrinated in naval folklore that Commodore John Paul Jones is interred here.

I had with me an illustrated guide to the 338-acre campus, and while I'd studied it many times before and seen the glittering names that identified the halls, to be actually standing there, in the middle of all that history, was to me a humbling experience.

There was Ricketts Hall, named for graduate Admiral Claude V. Ricketts, the gunnery officer credited with saving the battleship USS *West Virginia* after she was hit and burned at Pearl Harbor.

There was the Halsey Field House, named for Fleet Admiral William F. "Bull" Halsey (Class of 1904), WWII hero of the South Pacific. Rickover Hall, named for Admiral Hyman G. Rickover, father of the US nuclear navy (Class of 1922).

I stood in front of the Nimitz Library with its 600,000 books—all in the name of Fleet Admiral Chester W. Nimitz, commander-in-chief Pacific Fleet and Pacific Ocean Areas, World War II (Class of 1905).

Directly behind Bancroft stands the gigantic King Hall, the midshipmen's 12,000-meals-daily dining area, named in honor of the five-star Fleet Admiral Ernest King (Class of 1901). Like me, Admiral King was from Ohio, a little town up on the shores of Lake Erie, about as far away from Maineville as you can get in my state and still be in America. His grave is in the Academy cemetery.

I noted the main road right through the North Severn Complex was named after the four-star Admiral Thomas Kinkaid, the "fighting admiral" of the great WWII carrier battles, commander Allied Naval Forces and the US Seventh Fleet, WWII (Class of 1908).

Dahlgren Hall was named for Rear Admiral John A. Dahlgren, the Civil War leader who revolutionized US naval gunnery with shell guns and muzzle-loading cannons manufactured in the Navy's first foundry, which he personally established.

Even the midshipmen lounge, the Hart Room, was named for a naval legend, submarine fleet commander Admiral Thomas C. Hart (Class of 1897), same graduating year as William D. Leahy, the first admiral to hold five-star rank and the first Chairman of the Joint Chiefs of Staff under President Franklin D. Roosevelt. Leahy Hall, named for him, is the Academy's office of admissions for new prospective candidates.

Every yard was steeped in storied moments and events in America's naval history, commemorated in buildings, monuments, memorials, and statues. Was I intimidated? Are you kidding! I stood six feet, three inches when I arrived in Annapolis. At the moment I walked into Bancroft Hall I felt about two feet, three inches. It was impossible not to feel overwhelmed, just standing beneath Bancroft's mighty rotunda, in the towering spiritual presence of the great commanders who had lived, studied, and worked here before.

But very quickly, a strange thing happened. Yes, they expected everyone to start jumping around, obeying commands, rules, and regulations.

But through it all, the emotional battering, the unreasonable demands, the mind-bending traditions, I sensed they wanted the best for everyone. They wanted us to step into the boots of the great ones, to become leaders ourselves, masters and commanders.

All 1,200 of us lining up for the summer indoctrination course were called plebes, from the Latin, whose modern translation means the lowest possible class of Roman citizen (*plebeius,* derivative *plebian*). It's a four-year course and we were instantly under the command of the second-class midshipmen, the juniors, whose task it was to transform us from civilians into military officers.

The Brigade of Midshipmen is organized into two regiments, each with three battalions of five companies. I considered it an amazing omen when I was assigned to the 14th Company, known variously as the "Friendly 14" or the "14th Company Tomcats." At the time I was still living and breathing the prospect of flying the F-14 Tomcat. I still had the picture from Little Miami High School.

To tell the truth, the running, jumping hell of that Plebe Summer is a distant blur in my mind. The midshipmen commanders bombarded us with instructions, and most of us hardly knew whether we were coming or going. We were, however, very definitely charging this way and that, up flights of stairs, around the campus, here, there, and everywhere, with hardly time to breathe, think, or decide, except we were made to do all three of those in short order, watched every moment of the day, yelled at every other moment, and laughed at the rest of the time.

From the very first meal we all had, sitting together at our designated table, it was like nothing any of us had ever known . . . *Sit up straight, do not lean back, eyes front and center, do not look at anyone else, KEEP YOUR EYES IN THE BOAT!* You may be forgiven for thinking that right here we're in some kind of nut country. But that's the way it is at Annapolis: rules there are not meant to be broken. They're meant to be obeyed *at all times.*

Any second-classman could ask a plebe anything he felt like at any time. No matter how fast any of us were running to an assignment. The cry of command may sound juvenile, but to us it was chilling. The crisp shout from a second-class midshipman, the guys in charge of us: "Hippity-hop, plebe stop!"

*Holy shit!* This was bad. And the exchange between us was worse.

"How many days to Christmas break?"

"Sir, one hundred and twenty-one days until Christmas break, sir!"

"Wrong!"

"Sir, no excuse, sir! I will find out, sir! Beat Army, sir!"

"Midshipman Lay, chow call go!"

(Oh, Christ, not that.) "Sir, aye aye, sir!"

This was bad. For this task I needed to go to the fourth floor in Bancroft Hall, a modest little building of 1,700 midshipmen rooms, nearly five miles of corridors, and about thirty-three acres of floor space, home to all 4,300 of us, and apt at certain times to become slightly congested—like Mecca at the Ka'bah in the middle of the Ramadan hajj.

But first I had to make sure I knew the answers to a whole screed of requirements, especially that one about the days to Christmas break. Having found out the necessary facts, I had to get to the appointed spot up on the fourth floor. You couldn't take corners like a race car when you're belting through Bancroft. You had to square them off as if taking part in a marching parade. It slowed you down to hell. Trust me.

Anyhow, all the midshipmen on chow call charged for their various stations, watching every step of the way for the big square silver tiles that mark the corridor corners. If you skidded around there and missed one, a second-class midshipman will see you, no matter how plainly desperate you are to reach your destination.

"Hippity-hop, plebe stop!"

Sweet Jesus.

"How many days to the Army/Navy game?"

"Sir, there are one hundred and fourteen days until Navy beats the hell out of Army, sir!"

"Shove off."

"Sir, aye aye, sir!"

Another flight of stairs. I was out of breath but still charged through this crowded madhouse, ducking, diving, squaring the corners, bellowing the omnipotent battle cry of the college every time I hit a silver tile . . . *Sir, go Navy, sir! Sir, beat Army, sir!* Reciting the chow call to myself, striving not to be late. Because that's darn near a hanging offense. And there were about three hundred other guys doing exactly the same. Can you imagine the uproar?

Somehow I got there, along with hundreds of others, standing on their respective silver tiles, waiting for the second-class midshipmen to appear. Just before ten minutes to noon, there was total silence throughout the building as we took our places. You could hear the clocks ticking. And then, at exactly ten minutes to noon, the entire place erupted. Hundreds of plebes stood rigidly at attention, shoulders back, arms straight, shouting their chow call at the top of their lungs, as fast as they could:

*SIR, you now have ten minutes 'til noon meal formation. Noon meal formation goes outside. The uniform for noon meal formation is working uniform blue Delta. The menu for noon meal is Mexican meal, taco shells with taco sauce, seasoned meat, onions, tomatoes, and sour cream, guacamole, chips, fruit salad, ice cream, iced tea, and milk. There are 112 days until Navy beats Army; 121 days until Christmas Break . . .*

At this point there usually would be ferocious activity as plebes made mistakes, their upperclassmen yelling, "Wrong!" It was barely controlled bedlam, in which dozens of plebes were shouting, "Sir, no excuse, sir! Sir, request permission to start over, sir!" And repeating the mantra of the menu over again.

The air was thick with shouts, insults, and commands: "I can't hear you! Start over!"

"Sir, you now have ten minutes to noon meal formation . . ."

"*How many minutes?*"

"Sir, nine and a half, sir! Sir, you now have nine and half-minutes to formation . . ."

"*What formation?*"

"Sir, noon meal formation, sir!"

"*Start over!*"

"*Sir,* you now have nine and a half minutes . . ."

"How the hell could I *still* have nine and a half minutes?"

"*Sir,* you now have nine minutes . . ."

"Can you read a clock?"

"Sir?"

"Are you asking me a question?"

"Sir, no, sir! Sir, you now have eight minutes to noon meal formation . . ."

"I can't hear you. Start over!"

And so it went on, until the final conclusion:

"*Sir,* the officers of the watch are: the Officer of the Watch is Lieutenant Brown, 30th Company Officer. The Midshipman Officer of the Watch is Midshipman Commander Stevens, vice honor chair. The major events in the Yard are . . . *none.* The professional topic of the week is submarine warfare. You now have seven minutes, *sir.*"

There are all kinds of traditions involved. Remember, the plebe is reciting this stuff right in the middle of his own area, in my case the 14th Company Tomcats. If I've got it wrong, and I'm being reamed for stupidity by the second-class midshipmen, the others, my company mates, will swarm out of their room and pack around me, all part of the unbreakable Navy tradition that we don't ever leave anyone just to cope by themselves.

It's a type of throwback to one of the great naval codes of brotherhood: in battle, or in operations of the gravest danger, we don't *send* anyone anywhere. We all go together.

Of course, the very thought of a nineteen-year-old would-be fighter pilot, standing in the corridor of this huge naval college yelling at the top of his lungs, lines involving tacos, tomatoes, and sour cream, possesses an element of the absurd. Consider for a moment the number of facets contained in each of these long traditions of discipline and "punishment" with which we lived on a daily basis.

That chow call had a very serious place in our lives. For a start, it taught us that there was no whispering or monkeying around in a mumbling or inarticulate voice. You snapped out the required information loudly, and fast, no mistakes.

In the Navy, should you suddenly find yourself taking command of a big, damaged warship, with injured men on board, and the hull shipping water, you'd better be heard by everyone. At Annapolis we learned that military art form of communication from the get-go. How to make yourself heard and understood amid the noisiest and most chaotic circumstances imaginable.

Those lines we learned, and comprehended, every morning of our lives, were important. Maybe they were about guacamole and chips, but they taught us all a rigid form of discipline, cramming information into our minds, remembering lists, even while we were on the run. The system forced us to say them over and over, as we spun right on the silver tiles, pounding the corridors, squaring the corners, no time wasting, every second precious and utilized.

It also drummed into us the ever-present concept of mutual respect, especially for our superiors, beyond our class year, which did, of course, include darn near everyone. Annapolis is almost entirely run by the midshipmen. Its Honor Concept is one of the pillars of that society:

> Midshipmen are persons of integrity. They stand for that which is right. They tell the truth and ensure that the full truth is known. They do not lie. They embrace fairness in all actions. They ensure that work submitted as their own is their own, and that assistance received from any source is authorized and properly documented. They do not cheat. They respect the property of others and ensure that others are able to benefit from the use of their own property. They do not steal.

Those are not just words. Annapolis does not just print and issue them. The United States Naval Academy engraves those words upon the heart of every midshipman. It's said the Navy system can deal with almost any transgression—except lying. Should you be crazy enough to attempt an untruth as a way out of trouble, you will be gone within hours. The Academy refers to the process quaintly: "being separated."

They also empower every midshipman on the campus with the right to confront someone they see violating the Honor Concept without formally reporting it. It's a way of developing honor and building trust. Brigade honor committees, composed of upper-class midshipmen, are responsible for the Honor Concept and possess formidable powers to protect it.

The Academy mission statement is uncompromising: "To develop midshipmen morally, mentally, and physically, and to imbue them with the highest ideals of duty, honor, and loyalty. To graduate leaders who are dedicated to a career of naval service and have potential for future development, in mind and character to assume the highest responsibilities of command, citizenship, and government."

They don't just hand over command of a half-billion-dollar guided-missile destroyer or strike fighter to any old graduate. And if you come out of Annapolis, you need the highest possible standards, because it is likely that sometime in the future many fellow officers, and indeed many thousands of your fellow Americans, may be entirely dependent upon your decision and your reasons for making it.

It's easy to see where these profound depths of ethics emanate: from the high command of warships in battle. It is untenable for any commander to be in any way subversive or even economical with the truth. The theater of war in which they operate demands 100 percent integrity and honesty. Nothing can be finessed, exaggerated, or omitted. No one can function in a life-or-death situation without full knowledge of the precise situation. And full knowledge of what's damaged, being repaired, or kaput.

Thus Annapolis, with those ironclad codes, is specifically designed to protect and inspire the greatest possible qualities of leadership. It's a place where a midshipman found guilty of even the whitest of lies will be regarded as forever suspect, because one day he may be the officer in whose hands everyone else's life depends. And the names Nimitz, Halsey, Kinkaid, King, Hart, Ricketts, Rickover, Burke, and Spruance stand eternally before us all.

And like all of them, we learned at this shining place, all of the rules, the ones committed to writing and the ones that were unspoken. Naval officers must think critically. They must discern fact from fiction. They must question basic assumptions and rapidly analyze vast amounts of information.

They must assess chaotic situations with clear logic. Their decisions may be made in stressful, or even lethal situations. The Academy never once stopped telling us that Annapolis was just one step along a path of lifelong learning, but it was *the* step, to enable all of us ultimately to enter the fleet as combat leaders.

I expect they hammered the same lessons into Chester Nimitz, "Bull" Halsey, Ray Spruance, and the rest. I expect they felt the same about the Academy as we do: one day you *hate* it, the next day you *love* it. The old midshipman adage is unchanging down all the years: Annapolis is one hell of a tough place to be at. But it's a great place to be from.

Nothing at the Academy is soft, relaxed, or easy. Everything is about accountability, independence, and self-reliance. When they deliver either academic knowledge or life's lessons—about four hundred times a day— it's like being given a drink of water through a hose, with one end attached to a fire hydrant, the other rammed down your throat.

Everything comes thick and fast, and through it all you're running, shouting, ducking, and dodging, trying to get to distant places, through the throng of equally panicked fellow fourth-class midshipmen, trying to remember how many days to Christmas break and whether pancakes were on the breakfast menu.

And then there was the marching. Lined up in strict formation, the plebes march everywhere. In my plebe year I marched more miles than Napoleon's Grande Armée advancing on Moscow. We had six different uniforms, and each one was compulsory for its allotted place in the curriculum. You plainly could not show up looking different from anyone else.

There were triple sweats, working uniform, summer whites, and service dress uniforms similar to those of US naval officers. Everyone wears gold anchor insignia on both lapel collars of their dress-blue jacket. The necessity to change from whatever you were wearing into the correct uniform for the next phase of the day induced nothing short of stark panic among us fourth-class midshipmen.

We were required to race back to our rooms to get sartorially assembled on the double. The speed essential for this was inevitably beyond impossible. The headlong flight of the plebe, returning to his home base, up the stairs and along the corridors, squaring the corners, and then diving into a new shirt, pants, and jacket was nothing short of an exercise in controlled pandemonium.

To this day I can jump out of my clothes and into new ones faster than any human being I know. One minute I'm standing there looking like a spare part from a junior college basketball team. The next moment I'm in a tuxedo, bright, shiny, and ready to go.

At Annapolis, this procedure required a certain amount of highly controlled discipline, the key to which rested with the age-old tradition of everything being shipshape. In one sense, that aspect of life at the Academy was a throwback to the days of sail, when everything had to be neatly arranged and stowed out of the way. I suppose it's unwritten, but it's the basic structure of the Navy, old and yet so new, ancient and yet so modern, the tried and tested ways re-created again and again, adapting every decade to the newest tactics in naval combat.

Our rooms in the great timeless stone bastion of Bancroft Hall were slick, functional, and jumping with computers and modern steel and wood desks and chairs. We each had our own areas, and next to our study desks were tall cupboards and open wardrobes for hanging our clothes. And as plebes, the lowest form of life, we were subject to inspections that seemed to occur every hour.

Every garment needed to be spotless, pressed, and placed in its correct spot. At first we thought this was like being in a girls' school, making sure our white dress shirts and jackets were correctly hung, in the exact right order. But there was a method to this neurotic-seeming scrutiny. It provided our first test of compartmentalizing our information.

And that's a rigid naval requirement, the art of not confusing two or more subjects: for example, accepting there's a gaping hole in the port bow of the ship and that a missile may be unexploded inside the hull, but that a fire is burning into the lower part of the superstructure.

The officer in command must (1) ensure the damage control team swiftly reaches the area with mattresses, sledgehammers, and heavy wooden beams to plug the gap in the hull where water is entering; (2) ensure the firefighting crews have attached the hoses correctly to the main water pipes; and (3) ensure the bomb disposal crews are into the bow of the ship with all of their equipment to disarm that missile, if it has not already exploded.

One disaster but three very separate problems. The commanding officer must have them compartmentalized accurately, dealing with each aspect of the problem individually in his own mind. No hysterics, just careful assessments and actions, order at all times. Always taking care of the damage, while at the same time preparing to fight off another attack, then locate the enemy and slam back at him with the ship's guns and guided missiles. All compartmentalized in his racing mind.

The first steps on that intricate learning curve happen on the first day at the Academy with the mass sorting of uniforms, placing them in the right order, and keeping them separate from one another. It's a system that will not allow your sweatpants to somehow get hung up on the same hanger as your dress-white jacket and cause even a moment's delay.

The Navy code was clear: personal items and all clothing must remain neat and orderly at all times. The second-classmen who ruled our lives ensured this by running inspections at all hours of the day or night. Any plebe with confusion in his wardrobe, his cupboards, or his stack of sheets and blankets could look forward to a week of chow calls, just to remind him permanently of the folly of disorder in the US Navy.

Even in sports, the aims laid down by the Academy's military philosophers were as urgent and far-reaching as any set of rules since the Israeli commander-in-chief made it down from Mount Sinai with the tablets of stone.

We don't just go out there and try to win. Hell no. We go out there and try to return in victory as a close-knit carrier strike group ready to conquer the earth. This isn't a football game, not here. This is an exercise in world domination . . . "We want our future officers to be team builders, and to learn how to motivate others to excel. We want them to keep going when the chips are down, and all hope is gone. We want them to compete on the athletic field, and to fight on the battlefield—*to win*."

They assure us that working as a unit to achieve a common goal is the essence of combat teamwork. This is the place for future officers to learn. Everyone is required not just to play on a team, but to strive to *win*.

Midshipmen are taught to study the other team's weaknesses and then bring their own strengths to bear to achieve victory. They must find a way to meet very high goals. "Our hope is simply that our junior officers, the midshipmen, will learn not only what teamwork, determination, and leadership mean, but the process of transcending these qualities into combat victory."

The Academy's demands are uncompromising: "Developing midshipmen physically is about hard work, stamina, physical, and mental toughness. Leaders must learn to fight, and never accept defeat, on the playing field, or on the battlefield. The idea is to crush the enemy, to see him driven before you."

*Sir, aye aye, sir!*

That last line of the sports mission statement is like the oxygen of life at the Academy: *Never give up. Believe in the impossible.* One day you may be required to attempt it, possibly in combat, where it may be necessary for you to make the final sacrifice. And this, sure as all hell, is the place to develop that mind-set.

THROUGHOUT ALL OF THESE endless twenty-nine-hour days on the eastern shores of Maryland, where no one had enough time to breathe, never mind do everything that was required, we tried our best to fight our corner. Not only did we complete our specialized naval work, we also had to complete a regular education as if we were at Princeton or Yale.

A couple of years back, the USNA graduated four Rhodes scholars, the most of any college in the nation. Couple of years before that they graduated three to Oxford University.

British philanthropist Cecil John Rhodes knew a thing or two about people. He insisted that in addition to pure intellect, qualities of character and leadership must be considered for his coveted scholarships to Oxford and Cambridge Universities in England. Guess that put our guys out in front before the judging even began.

Despite the massive workload foisted upon the midshipmen on a daily basis, everyone who graduates receives a bachelor of science degree. And believe me, they've earned it. Standards are exemplary. Our days started early, at six a.m. for PT—that's hard physical training. Morning formation was at seven, morning classes at seven forty-five. Noon formation was at 12:05. There were afternoon classes, evening studies, with "Taps" and lights-out at eleven.

For us there was no such thing as slacking or goofing off. Which probably comes back to the Honor Concept. We just did not, could not, kick against the rules and the time allotted for intense study. We had to obey.

Remember that the laws of mathematics, physics, and other sciences are enshrined in this place. Half of the engineering discoveries in the world have been instigated and perfected by various military departments, especially the US Navy.

Just look at the list of possible majors for midshipmen in the Division of Engineering and Weapons: aeronautical engineering, astronautical engineering, electrical engineering, general engineering, mechanical engineering, naval architecture, ocean engineering, systems engineering. It's like MIT with boats.

The Division of Mathematics and Science, where I studied for my major, offers chemistry, computer science, general science, pure mathematics, mathematics honors, oceanography, oceanography honors, physics, and quantitative economics.

In the Division of Humanities and Social Sciences, a field where Annapolis has been ranked number one in the nation, they offer economics,

English, history, and political science, all of them with separate honors courses.

By naval design, there seemed to be a thousand decisions to make every day because future commanders may need to make one that really matters one day. They must get used to that thought process, under stress and with a zillion distractions.

When a ship gets hit by a bomb, like USS *Cole,* or by seven aerial torpedoes and two bombs simultaneously, like the super-dreadnought *West Virginia* at Pearl Harbor, you need guys who can cope with big trouble, raging fires, billowing black smoke, and loss of life, all at once.

Obviously it can be overwhelming. Which is why Annapolis spends a million hours producing guys who will not get overwhelmed—by anything, not in the air at supersonic speed, on the surface under fire, or under the surface listening to the pings of the sonar.

They're known as US Navy battle commanders, and thousands of enlisted men rely on them whenever and wherever there's major conflict. On the arm of each and every one of them, right above the stripes that denote rank, there's a single golden star that forever signifies the officer not only has been granted command, but is trusted implicitly by the highest US naval authorities.

If that star was awarded by the admirals at the United States Naval Academy, then that commander stands tall, as a leader of men, an officer who crashed his way through the Annapolis system, proving himself again and again, academically, physically, and personally.

Which is why the Navy suffered a resounding, yet silent, feeling of no-confidence when that command authority was taken away from such men.

It takes four years of solid work and application to graduate from Annapolis, four years in which midshipmen must accomplish more than any other students in the nation, except possibly those at West Point and the Air Force Academy out in Colorado Springs.

By now you might think I really should have gone there instead, perhaps to become a fighter pilot rather quicker, without all the warship data that was so ferociously instilled in us. But my picture of the Tomcat had an aircraft carrier in the background, and the word "Navy" was painted starkly on the fuselage, right behind the big white star in its blue circle, set within red and white stripes. It gave me unexplained chills when I was fourteen. Matter of fact, it still does.

Looking back I can only wonder at the brilliant formality of the teaching at Annapolis, and the fact that we were somehow coerced into absorbing that much knowledge. And in a strange way they also added instructions and teachings that we managed to learn in our subconscious. One of them involved the unquestioning, instant acceptance of an order, a concept of obedience long outlawed and cast far out into the darkness of American corporate life.

They had a curious way of communicating this critical requirement into the psyche of a future naval officer. They simply handed us a letter shortly after we arrived in Annapolis. It contained nothing more than an essay written in the last year of the nineteenth century by the American writer, artist, publisher, and philosopher Elbert Hubbard.

It was, of course, his epic "A Message to Garcia," a work well known to us, but these days highly unfashionable among civilians, many of whom probably think it infringes upon their human rights to gripe and moan. The work is scarcely read in regular US colleges.

It was written by a man with no naval background, unless you count the unfortunate manner of his death. Elbert and Alice Hubbard were aboard RMS *Lusitania* when she was torpedoed and sunk by a German U-boat (U-20), eleven miles off the Old Head of Kinsale, County Cork, Ireland. Almost 2,000 people were lost that day, including the sage who wrote, perhaps inadvertently, the essay that has become a mini-bible in the folklore of military command.

I intend to quote the brief essence of the story, "A Message to Garcia," and then examine its colossal implications, for it cleaves an ax down the divide that stands between naval standards and those of corporate America. *Go for it, Elbert. With a little mild editing, my pages are all yours:*

"In all this Cuban business there is one man stands out on the horizon of my memory, like Mars at perihelion. When war broke out between Spain and the United States it was very necessary to communicate quickly with the leader of the insurgents. General Garcia was somewhere in the mountain vastness of Cuba, no one knew where. No telegraph message could reach him. But the President must secure his cooperation, and quickly.

"What to do!

"Someone said to the President, 'There's a fellow by the name of Rowan will find Garcia for you, if anybody can.'

"And so, Rowan was sent for, and given a letter to deliver to Garcia. I have no special desire to tell in detail how 'the fellow by the name of Rowan' took the letter, sealed it in an oilskin pouch, strapped it over his heart, and, in four days, landed by night off the coast of Cuba, from an open boat, and disappeared into the jungle.

"But, in three weeks, he came out on the other side of the island, having traversed a hostile country on foot, and delivered his letter to Garcia."

Right here Hubbard pauses, then writes, "The point I wish to make is this: President McKinley gave Rowan a letter to be delivered to Garcia: Rowan took the letter and did not ask, 'Where is he at?' By the Eternal! There is a man whose form should be cast in deathless bronze, and the statue placed in every college in the land.

"It is not book-learning young men need, nor instruction about this and that, but a stiffening of the vertebrae, which will cause them to be loyal to a trust, to act promptly, concentrate their energies: do the thing—Carry a message to Garcia!

"General Garcia is dead now, but there are other Garcias."

Hubbard concludes his discourse with a paragraph of pure enlightenment, lightly disguised as a turn-of-the-century rant, and beloved of all Annapolis graduates, since it embodies the very core of their warnings to all midshipmen.

"No man," Hubbard wrote, "who has endeavored to carry out an enterprise where many hands were needed, but has been well-nigh appalled at times by the imbecility of the average man, the inability or unwillingness to concentrate on a thing, and do it. Slip-shod assistance, foolish inattention, dowdy indifference and half-hearted work, seem the rule.

"And no man succeeds, unless by hook or by crook, or threat, he forces, or bribes other men to assist him; or perhaps, God in His goodness, performs a miracle, and sends him an Angel of Light for an assistant."

At Annapolis, that particular Angel of Light is expected to be in residence at all times, right on our shoulder boards, next to the golden anchor, which confirms each one of us currently has the honor to be a midshipman at the United States Naval Academy.

Old Elbert might have been a civilian, but more than a century later his words are held in the highest possible regard. We were ordered to read his essay, absorb it, take note of its somewhat brutal but clear message, and, metaphorically, take the son of a bitch to Garcia, wherever the hell he may be.

The second part of Hubbard's essay involves a bet he wished to have with his reader. And he's offering heavy odds against. "Summon one of your clerks," he wrote, "and make this request—'Look in the encyclopedia and make a brief memorandum for me, concerning the life of Antonio Correggio.'

"Will the clerk quietly say, 'Yes, sir,' and go do the task?

"On your life, he will not. He will look at you out of a fishy eye, and ask one or more of the following questions:

"Who was he?

"Which encyclopedia?

"Where is the encyclopedia?

"Was I hired for that?

"Don't you mean Bismarck?

"What's the matter with Charlie doing it?

"Is he dead?

"Is there any hurry?

"Shall I not bring you the book and let you look it up yourself?

"What do you want to know for?

"And I will lay you ten to one that after you have answered the questions, the clerk will go off and get one of the other clerks to help him try to find Correggio, and then come back and tell you there is no such man. Of course, I may lose my bet, but according to the Law of Average, I will not.

"Incapacity for independent action, moral stupidity, infirmity of the will, unwillingness cheerfully to catch hold and lift, are the things that put pure Socialism so far into the future. If men will not act for themselves, what will they do when the benefit of their effort is for all? Certainly not deliver the letter to Garcia."

He concludes with a characteristic flourish: "My heart goes out to the man who does his work when the boss is away, as well as when he is at home. And the man who, when given a letter for Garcia, quietly takes the missive, without asking idiotic questions.

"Because civilization is one long, anxious search for just such individuals. Anything such a man as Rowan asks shall be granted. His kind is so rare that no employer can afford to let him go. He is wanted in every city, town, and village, in every office, shop, store, and factory. The world cries out for such a man. He is needed, and needed badly, the man who can carry a message to Garcia."

I doubt that Elbert Hubbard ever dreamed that one day, in the finest military college in the world, his words would be legion. And within its walls, there would be 4,400 midshipmen, any one of whom could be counted upon to cross that hostile territory and take the message to General Garcia. No complaints. No idiotic questions.

And to Hubbard goes all the credit. That essay of his, read assiduously by every new intake of midshipmen, had a lifelong effect on every one of us. At least on everyone who made it to graduation. The ones who didn't, I'm sure, became perfectly decent and proper members of society. But they might not have delivered that letter to Garcia.

I HAVE CONCENTRATED on the early part of my time at Annapolis, because that's when they set about changing us, and those changes signified a completely different set of values from those present in regular corporate life.

We were taught to work in teams, and we were taught to help anyone who was finding the going just too tough. Any failure reflected on us all. It was in no one's interest to work alongside the weakest link. And we did not outlaw him, we made him better. We did everything we could to bring that midshipman up to standard. No one could afford to let the chain link break, so we strengthened it.

In corporate America, there is far too much rivalry among people working in the same divisions for the same company. There are too many people devoted to their own image and ego. Wall Street's financial institutions are full of people who would rather see the ship go down than come out looking bad themselves. Did you ever see a more gigantic barrage of excuses hurled asunder than when the financial crash came in 2008?

You could have been trampled in the stampede, as executives rushed for cover, denying, lying, crying, sighing, pretending it wasn't happening. BAM! Down went Lehman, and the biggest execs in the entire place were whining that Hank Paulson should have saved them. They were actually insulting him, saying that it was all his fault, the collapse of the US economy, as if he had issued the subprime mortgages to guys who never could have paid it back.

Can you imagine, in your most reckless dreams, that the Navy would have tolerated for one split second that excruciating form of cowardice and excuse-making?

I'll tell you what would have happened in the Navy, if the *George Washington* had been hit by one of Saddam's missiles. We'd have court-martialed the American CO. Hauled his ass right in front of a tribunal and demanded to know how the hell he had managed to be that careless. And rightly so.

We would not have gone running to the Secretary of Defense and accused him of making the ship too big or too weak or too unprepared. In essence, that is what the Lehman chiefs actually did: blamed a man who had nothing to do with their catastrophic failure.

I'm not for one moment saying the Navy conducts witch hunts for people and always needs a scapegoat. But when something goes awry and we lose a warship, we hold its commanding officer to account. He is very carefully interrogated. No one complains. Because the CO himself expects nothing else. He is the officer in charge, and since his earliest days at Annapolis, the most important words in his life were "accountability," "independence," and "self-reliance."

Those are words by which we all lived, in probably the most demanding profession on earth. The gambling of vast sums of other people's money in the derivatives market before 2008 was not somehow intellectually superior. It was, if anything, a darn sight easier than taking care of a billion-dollar aircraft carrier with 5,000 Americans embarked, thousands of miles from home and flanked by hostile shores.

And when push came to shove, Wall Street's financiers gathered up their possessions and fled the datum. The commanding officer of a US warship would not have been awarded that option. He would have been required to face the music, answer the questions, accept criticism, and possibly been exonerated. But there would have been no alternative, no evading or avoiding. If blame was there, that commanding officer would have taken it. *No excuses, sir. I accept responsibility.* The way we would have expected. The way they taught us on the eastern shores of Maryland all those years ago.

Do not think the questioning would have been soft. It would have fallen some way short of the Gestapo but nonetheless would have been classified as rigorous. The CO could have expected:

"At what time did the missile hit?"

"And where were you in those precise moments?"

"How soon did the AWO (air warfare officer) spot the incoming weapon?"

"Precisely what time were the chaff launchers fired?"

"When was the precise moment you knew your ship had been struck?"

"Was there any warning during the preceding hours that such an enemy strike may have been planned?"

"Did the carrier have time to alter course?"

"What was your first order upon learning the carrier was taking on water?"

"Who was responsible for activating the fire crews?"

"Where precisely was the AWO when the missile hit—may we assume at his screen in the ops room?"

"What was the speed of the ship in the minutes immediately prior to the hit?"

"What time did you receive the initial reports from fire control, and damage control?"

If those chancers who run the Wall Street investment banks had been subjected to this kind of stuff, I suspect they might have needed a few spare pairs of pants.

And the question should be asked: Who would you prefer to be in charge of those high-income divisions of the banks, supervising the equity traders, the bond traders, the brokers, the mortgage executives, the guys on the huge-spending commercial and residential property floor?

Would you take the dyed-in-the-wool corporate CEO, invariably a cunning man, accustomed to taking big risks on behalf of other people, while reserving a personal place in the lifeboat?

Or, perhaps a US Navy commanding officer, perhaps even a carrier strike group commander, with several billion dollars' worth of oceangoing hardware under his authority?

In matters of other people's money, and other people's wealth, I know which way I'd jump. I'd take the man whose byword was "integrity." I'd take the man who had never told a professional lie once in his life. The man who regarded dishonesty as a fate way beyond mere disaster. A man to whom honor was everything, and who would stand by his word under every possible kind of stress. To the death if necessary.

I happen to believe the military high command is superior to its civilian counterpart. The crash of 2008 was constructed on a seething bed of lies, with a culture of risk-taking that no naval commander would have even considered. Trust me, if the US Navy's great commanders had been in charge, that crash would not have happened. It could not have happened. They would not have allowed it to happen.

I accept that many people might not have made so much money. But the world's economy would not have collapsed either. I think of all those "executives" of the opening years of the twenty-first century, starting with Jeff "Slammer for Two Decades" Skilling, who presided with sensational dishonesty over Enron's train wreck of a stock collapse from $90 to 30 cents.

And how about the CEOs of Global Crossing, Qwest, NTL, Adelphia Communications, and WorldCom? All of those companies crashed into bankruptcy, and in their death throes, issued convertible bonds to raise money in a flagrant attempt to bamboozle investors.

In short order we had the CEO of Bear Stearns, Alan Schwartz, assuring investors, "Our balance sheet, liquidity, and capital remain strong," right out there on CNBC. Two days later Bear Stearns effectively went bankrupt.

CitiGroup was no different. Hurtling toward possible bankruptcy with a near-suicidal portfolio of leveraged buyouts, CEO Charles "Chuck" Prince made one of the most infamous statements in Wall Street history when he told the *Financial Times,* "As long as the music is playing, you've got to get up and dance—we're still dancing." It was widely seen as emblematic of US banks' total failure to come to grips with the onrushing financial crisis.

Stan O'Neal, the first African-American ever to head a Wall Street firm, was forced to resign as CEO of Merrill Lynch but paid himself almost $100 million in 2006–2007, right before Merrill announced losses of $8 billion.

And how about Angelo Mozilo, cofounder of the vast Countrywide Financial Corporation. To avoid a fraud trial, and possibly jail, he paid the biggest financial penalty ever levied against a senior executive of a public

corporation—$67.5 million—for misleading investors about risky mort-
gages, deliberately disregarding his duty to them, by hiding information.

Ken Lewis, CEO of Bank of America, scarcely covered himself in glory
by buying Countrywide and then, later, paying $50 billion for Merrill
Lynch, which almost immediately lost more than $15 billion in one quar-
ter. The two purchases cost Bank of America tens of billions of dollars
and smashed its balance sheet to smithereens. A legal dust storm swirled
around Merrill's charging-bull emblem as both the SEC and New York
Attorney General Andrew Cuomo decided whether to charge Lewis for
misleading shareholders.

The world's biggest insurance corporation, AIG, saw its CEO, Martin
Sullivan, forced to step down after the corporation's stock market value
plunged from $100 billion to $4.2 billion. Andrew Cuomo described the
private-jet-riding Sullivan as responsible for "unwarranted and outrageous
executive expenditure" and blamed him for gigantic losses. It initially cost
the US government $85 billion—before rising to $182 billion—to bail out
AIG. At the Financial Crisis Inquiry Commission hearing in Washington,
the panel expressed astonishment when Sullivan claimed he did not know
about problems in the AIG portfolio. CNBC named him "one of the worst
CEOs of all time."

Brad Morrice, CEO of the massive mortgage-lending juggernaut New
Century, was charged with fraud after presiding over a stock-market price
crash from nearly $66 a share to 10 cents in 2007. This was the second-
largest mortgage house in the United States, and Morrice was once named
by the accounting giant Ernst & Young as America's Entrepreneur of the
Year.

I guess they all must have been reading from the same hymn sheet. A
decade later, New York prosecutors, backed by Cuomo's office, announced
they would charge Ernst & Young with civil fraud for helping to conceal
Lehman Brothers' financial catastrophe in 2008.

That Wall Street was grinding on the rocks of its own dishonesty in
2007–2008 is beyond question. Some extremely important financiers were
issuing stern warnings here, there, and everywhere. People were quitting
in fear; others were fired simply because of their caution, because they
marched to the beat of a different drum—the one that pounded out the
message of outrageous profit in the boardrooms.

But the existence of pure dishonesty is inescapable—and by that I mean corporations like Lehman issuing a new corporate bond mere months before going spectacularly bust, with debts large enough to have collectively sunk most of the nations in sub-Saharan Africa.

They just went right out there and tried to sell their own debt to other financial institutions, when the boardroom must have known, by all that was holy, that everyone was going to lose damn near everything in the not-too-distant future.

Any investors buying Lehman shares or bonds at that time might as well have taken a walk over the Brooklyn Bridge and cast their bread upon the waters of the East River. And the multimillion-dollar bonus guys in that venerable old banking corporation plainly knew that—unless they were imperially stupid as well as dishonest.

There have been many discourses on the Wall Street crash, and I confess to reading most of the serious accounts of the disaster. When I have a moment to reflect upon them, I am driven always to my recurring theme in this chapter: that the behavior of too many people in this strictly American saga should be filed under the heading "dead suspect."

Their actions, which caused so much sorrow and heartbreak, must bring sharply into question the whole ethos of greed and its progressive path to evasion, obfuscation, and then downright lies. I will, I am sure, be accused of misunderstanding the necessity to accrue profits to survive. But I dismiss that because it seeks to cloak the practice of lying into some kind of weird obligation toward "the greater good."

In the end, the truth will come out. It always does. The United States armed services know that. Collectively they swear by its wisdom and demand that all of its commanders and troops follow the mantra. The truth is the basis of all civilization. The world's most appalling dictators, who are apt to ignore that, usually find out the hard way, either in life, which is bad, or in death, which is probably worse.

No amount of bleating and whining will ever let Wall Street off the hook. They darn near single-handedly screwed up the world. It would not have happened if they'd taken a very strong pull on what was becoming a runaway horse.

That way they might have listened to the wiser heads around them— the guys who were watching the market and trying to get out of the sub-prime fiasco as far back as early 2006. So far as I can see, the whole place was careening along on a flatbed raft of untruths. The very paper the subprime mortgages were written on was founded on a lie, an enormous lie, as applicants filled in the "income" square with untruths the size of a New York state penitentiary.

This was the age of the $400,000-a-year mailman, the $250,000-a-year supermarket shelf stacker. The applicants knew they were lying, the mortgage salesmen both knew and encouraged them to continue lying, and the mortgage brokers themselves knew they were lying, unless they were all insanely stupid. But no one cared, no one made one move to stop it, until the roof started to crash down in 2007.

Even the ratings agencies, particularly Moody's, Standard & Poor's, and Fitch, the guys who were handing out AAA ratings on subprime mortgage–backed bonds, were right in the thick of it. A triple-A rating is the equivalent of that issued by the US government, which has never defaulted one dollar on a government security in all of its history. It's the blue ribbon of reliability, the gold-star accolade awarded to a debt obligation that is without risk. At the time, of course.

These guys were handing them out to recommend bonds created by Lehman and Merrill Lynch for thousands of mortgages issued to people who had no chance whatever to repay the money, principally because they were broke. In the trade they were called NINJA mortgages: huge house loans issued to people with no income, no job, and no assets.

Top Wall Street execs must have known the mortgages would never be repaid. But they never let on. Until, in the end, even the ratings agencies rushed for cover, issuing reassessments of bonds they once had rated as AAA. They were downgrading certain bonds from AAA to junk in one jump. Moody's desperately tried to deflect scrutiny of its balance sheet, which in the first six years of the new century had gone from profits of $800 million to profits of more than $2 billion.

Reason: massive fees from the investment banks, paying them to hand out those triple-A ratings. S&P and Fitch weren't much different.

The three agencies were supposed to understand risk and reliability, with their quasi-government auras. And now they were effectively presiding over a financial catastrophe of their own making. No one in their right mind would have dreamed of purchasing all those securitized bonds without the once-priceless AAA imprimatur of Moody's, Fitch, or S&P.

And boy, did they ever backtrack in a hurry when it was plain the game was up. By the end of January 2007, they'd downgraded nearly 1,500 mostly subprime CDOs (collateralized debt obligations) in the United States.

This chapter, however, was not designed to gloat over the failure of so many formerly revered corporations in the financial world. It was written on the subject of character and honesty.

I do not believe that if the men who command our nation's battle fleets had been in charge, they would have permitted the subprime fiasco to get off the ground. God knows, in America's finance houses there were a thousand times more lies told in those three or four years than in the first 160 years of the Naval Academy's existence.

The crash of 2008 was founded on a labyrinth of untruths. And the peerless images of Chester Nimitz, "Bull" Halsey, Ray Spruance, Arleigh Burke, Ernest King, Claude Ricketts, and Hyman Rickover stand, as ever, selflessly before me.

Would they have allowed it? Were they anything like the above list of American CEOs? You may answer those two questions for yourself.

## CHAPTER 4

# The Golden Star of Command

Thirty or forty smartly dressed midshipmen, each of them determined to become a serving officer in the US Navy, either resigns, suffers a nervous breakdown, or runs for his life before completing that first year as an Annapolis plebe.

Everything about the place drives young men and women to levels of stress and feelings of helplessness that have to be tackled and overcome. Most make it through, but some cannot. There's nothing average, easy, or even normal about the way the Academy hammers home the lessons. It's a program designed to develop those who can cope with the highest responsibilities of command, just as it says on the prospectus. There is nothing comparable in civilian life.

Not many US college students are forced out of bed at six a.m. to begin their day with physical training regardless of rain and freezing cold. Midshipmen do not get long, lazy summer holidays involving baseball, beaches, and girlfriends.

Most of my sports programs were compulsory, the football and basketball. We had to learn to box, and to swim, and to jump from a ten-meter diving board, and we had to run a mile in under five minutes and thirty seconds. We had to learn to sail, and we spent hours out on the water in forty-two-foot yawls.

At the conclusion of my plebe year, I was deployed to a destroyer in Hong Kong, classified as an enlisted man, given a couple of sets of dungarees, and ordered to start work scrubbing, cleaning, polishing, and swabbing the decks. I thought at the time it was one of the more diabolically unreasonable programs with which I had been presented.

But we all knuckled down, and the warship made its way through the waters of the western Pacific, steaming into the Yellow Sea to visit Korea, then sailing south to Japan, where we pulled into Sasebo, way down in the southwest of the islands.

Looking back, the deployment was designed to provide us with a unique insight into the life of an enlisted man. We were mostly destined to become officers, and in the opinion of the US Navy it was essential that we understand precisely what the other ranks went through, their attitudes, hopes, and ambitions.

I know of nothing in corporate life so thorough, so guaranteed to achieve its purpose in the field of executive-employee relations. Senior naval officers, however stern and uncompromising, usually have a kindly weather eye for the plight of the enlisted men, principally because they have all been there. And that experience is priceless. Remember, when danger threatens, we all go together. That officer-enlisted relationship really matters.

The long working journey that summer also had another purpose. It taught us the ingrained naval officer's skill of mastering geography, being unfazed by vast distances, instantly feeling at home in foreign places. In most of us, it instilled a lifelong interest in navigation, and the sea, and the stars, and the difference between the chart and the real thing.

In my opinion Annapolis crams about six years of learning into an intensified four-year degree course. There was no respite. Aside from the constant examinations, testing, and grading, and the normal educational requirements in mathematics, economics, science, naval history, world geography, and English grammar, we also learned the rudiments of aerospace engineering, electrical engineering, and general naval engineering, as applied to warships.

We learned to drive them, and we learned the basics of gunnery, guided-missile warfare, radar, and sonar. I guess a guy who may end up commanding a warship may as well understand how it works, from top to bottom. In the Navy, the commanding officer is held responsible for everything, especially getting hit by the enemy. Never mind, "I didn't know anything about it."

By the end of my second year—that's midshipman third class—I was becoming keenly aware that I had never even set foot in a fighter aircraft. But they kept us so busy I had little time to worry. In that year they called us youngsters and we got a few privileges. Aside from being generally more respected, simply because we had completed the rough-and-tumble of plebe year, we were permitted to watch television or movies, and even to listen to music.

At the end of that academic year, when the rest of the US student world is taking an extended holiday, we went on another deployment known as PROTRAMID—that's Professional Training of Midshipmen. Again it's intensive, involving stints in surface ships, submarines, helicopters, and finally aircraft. We'd been up in the Northeast for several weeks, but now we all flew down to Pensacola, Florida. There they proceeded to bombard us with Navy flight information, which, needless to say, I loved.

Pensacola is both an air station and a deepwater US Navy port. It is rightly considered the Cradle of Naval Aviation, and it's the principal training station for midshipmen with fighter pilot ambitions. An aircraft carrier is always on station for anyone sufficiently advanced to undertake a carrier landing. But for me that was a long way off. I'd never even sat at the controls of an aircraft, far less attempted to bring a strike fighter home. Still, I had my Tomcat picture. Never left home without it.

There was a whole lot more activity in the sky than anywhere I'd been before. Pensacola is an enormous base with almost 10,000 military and naval personnel. Fighter aircraft were taking off and landing at all hours. I still remember the kick I got out of watching them streak across the Florida skies, swearing to God I'd be up there with them before I was much older.

And once more, as so often in the US Navy, we were walking in the footsteps of the mighty: Ted Williams was once a flight instructor here; Ensign Neil Armstrong was a Naval Aviator, made his first carrier landing right here in Pensacola. Colonel John Glenn was a Naval Aviator here, although he later flew combat missions as a US Marine pilot in Korea.

That deployment to Pensacola will always have a special place in my memory, mainly because it was the first time I was actually in flight with a Navy instructor, flying along the long, sandy Florida shore, staring at the green waters and watching the instruments.

Toward the end of our course, the leaders of our group were scheduled to take our first flights, where we were actually at the controls. I can say it was, without question, the most important moment of my entire life.

My instructor climbed into the Beechcraft T-34 Mentor, the Navy's single-engine turboprop trainer, and positioned himself in the rear seat. For the first time in my career, I climbed into the cockpit, right there in the front seat, and prepared for heaven.

I taxied to the takeoff area, and the instructor gave me a few last-minute orders. I held the brake and began to open the throttles, and then I heard the command that would confirm my life's ambition was not so far away: "Okay, Jeff, let's go."

I hit the gas and the white-painted aircraft with its orange wingtips raced down the runway into a light sou'wester gusting in off the Gulf of Mexico. Already I felt that Naval Aviator sensation of doing a thousand things, watching the airspeed, watching the revs, maintaining a light touch on the stick, eyes on the runway ahead. I remember easing it back just a fraction, and I really remember the feeling of pure elation as we left the ground and headed into the endless blue skies above the base, climbing higher, the wind beneath my wings.

Of course I realized I would be flying at about a quarter of the speed of a Tomcat, but it did not affect my exhilaration, and the cornfields of Maineville suddenly felt far, far away.

I locked onto our course of one-eight-five and headed south down Pensacola Bay, and out toward the waters of the Gulf, climbing to our cruising altitude of 6,000 feet. I thought this was the best day anyone could ever have. My instructor was a real good guy, and he let me move the aircraft around for a couple hours before permitting me to come in to land, handling the controls all by myself. He never said a word to me. Didn't have to.

By the time I climbed down from the cockpit I thought I *was* Major General Chuck Yeager, first man through the sound barrier.

Then another year began. And we passed a major landmark. For your first two years at Annapolis, you can leave at any time, pull the plug on your career as a naval officer. If you spend one night at the Academy at the start of the third year, you're in the US Navy, committed for five years, in uniform, and everybody knows you're in.

Anyone who wishes to get out after that first night, well, you're all done as an officer. Stung by the enormous amount of time and money spent thus far on your "career," they instantly send you to the fleet, assign you to a ship as an enlisted man, and you can start chipping paint for the next couple of years. From that moment, there's no escape.

For the rest of us, the pace heated up. By now my year was in charge of the plebes and we bounced them up and down as we ourselves had been indoctrinated into the Navy when we first arrived. But at the end of that third year, despite our onrushing seniority, we still were not permitted to go home and goof off.

No, sir. We set off on a summer-long sailing cruise, heading out to sea in our eight forty-two-foot, two-masted yawls. It was a long and fabulous journey, down to Norfolk and then all the way to Martha's Vineyard for several days, before cutting across Buzzards Bay, through the Cape Cod Canal, and into Boston. We ran into some rough weather in Massachusetts Bay and I remember wishing I was better at sailing, more certain of myself in heavy seas.

But we all improved during the journey, and then we sailed south to take part in the Navy's Fleet Week in New York Harbor. We arrived via Long Island Sound and the East River and sailed in formation past Governors Island, from where President Reagan was watching the parade of ships.

We were in two lines of four boats, and as we drew level with the president's vantage point, we suddenly cracked open our eight spinnakers simultaneously. The huge single letters on each of our 'chutes spelled out "Fly Navy." The fourth boat in our front line displayed our big gold star on its dark blue background.

We were later told the president was hugely amused at our slick, patriotic antics, and gave us a very sharp salute. He did of course *love* the US Navy, with that ambition of his for six hundred highly trained ships. Well, guess that was only 592 he had to worry about now. We were cool.

Soon we turned south again, for the long sail back to Maryland. We left New York, in a stiff breeze that blew along the Jersey shore, before we ducked into the Intracoastal Waterway at Manasquan. On that wonderful wide stretch of a tidal bay, protected from the broad Atlantic by the long chain of islands along our port side, we sailed south, west of Atlantic City.

We sailed more than a hundred miles through the waterway, all the way down to Delaware Bay, the enormous estuary where one of America's greatest rivers flows into the Atlantic Ocean at Cape May. From there we turned north up the river, then picked up the Intracoastal again, cutting across the huge Delmarva Peninsula, and into our home waters in the northern reaches of Chesapeake Bay.

Our little fleet all sailed together under the Chesapeake Bay Bridge, and we cracked out our "Fly Navy" spinnakers, when we caught a stiff southeasterly breeze on our hard starboard turn, up to the Academy's Santee Basin, headquarters of the best sailing team in US college competition. If we weren't sailors by now, we never would be. That long journey was so much fun I darn near forgot about the old F-14. But not quite. To this day I've never done that.

We had sailed for well over 1,000 miles, and I point this out to illustrate just how thorough the US Navy is about training its select corps of officers. If they're even contemplating the prospect of one day putting a midshipman in charge of a warship or a submarine or a big strike fighter, they intend to find out everything there is to know about that candidate.

They regard it as an absolute imperative that any officer who graduates from the Naval Academy is competent in a small boat and knows how to sail, navigate, and take command. Having taught us all the rudimentary lessons about seamanship, and approximately how to behave in bad weather, the instructors did precisely what you would expect. They sent us out to sea on a 1,000-mile voyage just to make sure everyone knew what they were doing—and would step up to the task should their warship ever be hit and the survivors forced to abandon.

My own career path was not so far away from anyone else's. If some bastard managed to bomb the carrier in which I was plying my future profession, I'd probably get just as wet as the rest of the crew, and as a lieutenant commander might possibly be expected to take command once we headed to the lifeboats. I might even have to bail out, or even ditch from an aircraft, and if a boat was within reach, the Navy would expect me to understand perfectly what I must do.

At the time of writing this, I have been working in the civilian world for more than five years. I have seen many corporations from almost every angle, and I have seen nothing to match the Navy's thoroughgoing, systematic, and painstaking methods of assessing their human resources. There's nothing like it in corporate America. A few progressive corporations may think they have a grip on the subject, and some of them employ psychiatrists to make careful diagnosis of candidates, at the conclusion of which they have some kind of an opinion.

That would involve far too much guesswork for the Navy. When they graduate an officer, they need to know, beyond any shadow of a doubt, they have the right man; that he has fought his way through the Dark Blue Obstacle Course and come out whole at the end of it. The Navy needs to see him in action for several years, to watch him under pressure, in the face of adversity, and in his demeanor as a leader of men.

Only then will they award him that coveted golden star of command, which will remain on the sleeve of his uniform for all the days of his working life. Most important, that star does not just denote learning and competence; it is the public emblem of the Navy's belief in the officer.

And that, on both sides, is a matter of honor. In the US Navy, honor is the most cherished commodity there is. The concept exists marginally in the corporate world, but it's not the same.

The Academy's final year is easily the best, principally because everyone at last knows what they are doing, and why. The great traditions of the place come into even sharper focus. The life-and-death struggle (to us) to beat Army in the final annual football game in Philadelphia becomes almost as vital to the midshipmen as for the players, resplendent in the finest uniform in the country: the blue and gold of the US Navy.

At last we understand precisely what that means—and not just the knowledge that the football helmet is designed to replicate the massive golden dome above the Academy's 100-year-old chapel, but the aura of sacred trust that exists in this most holy of places.

The enormous United States Naval Academy Chapel, set on high ground at the south end of The Yard, is one of the wonders of America. It seats 2,500 and beneath its stunning stained-glass windows provides a place of worship for both Catholics and Protestants. The two anchors that flank the entrance once belonged to the Navy's first armored cruiser, USS New York.

Entombed within the crypt is the body of Commodore John Paul Jones, the black-and-white marble of the sarcophagus supported by bronze dolphins, and his final resting place made unforgettable to all of us by the simple chiseled words, "He gave our Navy its earliest traditions of heroism and victory."

Inside the main chapel, one pew is cordoned off in blue velvet and, before it, one single candle burns eternally, dedicated to all prisoners of war and those in dark blue still missing in action. The words that dominate the altar are those of the Navy hymn: "Eternal Father Strong to Save, and, in this place at least, its heartrending cry, For those in peril on the sea."

I understand other colleges' uniforms inspire a kind of Neanderthal worship. But there is nothing quite like those of the Naval Academy, nothing even remotely like the blue and gold, the colors of the greatest ocean-going fleet the world has ever seen.

No other establishment can match that overwhelming sense of goodness and belonging, the pride and the loyalty, the sense of being a part of something so much greater than self. The Navy's deep roots in religion and heroism, real heroism, set us apart.

And at the Army-Navy game, when we sing the Academy's anthem, "Navy Blue and Gold," I swear to God every last one of us, past and present officers, is in tears, as the incomparable words echo around Lincoln Financial Field in Philadelphia . . .

> For sailor men in battle fair
> Since fighting days of old
> Have proved a sailor's right to wear
> The Navy Blue and Gold.
> *Beat Army!*

Wherever I am in the world, whatever the time, I always attempt to watch the game. Even if I'm just at home, when those stardust words split the skies above Philadelphia, I spring to my feet and stand tall. The astounding thing is that at that moment former midshipmen, on active duty, perhaps retired, relaxing at home, wherever that may be, are all on their feet, bound by that unbroken brotherhood that still binds us all together, decades after we have left the shores of Maryland.

I realize that great universities all over the United States have strong alumni associations and strong links to their graduates that last a lifetime.

But I know of nothing that compares to the achingly powerful emotional pull the Academy forever exerts on its sons and daughters. There is nothing quite like that, anywhere.

And as those strident notes finally die away, and the thousands of midshipmen in the stadium raise the roof with that yell of "Beat Army," all those timeless mantras come cascading in on us. The years melt away, and the ironclad laws of the Academy once more whisper through our minds: *never give in . . . believe in the impossible . . . accountability . . . self-reliance . . . commitment . . . loyalty . . . honor.*

They may be just words to everyone else, but to us they are a statement of the highest possible ideals, which like the golden star on our sleeve, we carry with us throughout our lives. No one ever forgets where they learned them.

My final year at the Academy passed swiftly. Examinations were taken and mostly passed—I finished about halfway. From there we all hurtled toward Commissioning Week and graduation day: when a midshipman formally becomes a line officer of the US Navy. That's what it was all for.

Most people think of graduation day at Annapolis as the moment when all those kids hurl their hats into the air and probably never find them again. Half right. That's the moment we hurl our caps in the air, but most times we do not even bother to look for them again.

Because at that moment, the old midshipman's cap with its small anchor has become obsolete. From that moment we're all commissioned officers, ensigns. And that permits us a brand-new cap—with a leather band, white top, and shiny black bill. There's a wide gold band from temple to temple. The central cap badge comprises the Navy ceremonial shield, with two big gold anchors and a silver eagle.

On the sleeves of the dress uniform, the thin stripe of the midshipman is replaced by the solid gold stripe of the ensign, right below the big gold star of command. The ensign's shoulder boards were similar—the thick, dark blue, fuzzy felt, the heavy five-pointed gold star and stripe.

We wore it all with immense pride, our white officers' uniforms with the gold buttons and that flash of dark blue on our shoulders. I cannot describe how much it meant to each and every one of us. Suffice to say, out of every 1,000 US high school grads who contemplate a career in dark blue, we were told that only one would actually dare to apply to the United States Naval Academy.

An indifferent world may pass us by. It does not matter. We alone understood what it meant to have been commissioned from this place into the US Navy. We were also told by our instructors that the bottom ten passes from our examinations would probably finish in the top ten at any other college in the country.

One man in the entire country understood as well as anyone just what went through the minds of his audience on that sunlit day in late May 1987 when we graduated. Vice President George H. W. Bush was in attendance to present us with our diplomas and commissions, each one signed by President Reagan and the Secretary of the Navy and embossed with the seal of the Academy.

We realized that Vice President Bush would make only the first one hundred presentations personally, and thereafter Admiral Charles Larson would complete the last 1,000. Former Navy Lieutenant Junior Grade Bush conducted the first part with immense grace and good humor.

But when the one hundred were up, we waited for him to step down into his chair, and we all saw him smile and shake his head. Admiral Larson looked momentarily baffled when the vice president said, as we later learned, "Sir, I'm staying up here on this stage until I've presented every last diploma. I know what this means to them."

Thus spoke a Naval Aviator, a decorated hero of WWII, the former Ensign Bush, who, with his aircraft hit by intense flak, on fire, flames belching out of the starboard engine, pressed home his attack on the Japanese positions at Chichi Jima. He released all of his bombs, pounded his targets, and then bailed out into the ocean, where he remained in a rubber raft until a US submarine, USS *Finback,* arrived to pick him up.

The vice president who awarded us our commissions that day was, at age eighteen, the youngest Naval Aviator in history. He received the Distinguished Flying Cross and three Air Medals. He'd flown his combat missions from the fast carrier USS *San Jacinto* and taken part in the Battle of the Philippine Sea.

He understood the golden star of command and that this was one glittering day in our lives. He also understood that with our great privilege would come awesome responsibility. There was the joy, and the gravity.

He, in company with so many other great men at that ceremony, grasped the moment when promising young men turned into warriors.

He presented the last of our 1,100 diplomas with the same effortless nonchalance with which he had handed over the first. The big handshake, the warm smile, and kind words. It was a very long, all-day ceremonial ordeal, but not to him. George 41. I thought then, as I think now: what a man, and what a brother officer for all of us.

It's funny how I recall my last hours at the Academy as vividly as I remember the first. Once more I wandered around taking one final look at the great landmarks of this living shrine to naval excellence, this nursery for admirals, this sailor's school that owes so much to history.

I stared up at the uncompromising expression on the bronze face of the Shawnee Indian Tecumseh, our statue of the figurehead of USS *Delaware,* the seventy-four-gunned nineteenth-century US ship of the line. The wide plaza in front of Bancroft Hall is named for him. Every parade began here, and every night of my midshipman life for four years I had heard the melancholy yet defiant notes of "Taps" ring out from here at precisely eleven o'clock.

I walked over to the Nimitz Library. Then across the plaza where we mustered daily for our noon meal formation. I knew, with an unutterable sadness, that I would not pass this way again. I walked on, into Bancroft Hall, this yawning Tower of Babel in which I had tried to fight my corner for four long years.

I stood below the rotunda, and then I walked, all alone, up the long, wide steps to Memorial Hall to pay my last respects to the former midshipmen who had given their lives on operational duty on behalf of the United States. All of their names are inscribed in the hall, and my new responsibilities as a commissioned officer seemed, for the first time, to bear down upon me.

Slowly I walked back along Bancroft Hall's vast corridor for the last time. Afterward I went in search of my beloved red Mustang GT and tossed my bags into the space behind the front seat. Very deliberately I drove toward the main gate, and as I left the Academy for that last time, I could see the golden dome in my rearview mirror. It was my last sight of the campus, and a bright confirmation that here at least there was a higher calling than personal ambition.

They always told us that Annapolis was not about you. It's about your team. And somehow, as I made my departure, I knew for certain that God was in his heaven and I had done my darnedest to live up to the ideals of the United States Naval Academy. I still had my picture, and now I turned south once more to Pensacola, one more step toward the strike fighter aircraft that were, I hoped, somewhere awaiting me.

On the passenger seat, right next to me, was the jacket of my blue dress uniform, the gold star strategically placed so I could see it at all times on the long journey.

SEVERAL HUNDRED BRAND-NEW US Navy ensigns surged out of the Academy on that sunlit May day, determined to taste freedom for the first time in four years. Before them stretched a long summer, and there was no compulsion to make any definite career moves until fall.

So we scattered to the four corners of the country for warm weeks and sometimes months of vacations, family, and girlfriends, free at last from the shouts and commands of Annapolis that had transformed us from half-educated kids to leaders of men in four arduous stages.

I too sensed the pure relief in that headlong rush to liberty, but I could not join my buddies in their exodus to our country's beaches and mountains. I headed straight for the runways of Pensacola, to the gun-barrel-straight concrete and asphalt launch pad of Forrest Sherman Field.

In a sense, this new deployment was like a home away from home for me. Admiral Sherman, for whom the Pensacola airfield is named, was a stalwart of the Naval Academy (Class of 1918), and the sports field out on Hospital Point was also named for him, as were *two* modern guided-missile destroyers. Indeed, he was the youngest-ever chief of naval operations.

A Naval Aviator and Pensacola instructor, Admiral Sherman holds a revered place in the annals of US Navy legends, lionized for his command of the aircraft carrier USS *Wasp,* when she was hit and sunk by a Japanese submarine on the way to Guadalcanal in 1942.

Three torpedoes smashed into her hull and all but incinerated the forward section of the ship. With gasoline blazing furiously, her bombs and missiles exploding, aircraft wrecked and crashing through the decks, and almost two hundred men killed, the *Wasp* was instantly into her death throes, listing hopelessly, twenty degrees. Captain Sherman gallantly tried to steer her aft to put the wind on her starboard bow, to contain the fires, but he was compelled to abandon.

With black smoke billowing more than a hundred feet into the air, Captain Sherman refused to leave his ship until every last wounded man was evacuated into the lifeboats. Almost 2,000 men were saved by the accompanying US destroyers, and Forrest Sherman was the last man to go, sliding down an escape line off the stern of the ship to the last lifeboat.

This might, in the fullness of time, be considered an act of selfless and disciplined courage. But Captain Sherman would not have considered it so. To such former Academy graduates, the safe evacuation of the entire crew comes with the territory. Captain Sherman would not have dreamed of finding his way to a safe boat and watching from below while the others escaped. He would rather have died than do that.

Powerful explosions from the dying *Wasp* boomed long into the night, and the still-burning carrier sank by the bow shortly after nine p.m.

Captain Sherman was awarded the Navy Cross, and the citation said simply, "For extraordinary heroism." Wherever you looked in this organization, there were some hellishly big boots to fill. In WWII, Pensacola-trained Navy and Marine pilots sank sixty-three German U-boats, 161 Japanese warships, and brought down more than 8,000 Japanese aircraft.

I was on my way to a place where they would swiftly find out whether I had the right stuff to fly those F-14 Tomcats. I knew it could only be achieved step by step. First of all, the ability to fly a fast jet aircraft, then the landings, then the carrier landing, then the carrier takeoff, then the diabolically tricky night landing on a carrier, the most nerve-wracking test of skill there is for any pilot, however experienced.

Many are called but few are chosen. I knew all about that. But I have to say there was never one shred of doubt in my mind that I would be one of that last crowd. Chosen. No bullshit. I was born to do this, way back there, alongside that old cornfield in southern Ohio.

I drove down to the northwest corner of Florida all alone. There are several ways to get to Pensacola, but I gunned the Mustang straight through Georgia and crossed the state line into Alabama. From the city of Montgomery I stayed right on Interstate 85, the highway down to Mobile, but I hung a left before that, found Route 29, and that's a straight shot into the US Navy's principal air training operation.

The next day I met my good buddy Tim Roylance, with whom I'd gone through the Academy, and we drove out through the long sand dunes on that wild stretch of the Gulf Coast to a little place called Perdido Key, where we rented an apartment right on the beach. That was home for several months, five miles from the base.

Through the summer into October they drilled us in ground-based academics, study of the weather, aerodynamics, engineering classes, and the rudiments of power plants, hydraulics, maps, charts, navigation systems. I'll say one thing about the Navy: they march their future battle commanders right in at the very bottom of the pile.

It's not enough that you know. They have to know that you know. The tests and examinations are relentless. They would not have cared if I were a rear admiral and a blood relation of the Red Baron, I still had to start at the lowest point. Just so they could be sure that when I took command of a strike fighter, I really knew what I was about.

In corporate America, guys right out of college with good degrees are able to join firms, especially in finance, quite high in the pecking order. In fact, corporate America is full of relatively smart young guys, "executives" with hardly any experience in the real world. Today, book learning, master's degrees, and doctorates are what matter. And I guess it works okay—at least I thought it did before September 2008.

But it does not work for the Navy. They take one look at your academic results, then stow them in a locker and make you start over, ground zero. Nothing's proven yet, so get moving, kid, and you can aim as high as you want, but you'll climb every mountain to get there.

Every step of the way we'll mark you, test you, add up your scores, take note of your weaknesses, and watch your every action, night and day, until we know beyond any doubt that you're our guy. Only then will we approve your career path. Never mind magna cum laude. It's the supreme approval of your peers we're looking for. And in the Navy we never forgive the weakest link. We all help anyone who's struggling, but either he shapes up or he's history, and we don't care if he's magna cum stupendo.

It was impossible to escape the suspicion that there was a colossal lack of worldliness in the ivory towers of Wall Street in the fall of 2008. The entire edifice of the subprime crisis tottered not only on a gossamer bedrock of lies, which everyone decided in their pitiful lack of wisdom to ignore, but there was a glaring lack of chief petty officers, guys who'd worked at the coal face of the industry.

Where were the executives who should have been saying, "Here...let me have a look at a few of those mortgages. Show me the original papers. What's this $40,000-a-year character doing with a brand-new four-bedroom house? The guy drives a frigging bus for a living. Something's wrong here. How the hell can he be paying $3,000 a month? He probably earns about 600 bucks a week."

With Lehman Brothers, Bear Stearns, and Merrill Lynch all steaming straight toward the iceberg, there seemed to be no apparatus for a reality check. Someone to sound the alarm. Hell, by the end of 2006 with one or two critical price indices on the move, the Navy would have summoned everyone to *battle stations!*

If we'd been running the show, our mortgage department would have contained half a dozen guys who'd actually written mortgages, sold mortgages, or worked in some little local bank that made mortgage loans. You think we bring $50 million strike fighter aircraft in to land with landing signal officers on the carrier's stern who've never been fighter pilots?

I cannot accept that the US Navy system of checks and balances would have permitted these Wall Street trading maniacs to be out there buying and selling billion-dollar bonds, backed by mortgages with more holes in them than USS *Wasp* on the voyage to Guadalcanal.

They could not, all of them, possibly have remained 100 percent ignorant of the quicksand they were marching over. Not even the CEOs, who lived above the fray in gleeful anticipation of their gigantic Christmas bonuses, could have been bereft of all inside knowledge.

And surely most harrowing was that they were selling potentially worthless bonds to major international clients. Deliberately and cold-bloodedly. I suppose there was a certain poetic justice when they were all caught, simultaneously, with their trousers around their ankles, loaded with very, very pricey CDOs and no more customers.

But there was a moral duty incumbent upon them to play fair with their own clients. And this was cast aside, first in the frenzy for profits, and then in the even greater frenzy to save their own skins. They cast their clients adrift, seeking only to save themselves and let the rest of the world go to hell.

The 2008 collapse, first of Wall Street and then of the rest of the global financial system, would have represented to the US Navy a shattering defeat on the battlefield, the loss of a war, perhaps even the loss of the nation's freedom. Because we are America's war guardians, the nation's lifeguards against the rage of international conflict. For more than two hundred years we have defended and protected American traditions.

It takes a certain kind of man to comprehend that level of responsibility, not just with military might, but with ethical and moral righteousness. For us the concept of failure is far beyond anything we have ever been taught. Failure is unthinkable. But so is the concept of softening our will.

I am sure many admirals have said it just as well. But we should remember the words of General Douglas MacArthur on the subject of defeat in his farewell speech at West Point: "The long gray line has never failed us. Were you to do so, a million ghosts in olive drab, in brown khaki, in blue and gray, would rise from their white crosses, thundering those magic words: Duty, Honor, Country.

"In my dreams I hear again the crash of guns, the rattle of musketry, the strange mournful mutter of the battlefield. But in the evening of my memory I come back to West Point. Always there echoes and re-echoes: Duty, Honor, Country."

Those are not the words of a Wall Street type. Those are the words of one of us: General MacArthur, a graduate of the United States Military Academy, a leader of men, and in his own magnificent way, a front-line guardian of our ethics, standards, and highest ideals.

This is why true excellence in the military, the Navy, or in the best of our corporations can only come from within, from a place where boards of directors react to an honor code and try to do the decent thing, tell the truth, and demonstrate character.

The general had stringent views on that, and a very fine definition of things that build your basic character: To become "strong enough to know when you are weak, and brave enough to face yourself when you are afraid . . . to be proud and unbending in honest failure . . . to face the stress and spur of difficulty and challenge; to stand up in the storm but have compassion on those who fall."

I had a long career in dark blue, and during that time I met many senior commanders who fit those ideals. To us they were words and meanings to which we were accustomed. They were ideals to which we understood we were expected to live. However, I fear those moral standards in corporate America have died.

In these early years of the twenty-first century there is something curious and otherworldly about them, at least when spoken in the context of big business. That ought not to be. The morals of Gordon Gekko in the movie *Wall Street* may very well have made him richer than General MacArthur, and he probably had a superior art collection. But the tycoon was only a pale shadow of the man himself.

Back at Pensacola, the examinations lasted for eight solid weeks. We took tests all of the time, right to the end. It had to be one of the most competitive sections of the Navy there was. And the problem was that if you were determined to become a fighter pilot, you needed a stratospherically high grade, and everything you did was marked. You needed every one of those marks you could lay your hands on. Therefore, regardless of the subject, you had to score high every time or risk slipping down the pecking order.

We had intensive courses not only in aviation and cockpit simulators, but in swimming and a whole variety of pool tests, I guess just in case we ever had to ditch into the ocean. It's always the same in the Navy. They want to watch you save your own friggin' life a few times, just to make sure you don't drown after they've spent several million bucks on your flight training.

Those tests were heavy. One of them involved strapping us in a simulated cockpit and then sliding it down a chute into the water and settling twenty feet below the surface. The first rule was not to panic, and then we had to disconnect the lines and various electronic connections and somehow get out. Guys really panicked down there, and the instructors were very stern.

They instilled in us the need to cope with failure, to understand where we had screwed up, and why. Constructive criticism was their watchword, and they made very certain we understood precisely where they were coming from. They made it clear that a person who cannot accept and then learn from mistakes was probably useless anyway. I remember one of their phrases: "We are going to teach you how to learn."

As always in the Navy, flight school was organized right down to the last detail. Part one was essentially indoctrination. Part two involved a move out to Corpus Christi, way down the Texas coast beyond Houston, about seven hundred miles from Pensacola. We'd be there in October, for primary flight training, learning the basics in notoriously windy conditions. Part three (intermediate) involved another move, this time up to Meridian, Mississippi, a couple of hundred miles north of Pensacola, up on the long Alabama border. We were scheduled to arrive there in May 1988 and remain there until graduation from advanced jet training, where big decisions are made. This would end on August 4, 1989. That was the day I would get my beloved Wings of Gold.

Meanwhile, we all slogged through indoctrination, pounding away at the obstacle course, becoming super fit, mastering the classwork. In the Navy they don't just want you to understand how an aircraft jet engine works, they expect you to take it to pieces and rebuild it in your lunch hour. Well, not quite. But again, you get my drift.

If that big Pratt & Whitney sucker shuts down suddenly in flight, a Naval Aviator needs to know what happened, and why, what to do now, and whether it can be fixed. There's only one way to gather that knowledge, and that's an intensive practical study of that complicated piece of engineering, and about two hundred tests to prove you're paying attention.

Fifteen doctorates and a couple of master's degrees won't help you. You just need to prove you know. As long as you achieve a nice little pass grade of 100 percent minimum, everybody's cool. Needless to say, not everyone received a free pass out to Corpus Christi. The course is just too demanding for some would-be jet pilots, even guys from Annapolis. They had to make fast career rethinks, but the Navy provides many options, mainly back to the fleet.

Tim and I sailed through indoctrination and drove down to Corpus Christi, Truax Field, for the next phase of flight training. This is where we all get seriously airborne, and as usual I was there early, before almost everyone else, assigned to Training Squadron 27, the Boomers. Not as in babies, but as in sound barrier, strictly sonic.

Of course I was not yet scheduled to blast my way through the aviator's equivalent of the four-minute mile, since our first aircraft would be the T-34C Mentor, the latest model of the six-decades-old Beechcraft trainer, now constructed for the Navy by Raytheon in Wichita, Kansas. Top speed: 280 knots.

Only two summers ago, back at Pensacola, I'd had a few goes in a T-34, and they were very sharp, white with orange wingtips, and parked in a straight line out beyond the hangars. They were obviously one of the great aviation training aircraft; otherwise the Navy would not have stuck with them for so long.

Generations of Naval Aviators have learned the basics in the T-34 Mentor, thousands and thousands of them. It all started not long after the Japanese bombed Pearl Harbor and the US Chiefs of Staff realized they needed a massive influx of pilots to deal with the "rising sun" in the Pacific. Corpus Christi was the chosen spot for the training to begin. President Bush (George 41) was in the third graduating class.

By the end of WWII, Corpus Christi, with its six auxiliary fields located around the main area, comprised 20,000 acres, with almost 1,000 buildings, hangars, shops, barracks, and warehouses, with four asphalt runways, one of them 8,000 feet long.

It is a gigantic place, the largest Naval Aviation training facility in the world, so big it contains the Corpus Christi Army Depot, which is in turn the largest helicopter repair facility in the world.

The T-34C is a single-engine two-seater turboprop trainer. In a way it was a familiar sight for Tim and me, because one of them hangs from the ceiling in Chevalier Hall back in Pensacola, right there above the wide marble corridor of the aviation technical schools building.

Once more we had to settle down to study both this aircraft and its simulator, right down to the most minute detail: the innermost functions of the engine, the radio systems, the airspeeds for takeoff, cruising, and landing, the start sequence, the computerized power plants.

We had to understand *everything*, including the warning lights. And with these routine mini-electronics it was necessary not just to know there was a problem when the "idiot light" flicked on, but also to know when precisely the light was supposed to be on, and if not, why not.

I refer to the "idiot light" because in aviator's parlance, if you don't realize there is something awry with your aircraft until the light comes on, well, you'll probably fail anyway. The Navy instructors would probably consider that to be either slack, idle, or incompetent—most likely all three. Certainly not the ultrasharp demeanor expected of a potential strike fighter pilot.

They took no chances with guys who were suspect. They actually programmed these little warning lights to come on right out of the blue, signifying there was a fire somewhere in the aircraft. If you say it fast, there's no problem: "Fire light's on." But if you think about it a bit more carefully, your instructor has just informed you the friggin' aircraft has caught fire and you're making 250 knots three miles above the ground, and the son of a bitch might explode. *Holy shit!* Even if it's just a simulator, they really want to see you in action, dealing with it, carrying out the correct procedures. No screwups. A lot of guys were really shaken by that flickering fire light.

The checklist was pages and pages long. You had to learn it and oftentimes recite it to the instructor, right out loud, word perfect in front of everyone. Thankfully those techniques had been drummed into us back at the Academy. When your Corpus Christi flight instructor demanded you demonstrate your knowledge, it was like a chow call with afterburners.

In addition, there were two books, crammed with information you needed to know. One we called the Big Blue Pill (our flight manual), and then there was a small abbreviated version, which you carried with you at all times. In the Big Blue Pill, there were certain passages, some of them quite long, that were printed in bold type, and those you had to memorize, top to bottom.

You could be asked at any time to recite any part of the Big Blue Pill printed in bold. Might even be the technique for a parachute jump, when you're working on something entirely different. You simply had to be adaptable, diligent, concentrated, and ready for anything at any time.

If you fell short of these standards, in the eyes of the instructors you would never be A+, and that would prevent you from becoming a jet fighter pilot. With them it's A+ or nothing. Like I said, you need every single mark you can get. There are marks for those little recitals you give to the instructors. There are marks for everything. And if you want to go all the way to TOPGUN, you must earn every last one of them.

We studied all day and halfway through the night from October right through Christmas and into the new year. And then, on February 22, the schedule was posted all over the base, in particular on the squadron notice board, the one that issued our life's instructions every day of the week.

There were the magic words. Not General MacArthur's "Duty, Honor, Country." But in their own way, just as magical: "Ensign Lay will fly tomorrow with Lieutenant Summerfield. Brief: 0830. Takeoff: 1000. Landing: 1230."

This was the first time I'd ever been on a flight schedule. You probably realize by now I was early for everything. For this I was especially early. I needed to be in the Ready Room, prepared and organized for the brief, by around eight fifteen. Looking back, I think I arrived shortly after midnight, the way you do after nearly dying of excitement.

I definitely knew two things: First, I had to be completely clued up on everything the lieutenant might ask me. Second, if I should somehow blow it, turn up late, and offer something truly lame like, "I guess I didn't sleep well," his reply would be succinct. Something like, "How many miles is it back to Ohio? You're all done as a pilot."

The truth is, if you haven't come fully prepared, you cannot have been listening for the past five months. The US Navy is in the process of organizing you into an air wing commander, and they don't leave a lot of margin for error. None. The Ready Room is small, with a whiteboard on the wall.

"Okay, Jeff. Gimme the weather."

"Scattered clouds, sir, at 3,000 feet, winds gusting to twenty knots out of the southwest, temperature: fifty-four degrees, rising to sixty-one by noon."

"Runway?"

"Runway One Seven, sir."

"Call sign?"

"Boomer three-one, sir."

The instructor then took me through every last inch of the procedures: ground checking of the aircraft, preflight, emergency real and simulated, engine speeds, the cockpit dials, takeoff and landing speeds, the ones we'd learned over and over since October. But that's the Navy way. No mistakes.

"Okay, Jeff, our mission today is out to Bravo II. We'll be flying east. If we need to bail out, you go left, I go right."

"Yessir."

"Our emergency today is engine fire on the start. What's the boldface?"

As it happened, I knew the boldface from the Big Blue Pill backward, forward, and sideways. I could have recited it in my sleep. I could have recited it if they'd been lowering me into my grave. I probably would have recited it before I requested St. Peter to open the Pearly Gates.

That Big Blue Pill, NATOPS (Naval Air Training and Operating Procedures Standardization), describes everything in the world of military flying, and it's finicky to the final degree.

However, it's worth knowing that shortly after WWII, the Navy managed to lose 754 aircraft in 1954 alone without even being in conflict, never mind in a world war. Right here I'm talking training. Young pilots were crashing and ditching all over the place, averaging around two smashed aircraft every day at the dozens of naval air stations all over the globe.

It was that program, the one contained in the turgid pages of NATOPS, that stopped it. Over the years we reduced the losses to only twelve, one a month. That, by anyone's standards, was a superb improvement. Not good enough, of course, but still incredible.

This was, broadly, why I was standing here reciting its paragraphs with life-and-death due diligence. NATOPS is taken extremely seriously.

At nine thirty, after one hour of intensive briefing, Lieutenant Summerfield and I walked out to the maintenance area where the aircraft was waiting. It looked kind of different from the others, still white with orange wingtips, but its front end was painted like a tiger shark's head. The big, jagged white teeth painted carefully in a line made it probably the most ferocious-looking T-34C ever to fly. Naturally, I took this artistic war paint as some kind of an omen, even though I knew the aircraft was just a trainer.

We walked around and made the preflight checks: props, wings, and undercarriage. Then I climbed up into the front seat and went immediately into the start sequence, all the time with the constant interchange of the briefing with the instructor.

We were on FAM-1—that's "familiarize yourself with the instruments." We had a short exchange about the last ten fixed problems there had been with this aircraft. Then we checked once more the takeoff and landing speeds, everything precisely by the book.

We taxied up to the radio tower. Runway one seven. "Permission to takeoff?" And suddenly we were a go. I was strapped in, and I gunned the

T-34 down the runway, feeling the liftoff, pulling up the landing gear, then the flaps, rising into the Texas skies, pulling back the stick, bringing the aircraft to life, heading down to the sea, the way Navy pilots always do, ripping that bloodthirsty shark through the gusting winds high above the vast flatlands that engulf the Corpus Christi naval air station.

It was, without a doubt, the coolest thing on earth. I wasn't driving an F-14 yet, and despite the teeth, the aircraft itself was strictly pacifist. But to me it was as dramatic as the first flight of the space shuttle. I was up there, in my US Navy flight suit, and that chilling word, "Navy," was painted on my fuselage.

Okay, it wasn't even a jet, far less a strike fighter. But I did not care. In that moment as I banked east and then flattened out, I had arrived. I think Lieutenant Summerfield understood that, because he never said a word; he just left me to smile in my own personal version of heaven for ten minutes.

Granted that tiny window of privacy, I reflected on just how far I had come from rural Ohio to this level of naval responsibility. I was, after all, the first member of my family to go to college.

The flight, and especially the landing, went perfectly, and I repeated the exercise thirteen more times before I flew by myself. And then on March 25 it was posted on the board: "Ensign Lay will fly solo tomorrow."

The next day I briefed myself. Then I was free, all alone, accelerating up into the clear blue yonder, no one yelling at me, no "come around," no chow call. I was at the controls of a Navy aircraft, trusted by my superiors to be there. They'd been building me up for this moment. In just a few weeks they'd taught me everything there was to know about this T-34C.

I was the pilot in command. I was yelling with joy, all by myself up there in the sky, a mile above the ground, zooming down to the beach, flying along it, back and forth. Since I'd first pulled on my working blues at Annapolis, I'd experienced a few very big deals: becoming a commissioned officer in the US Navy, getting my degree, making it to flight school.

But there never had been a bigger deal than this. Nor would there be in the foreseeable future. Not even a couple of months later, after they'd marked every takeoff, every landing, and darn near every footstep we'd taken.

Not even when they announced on the squadron notice board that I'd finished first in my class. Not even when a very senior officer told me they considered me the young pilot most likely to make it through to TOPGUN. There simply is nothing quite so exhilarating for any pilot as that first solo command.

I MADE MY LAST FLIGHT at Corpus Christi on May 25, 1988, collected my grades, moved out of the beach house, and drove in tandem with Tim directly to the earliest start date possible at Naval Air Station Meridian, Mississippi, then home to one of the Navy's only three Jet Strike Pilot Training Bases.

This was not just a new home. We were about to fly a new aircraft, a twin-turbojet 521 mph T-2C Buckeye, built by North American Aviation in Columbus, Ohio. My first jet aircraft, built in my home state, named after the Ohio state tree and after Ohio people: Neil Armstrong, Colonel John Glenn, and I were all Naval Aviators, all dyed-in-the-wool Buckeyes. At least that's how I saw it as I sped through east Texas toward the Louisiana border. You may have guessed, I'm real big on omens.

They assigned me to Training Squadron 19, the Attack Frogs, and we commenced flight training in the new aircraft on July 25 after the usual two-month study period, during which we proved we could, if necessary, take the old Buckeye to pieces and put it back together.

I made my first solo flight on September 14, 1988, and it was a complete blast, flying three times faster than the T-34 Mentor. Then they started to teach us the rudiments of dogfighting, flying patterns, and spin training, out there to the west of the city of Meridian, between 10,000 and 20,000 feet above the pine trees.

For some reason Meridian is one of the thunderstorm capitals of the United States, subject to sudden rainstorms, squalls, and general driving rain. It's very challenging, and those difficult weather conditions somehow make you better. Everyone says fighter pilots trained in Meridian are always better than their counterparts from other states.

With the constant takeoffs and landings of Navy aircraft, Meridian was an inspiring place to be. I remember that fall so well. It was hotter than hell and as the weeks went by nothing cooled down, especially the pressures and tensions.

The course developed into a kind of ticking clock, as we headed resolutely toward December. I knew in the first part of that month I would be required to answer a very serious question. The emblem on the Meridian air base patch is, tellingly, an aircraft carrier, and this inevitably was the target, our first carrier landing.

A brand-new magic word was popping into our vocabulary: Lexington. That's USS *Lexington,* the oldest aircraft carrier in the world, WWII's legendary CV-16, the "Blue Ghost," the wooden-decked warhorse whose aviators destroyed 372 enemy aircraft in the Pacific theater, plus 475 more on the ground, and 300,000 tons of enemy ships and cargo.

USS *Lexington* was the only US carrier ever painted dark blue—hence her nickname—after the grotesque Tokyo Rose four times announced the Japanese had sunk her "beneath the deep blue seas," only to see her come steaming over the horizon the following day.

In 1988 she was deployed at sea, off Key West, Florida. No longer a warhorse, she was now a trial horse, the official Navy training carrier for aspiring jet pilots. Like it was not sufficiently difficult anyway, they saddled us with putting a jet down on a living legend. Anyone who attended the Academy knew her war record as other students understand the Battle of Gettysburg.

In two days during November 1943, her aviators downed twenty-nine enemy aircraft. In February 1945 her pilots flew close support to the US assault force at Iwo Jima. The final air strike against the Japanese Islands was launched from her flight deck. In total, USS *Lexington* spent twenty-one months in unremitting combat.

And as a member of the Essex class, she was not so big as the modern-day Nimitz-class carriers, her flight deck just a shade more than nine hundred feet against the *George Washington*'s almost 1,100. She drew only thirty feet with displacement tons of 42,000, against the *Washington*'s 100,000-plus.

We had all been regaled with accounts of how tiny a carrier looks as the pilots come bucking home, through the shifting gusts and tropical thermals. And so far as we were concerned, the *Lexington* would be darn near invisible.

Most of us thought we'd probably need every last square inch we could get, when we finally lined our aircraft up for that first landing. I pictured it all in my mind: the flight deck looming suddenly nearer, the high speed, the myriad of winking lights on the instrument panel. I heard over and over in my imagination the short staccato orders of the *Lexington*'s landing signal officer . . .

"Roger Ball, Buckeye . . . twenty-six knots."

Jesus Christ. I am certain every one of us had nightmares about the forthcoming ordeal, controlling a fast jet as it screamed in toward the old wooden decks of the Blue Ghost.

## CHAPTER 5

# Dipping Our Wings to God

They flew us down to Key West on December 8 and we moved into the air station's bachelor officer quarters, the tallest building on the island, with its huge lettering on the side of the building, "Fly Navy," visible from Sloppy Joe's, Ernest Hemingway's old drinking hangout on Duval Street.

The following day, right there on the station notice board, they posted the flight schedule that announced my fate: "Ensign Lay will fly a T-2 Buckeye to USS *Lexington,* cruising 75 miles east of Key West, and make four carrier landings, and four catapult takeoffs."

It might have been fine for Papa to take the day off and go fishing, then drinking for a couple of days when he was supposed to be writing *A Farewell to Arms* at his home around the corner on Whitehead Street. It was not, however, okay for us to take our eyes off the ball, not even for ten minutes, in this enormous naval and military headquarters perched on the southernmost tip of America.

Next day, bright and early, on a warm, breezy morning, we attended our brief, and then three of us took off, in tight formation behind our instructor. All four of us were flying alone. Remarkably, the Navy trusted us so well, they sent us out to make our first carrier landing flying solo. The culture never varied. Full command of the aircraft, at a very young age.

I flew in the number two position of the formation, on the leader's right wing, climbing to 20,000 feet out over the ocean, leaving behind colonies of pelicans and iguanas.

The flight out to the carrier took a little more than ten minutes, and then we could see her far below on an azure sea as we circled around. My radio was tuned to the carrier's control tower now, and I knew to shut up and listen to the air officer talking to other pilots, out in front of us in the stack.

There was a lot happening and the radio was extremely busy. I could hear everything: "Skull one-one . . . take angels six . . . drop 2,000."

They were trying to move people down the stack, and we were boring a hole in the sky, orbiting, banking left, three to five miles wide and the radio never stopped. "Cougar three-one . . . Buckeye Ball, three-point-one . . . Skull one-one, *Charlie!*"

That last shout meant "Get your ass down here . . . get in the pattern . . . Let's *go!*"

But our lead man was Skull 11 and that was us. And when he heard "*Charlie!*" he immediately went around to a point off the carrier's beam, 180 degrees, and I followed him as he rolled out, then put his wings level. The other two followed me, and the leader dropped down to eight hundred feet.

We were making this long arc around the ship, and we were about five to eight miles behind, forty-five degrees off her port quarter. Our lead guy was going to break left—and I was counting to twelve, coming in fifteen seconds astern of him, standard distance for a stack of aircraft coming into the flight deck.

I was really aware of the airspeed. I was holding the aircraft steady, and while I was watching my leader, I wasn't strictly following him. No matter how experienced he was he could still screw it up. *Anyone* can screw this up, and the Navy encourages individual decision making. That way they have a fair chance of losing only one aircraft, not two.

I made my own adjustments, airspeed and altitude, and I watched him, flying up the wake of the ship, leaving it to his left. He was a quarter mile behind the landing area, and the LSO had him.

He called in, "Seven-two-one, Buckeye Ball, four-point-two."

The LSO on the stern instantly snapped back, "Roger Ball, Buckeye . . . twenty-six knots" (that's breeze over the flight deck).

I was in the middle of my turn. Even at this airspeed the aircraft was making three miles a minute. My heart rate skipped to about 2,000 revs per minute, and I calculated that I was good for another 135 degrees. Up ahead my instructor was just about to land. I was on my own, making only 120 knots right behind the stern.

I made my call to the LSO: "Seven-one-six, Buckeye Ball. Four-point-nine. Lay."

LSO: "Roger Ball, Buckeye . . . twenty-four knots."

The breeze had just dropped a couple of knots. Immediately I made several adjustments. I kept the wings level, landing gear down, hook up. They had to trust me now as I muscled up for my first touch-and-go.

I was making a million adjustments, my left hand hard on the throttle, right hand on the stick, and I was doing the math in my head: I know how much gas I have, and that means I need 118 knots. That's not 120, that's 118. Right about here you're awash in information. You just have to eat it up.

*Whoa! I'm too fast . . . throttle back a stitch.* I was looking at everything else, critiquing myself, correcting things, thousands of times, hands moving endlessly, never still. My eyes were never still, I was looking, listening, watching, checking the wake just below me. *Too far right . . . come back.*

Another pilot was behind me, not doing too good. I heard the LSO check in.

"Seven-zero-five, Paddles." (Very calm.)

"Go ahead, sir."

"I need you to concentrate on your instruments. You're rolling out on the wake, and ending up lined up left . . . Listen, there's a lot of wind over the flight deck today. I need you to keep your power up. You're pulling too much power coming off of that high crossing the ramp."

I could hear everything, and I couldn't afford to let it interest me. I knew how important the wind was. It's always pushing you down, and the ship is always moving away. You can't practice for this.

I was racing into the *Lexington*'s flight deck, accelerating straight at her in perfect landing attitude. The Buckeye's turbojets howled as I touched down, and I rammed open the throttles, holding her dead straight down the runway, gaining airspeed again, and then lifting her off fast, heading up once more.

Twice more I repeated the exercise, climbing, adjusting my airspeed, before the crosswind turn. Touchdown, and instant takeoff. Only then did the Navy instructors accept that I could touch down a jet on an aircraft carrier.

Their need for absolute certainty may border on the paranoid, but less than twelve months later, a student aviator of approximately my level of seniority misjudged a landing on the *Lexington* and lost control, and the right wing of his T-2 Buckeye smashed into the island, killing five people and injuring fifteen. At all times this is a hugely dangerous business.

You'll remember my concentration on the biggest moments in my life so far. Stand by. Here comes another one. This time I was bringing the Buckeye in to land, hook down, and catch the wire for the first time in my flight training. For me, that was big. Breathtakingly big.

Around I came, flying across the wind, waiting for the moment to straighten up for the downwind leg. I was checking the airspeed, checking my timing from the aircraft in front, taking my correct place in the pattern, counting to twelve, calculating the fifteen-second gap, checking my altitude, listening for the LSO. Everyone on the stern of the carrier knew I'd never done this before.

But first he shouted the command I'd waited to hear since I first saw my picture of the Tomcat climbing away from the carrier (ten years, three months, and four days, actually, give or take twelve and a half minutes—not that I'd been counting).

"Seven-one-six, Paddles . . . *Hook down!*"

That's the biggest moment in any Naval Aviator's life. Bigger than receiving your commission. Bigger than your first solo flight. Right now you're a Navy pilot bringing a turbojet in to land on one of the most famous US aircraft carriers ever built.

Down there was the Blue Ghost, and I knew they were all rooting for me as I reached out with my right hand for the hook lever and threw it down. I'd lived my whole life for the moment when I'd grab that hook for real, six hundred feet above the water. I didn't throw it down, I slammed that sucker down. Sheer elation.

Right now my airspeed was right, 120 knots, and I called in to the LSO: "Seven-one-six, Buckeye Ball. Three-point-one. Lay."

"Roger Ball, Buckeye . . . twenty-three knots."

The crosswind was gusting up there, six hundred feet above the ocean. The carrier was dead ahead but I was correcting every moment, trying to keep the long, white wake of the ship always on my left. I kept glancing down to check. The instruments couldn't help much now, and I was a tad too fast, and I was trying to hold the Buckeye in landing attitude. My heart was pumping faster than the jet engines.

I knew what was happening down on the stern. Everyone was watching as I came howling out of the blue summery skies. The LSO was about to bellow, "*Groove!*" to confirm I was close—"Stand by!"

Airspeed was right. Altitude was right. The ship's wake was right where it was supposed to be. I heard the LSO yell, "Short!"—*get away from the machinery.* I half expected him to add, "Watch it. This guy's a rookie." But he refrained and treated my landing like everyone else's.

One hundred yards out, I heard the call, "Ramp!" And balancing the Buckeye as deftly as a ballerina with flying boots on, I touched down, spot-perfect, right on the three wire, and the hook grabbed with dead certainty. The Buckeye was down. One second later, I was hurled forward in my seat straps as we were hauled in against the iron grip of the steam piston beneath the flight deck: 120 knots to zero in exactly two seconds.

The deceleration was jolting. I was trying to gather my thoughts, but already advancing through the steam was the familiar yellow-shirt.

He was signaling, holding his left thumb in his right fist, and motioning back and forth out in front of him like a guy in a sculling boat. His message was clear, and he was reading my mind, like everyone else. No one could hear above the howl of the engines, but his signal said, "Okay, Jeff. Pull power. That's fine. We got you. Calm down."

But he was in a major hurry. He made a clockwise windmilling motion with his right hand and arm, telling the guys on the wire to free me up. Then he looked straight at me and jammed his right thumb into the flat palm of his left hand, instructing me to get the hook up.

He stood in front of me and started moving both hands fast, wiggling them and then slowing, calm but steady, trying to get me out of the way, because fifteen seconds behind me another Buckeye was coming in to land. And the Blue Ghost needed to be ready.

I was still in the landing area, and back astern of the Buckeye I knew there was an LSO talking about me, calling the most familiar words in the fighter pilot's entire lexicon, as he straightens up for home: "*Foul deck!* . . . *Foul deck!*" (That was me. Still in the way, with a new aircraft bearing down at 120 miles an hour, about five hundred yards out, screaming in above the wake.) I had about five seconds to get the Christ out of the line of fire before they called out to abort the next landing. Still, I only had to do this three more times today.

As soon as I cleared the landing area, I checked my fuel, and the critical words were "Hold down"—that was our code, pilot to the purple-shirts— the "Grapes"—for fuel tank reading 2.3, meaning 2,300 pounds of fuel, calculated at 800 pounds for the landings, and 1,500 pounds to get home to Key West.

If you have much more, that's too heavy and may require an adjustment of the hydraulic piston on the wire, which essentially stops you. Any less, you need gas and you're entrusted to make that call. No one's going to check, because it's a command decision. You don't need to ask.

The Navy expects all of us to behave as commissioned officers, entrusted with their aircraft. *You have the golden star, and we've trained you for command authority at a very young age . . . Sort your gas out, kid, and make it snappy. Call for refuel if you need it.*

There is an undeniably brusque quality about our command operations, and we are apt to speak in telegrams, using one highly accurate word where civilians might need two dozen. We are trained to speak quickly and succinctly, like a succession of chow calls on steroids.

We are trained to use precise phrases, which everyone understands immediately. Unlike West Point, we have no time for the gray. We wear dark blue, and we communicate in black and white.

We do not operate with subtleties, winks, nods, or nudges. We say it right, first time, precisely like it is and like it is going to be. No bullshit. No gray areas. Otherwise we'd be nattering, and having conferences all day like civilian executives, half of them concerned with making sure everyone understands what some turkey is trying to communicate.

The US Navy has not been tarnished by modern management fads, nor indeed by management-speak. We could write a better handbook on management than they ever could. Because we have proved to be a "center of excellence" with old-fashioned "benchmarks" for "performance," "delivery," "risk management," "investment in people," and a quiet "moral courage," which Americans, perhaps above people of all other nations, understand only too well. And they *really* understand when it's missing or falls short.

Civilian obfuscation with weird expressions and phraseology is simply not our way. We do not have that luxury of time because, sometimes metaphorically, there's a thirty-five-ton jet fighter bearing down on us at high speed.

We operate along the same lines as Sir Winston Churchill when, as wartime prime minister, he was stung by the mounting shipping losses to the German U-boats and demanded a complete reorganization of the Royal Navy's entire Atlantic defensive strategies, battleships, destroyers, frigates, submarines, the lot.

He added, with a well-recorded growl, "And if it won't fit on one side of one sheet of paper, then it has not been properly thought out."

Like Winston's, our aims are always brevity and speed, and my first takeoff from a carrier was a prime example. Picture the scene. I'd been hauled out of the way of the oncoming air armada of training pilots, hauled down into the daisy line behind a yellow-shirt dragging me in on a tow bar, since the Buckeye has no nose-wheel steering. I was just supplying the engine power, very carefully, whenever he signaled. Fortunately, my heart had recently restarted, and I was in my right place in the line.

You might think after my early start, and three touch-and-go landings before my formal arrival, hook down, on the carrier, I might have been due a cup of coffee. Wrong. We're talking no break, no surrender, no goofing. *Get right back out there, on to the next event. Let's go. We're not screwing around here. Get down to that Cat, and get that Buckeye airborne.*

You've heard the expression "onward and upward"? Well, no civilian in all the world properly understands the true meaning of those words. At least not until they've served a few years in the US Navy. From touchdown to Catapult 1 we're talking five minutes.

The radio was on, and I was moving up in the daisy line. The tower wasn't happy with the next man for takeoff, and I heard them snap, "Rotate!" Hell, that was the guy right in front of me, and that short, sharp command meant his nose cone was up the chute, not set in the flyaway attitude, not tilted upward. If he left it like it was, he would shoot straight off the bow of the carrier like a goddamned bullet, with not enough lift, and hit the water.

Jesus Christ! I knew what they were saying to him, and he sure as hell did. This stuff had been pounded into our brains for months and months. It was unnerving to hear on the radio someone had done something really careless, a life-threatening omission. I was just trying to do everything right. I could do without the distractions! Typical of the Navy. One word to protect someone's life: "Rotate!"

This was, of course, the first time I'd been in a real takeoff line on a real aircraft carrier with real aviators, front and center. And all around me, these fire-breathing machines of war were moving in a delicate pattern, so carefully, inches here, a couple of feet there, engines roaring, the yellow-shirts signaling, calm but urgent. All in pursuit of perfection. Zero errors. They're too expensive.

Civilians cannot accept the concept of perfection. They have a trite little phrase: "Nothing's perfect." But the truth is, they're just too lazy mentally to achieve it. On the other hand, we are taught differently. The choreography on a carrier flight deck is perfection. Day after day, the gentle quiet maneuvers, among the hellish noise. That's perfect. At least it had better be. Or there'll be hell to pay.

I followed the signals, moving down to the catapult for the first time. I watched them get off in front of me, and then I was second in line, and I inched forward, and the JBD (jet blast deflector) came up smoothly, out of the deck, right in my face. Thick, white steam blew over the runway from the last takeoff, drifting up from the giant steam piston below. Through it I could see ghostly figures moving forward, signaling for the guys to hook us up to the catapult.

Quite suddenly the guy in front went to full power. The raging hot air blasted into the deflector, then came billowing over the top, buffeting against my vertical tail, causing me to shake and bounce every which way. The Buckeye jolted and danced around and, again suddenly, from below the deck there was a sudden *bam!* as the hydraulic piston released, and rammed forward like a cannonball, dragging the aircraft along the deck.

A split second later, there was another terrific *bam!* as the piston hit the water brake. *What the hell was that?* I thought we'd been hit by a cannonball. Out in front, I sensed rather than saw the other aircraft being hurled forward, in a violent close-up exhibition of pure power. I guess I'd never been this close, never before seen this view of those massive catapults in action.

An enormous hiss of steam sent a huge white cloud billowing over the runway, but through it all I could just see the aircraft race over the bow of the ship, but then I lost her, although I knew, from a thousand videos, she would sag down toward the water before accelerating skyward.

The JBD slid down, and through the white cloud a wraithlike figure in a yellow shirt came toward me on silent footsteps, beckoning me forward to the catapult, finger raised, slowly, like the Angel of Death.

Holy shit! This was it. Again I inched forward following the signals. I remember it was phenomenally quiet, with the engine idling, and I felt this overpowering sense of apprehension in the silence of the cockpit. I felt my life was somehow in someone else's hands. But again, everybody's life on the entire ship was in someone's hands.

I knew that somewhere under the fuselage there was an eighteen-year-old kid entrusted to hook my aircraft to the catapult. The Navy had trusted me to command this million-dollar aircraft, and the kid with my life. That's the way. We're always in someone else's hands, trusting each other, trusting the system, all of us with enormous responsibilities, mostly at a very young age.

The shuttle was fixed. I couldn't see if it was okay, but I knew what they were doing. I rolled forward, and they were still checking. There were green and white shirts, and the yellow in front of me. The "shooter" was still calling me forward, until we went to "tension" on the catapult.

His forearms were suddenly raised and crossed, and he was leaning back, and turning, checking over each shoulder that the runway was clear. Here was the signal. The fingers on his high right hand were shaking back and forth: *Go to full power.* The aircraft was straining against the leash.

Down below they were still checking the hydraulics. The very heartbeat of this ship had stopped. Everybody was looking, waiting for the sensational stationary slingshot that would hurl this new pilot forward.

I was pulling and pushing my controls for one last check that it was all go; the rudder, the stick, the revs, throttles open.

The shooter was still signaling full power, and now he pointed directly behind me. His signal demanded, "You good?" and then to someone else,

"You good?" I couldn't see any replies, but I knew what he was asking, and now he pointed directly at me.

This was another massive moment in my career, and I saluted formally, ramrod right forearm, palm flat. If I live to be ninety, I'll never tire of that moment. The salute to the shooter: *Okay. I'm ready to go.*

He returned my salute and went down on one knee, left arm extended. He glanced back once, and his arm swept down and touched the deck. I held the throttles open, and *bam!* Cat 1 exploded, the shooter ducked low, and the piston flung me forward, slamming me in the back. It would have knocked the air from my lungs, but for the harness and mask. Immediately there was that second *bam!* as the water brake slammed on, and the piston stopped dead right below my wheels.

The Buckeye's turbojets howled as it screamed toward the bow. I pulled the stick back a fraction as I launched out, flying high over the water. I was looking for my interval—that's the guy in front, who's supposed to be fifteen seconds ahead. He was there, and I followed him, and no one in the tower said a goddamned thing as I moved through the most important takeoff of my life. No one ever does in the Navy. Unless you screw it up.

So we tracked back around again, landed, and did it again. And again. The second one was just as good as the first. The third one was excellent. But nothing was ever burned into my mind like that first catapult shot from the Blue Ghost.

It's somehow like a tribal rite of passage, and I still wake up thinking about it, that brief and glorious moment when it felt like all the world stood before me. My greatest ambition was accomplished. I was not yet at TOPGUN, not yet at the controls of an F-14 Tomcat strike fighter. But, by golly, I was on my way.

I also remember the last takeoff. No one said anything, but as soon as I was airborne after catapult shot four, I heard, "Seven-one-six, tower. Signal divert, Navy Key West. One-three-five, seventy-four."

Which meant, "Don't come back, go home, fly southeast bearing 135 degrees. It's seventy-four miles." No one mentioned I'd completed three touch-and-go landings, four traps, four catapults, without a wave-off, without a bolter (that's missing the hook, then going for your life back down the runway to do it again). And no no-grades. Perhaps best of all, no mistakes on the radio.

We all returned to Key West after that somewhat grueling day on and off the *Lexington*. That night I received a call on the radio from my LSO, the guy who'd been with me the whole time, right from that first landing, and however good at his job he was, however skilled a pilot, he was not into poetry.

"Seven-one-six, Paddles."

"Go ahead, sir."

"You're a qual."

Calmly, feigning nonchalance, I replied, "Roger that, sir." I grabbed for the radio to turn it off for just five seconds so I could unleash a rebel yell, without everyone hearing me.

And how about that LSO? Having imparted the shining news I'd been waiting for most of my life, he just clicked off. Can you believe that? *You're a qual!*

There was nothing like "Well done! Jeff Lay, pilot of the future. You just passed the most stringent Naval Aviation exam there is, and what's more, you were in the top three among all of the ensigns."

Hell, no. *You're a qual.* Just a simple *you qualified for the next phase of the training. So get on with it.* I subsequently came to know that particular LSO quite well. A terrific guy, very special to me. Robert Frost he wasn't.

The intermediate phase was over, and I returned to flight school to start the final phase, the advanced section. They put those of us going forward into the TA-4J Skyhawk, where we learned the deadly serious business of combat dogfighting and bombing. We'd touched on it before. But this was much more intense, a highly developed, complex, and sophisticated form of air warfare.

The TA-4J is a version of that sharp little warrior of a thousand battles, the A-4 Skyhawk built by McDonnell Douglas. It's capable of carrying a couple of very lethal missiles under each of its delta wings and is powered by a single turbojet. Its official description is a carrier-capable, ground-attack, naval aircraft, and indeed has been used endlessly in such roles over five decades. However, the version we worked in was one of 550-odd special two-seat trainers, complete with the familiar white with orange markings.

We flew it all the time, while we learned and then polished our combat skills, and finally in July 1989 we finished the advanced jet course. In the three separate phases I had two firsts, and one third. I guess I was top of my year by miles. You often get that with workaholics who are obsessed with their subject.

They awarded wings to those of us with passes. At long last, I was a copper-bottomed, southern-fried Naval Aviator, but almost before I had time to have the wings attached to my uniforms, I was told in no uncertain terms that I had to earn them every single day of my service in the US Navy.

I was informed by a very senior instructor, "They are like the explosive bolts under your ejection seat, because those wings can be blown right off, taken away from you."

Well, they weren't the only things that could be taken away from me. Plainly, I knew how well I had done in the course. Everyone knew how well I had done. But the next diabolical shock of my career was on its way. And while I sat, I have to admit, in a mild state of self-congratulation, they requested my "dream sheet"—that's a kind of wish list, where you state in order of preference the career you are seeking now that you've qualified.

I did not need much space for my choice. It was to fly F-14 jet fighters. Just aim me straight at Fightertown USA—that's the legendary Miramar air base near San Diego, the place where they at last put you in the biggest, toughest, fastest strike fighter ever built: the Tomcat. And let's face it. If I, Number One Jeff, could not hack it down there at that wondrous airfield of the giants, who the hell could?

The answer was not long in coming. I received my orders within days. I had been selected to become an instructor in some godforsaken Texas air facility I had scarcely even heard of. Guys I'd just left in the dust were on their way to fly the Tomcats. They had not finished anywhere near me. One of them was the guy they'd had to shout to "*Rotate!*" Jesus Christ. And I'd worked so goddamned hard. No one in the entire US Navy had worked harder than I had.

I neither knew, nor cared, nor wanted to hear that the Navy had given me an enormous honor. I was absolutely devastated. More shocked and disappointed than I had ever been. They told me I had been the top instructor pick, as if that was supposed to impress me.

I'd have thought, after this long, they'd have known I just wanted to get into combat, to climb aboard the living, snarling incarnation of the twenty-year-old picture I'd kept with me like a secret talisman.

But slowly I came around. And the moral lessons I had been taught at Annapolis slowly crept up on me. *Service before self.* I am not here for personal glory. I am here for a higher purpose. I am part of a huge team. And they have assessed my abilities and decided that I was their prime choice to teach and train the new influx of young aviators.

I ventured out of my room and went to talk to some of my best friends among the instructors, and they were trying to impart something to me. President Reagan had set a course for a six hundred–ship US Navy with a fleet of brand-new aircraft carriers. He wanted to double our warfighting capacity at sea and in the air.

He was no warmonger, he just wanted the United States to become impregnable, especially from the increasing number of jihadist dingbats running around with bombs in the Middle East. We all, of course, loved Ronald Reagan.

Ships were being built in a big way. And so were strike fighters. President Reagan understood the world could be a very nasty place, with more than its share of evil, brute force, and chaos. This was not an archaic anachronism. This was a clear worldview by a very great president. And the Navy was short of instructors for the hundreds of new pilots they needed. The need was not just urgent, it was critical.

They had chosen me to play a major role in achieving President Reagan's wishes. I suddenly realized, with an encroaching sense of shame, I was casting aside the very soul of the US Navy, the precise mind-set that we are all taught to despise: a fixation with one's own hopes and expectations.

I know as well as anyone that as a commissioned officer, it must always be service before self. We'd all learned the same creed, and we all understood how important it was. Except, apparently, for me.

I did not need my instructor buddies to remind me. The old, familiar words were always there in my immediate subconscious:

*This organization does not exist for your personal glory. Its business is the defense, and the best interests, of the United States of America and its people. That's what you signed up for. That's what we taught you. We have given you the highest honor to which someone of your age could possibly aspire.*

I have to admit my buddies issued one short sharp reminder, typical Navy officers, an eight-word rewrite of my current life view: "That's our judgment of you. Go to it."

I was just twenty-five. These guys had just mended my broken heart. The Navy's decision to send me off to be an instructor was probably the best decision anyone ever made about me. Because I discovered I have a real penchant for teaching. I'm not only good at it, I actually love it.

Throughout my life I have known the greatest joy while teaching kids new things, at steering them on a new pathway of knowledge, watching them switch on, and get interested and then determined. Just as I did myself, all those years ago when first I began to learn the history of the US Navy.

I did not quite realize at the time I would be an instructor for only two years. But throughout my career, I have always returned to the art of teaching others. I mentioned this before, but my greatest thrill was on the day I realized I had taught a kid to be a better pilot than I was—an achievement I had never even suspected was humanly possible.

I resolved to stop feeling shattered by my new posting, because the Navy system rolls on unabated no matter what anyone thinks or wishes. They still mark everyone for everything, night and day: *Stand up and take your grade.* And I still wanted good reviews for all of my efforts.

Because I continued to harbor my F-14 ambitions, I needed great reviews, and fifty of us were chasing the approximate same dream. Innately depressed as I was, I resolved to make the best of it, and I just stood back and watched sorrowfully as guys who had finished in the lower half of my class in flight school went off to fly the Tomcats.

But remember, guys who had fought their way through years of training may have finished in the lower half of the US Navy flight class, but even that bottom section is a whole hell of a lot better than anyone else's stragglers. They were still excellent at their profession. But they mostly were not as good as I was. And I had to wonder, had any greater injustice ever been visited on any potential TOPGUN king of the no-fly zones?

*Shut up, Lay, and get on with it.*

They posted me to Naval Air Station Kingsville in Texas, the Navy's premier location for jet aviation training, specializing in the production of tactical pilots for the strike force pipeline. It's a huge place, flat, flat, flat, a kind of tumbleweed landscape, with big runways. The whole place works closely with the nearby Corpus Christi facility, my old home.

On the lush, grassy plains between the towns of Kingsville and Brownsville, everything is on the large side. NAS Kingsville stands next to the modest 825,000-acre King Ranch, home to a few cattle and quarter horses: 60,000 of the former and 300 of the latter. It's the largest ranch in the United States and makes the country very, very beautiful, simply because it's so unbelievably green.

And this, like many magnificent things in this world, was no fluke. The nineteenth-century founder of the ranch, Captain Richard King, worked out that the most important thing on any ranch is the quality of the grass and the pastures. He practically revolutionized those Texas plains. They still looked like a giant field of emeralds from the skies, and even when it's dark and you're cutting through the moonlit skies at five hundred mph, you can spot the glowing green of the King Ranch from miles away at 20,000 feet.

Like the naval air station, parts of the ranch are in Kleberg County, but its gigantic four parcels of land, known as divisions, stretch over another five Texas counties, forming a bigger total acreage than Rhode Island.

I was a lieutenant by now, and my charge for the next two years was to teach Student Naval Aviators to fly the T-2 Buckeye, how to land, how to fly a jet, how to fly formation, air-to-air gunnery. I was determined to make the very best of it, right up there over the King Ranch.

I arrived on the less lush but just as flat fields of the station in August 1989, and I would not leave until November 1991. That meant I would have to sit and watch the television when my former colleagues went into combat and fought Operation Desert Storm for President George H. W. Bush.

There's no point pretending it was not very, very difficult for me watching them racing above the desert in the F-14s. But I never said a word, just sat there in a kind of reflective, utterly unselfish, martyred silence, casting asunder all of my desires for personal glory. Well, nearly. Christ, I would have loved to have been there.

But, I have to admit, I really liked my new job. I was particularly good at turning around kids who were troubled and those who were struggling. The Navy had taught me patience and to leave my ego behind, and I took all the time I needed to bring these kids on, to take them up and give them a chance to fly, make them better.

Not all of them had been through the Annapolis mill, and some of them found it difficult. But there's always a way. You just need to touch the right button, give them ambition, impress on them that they can be as good as they want to be. This is America. Everyone's got a chance. Jesus, I was born next to a cornfield in Nowheresville, and one day I'm going to—

*Shut up, Lay. Get on with teaching.*

Working constantly on my compulsory good attitude, I took the students all over the place. I used to volunteer for anything. I'd fly Navy aircraft with the students to San Francisco, Cincinnati, Georgia, Florida, California, anywhere—I loved flying that much. Still they marked everything, every takeoff, every landing. I finished overall third among the instructors, narrowly, but I was the top lieutenant instructor.

My next move was to a sacred place in the folklore of Naval Aviation: NAS Miramar, first home of the Navy Fighter Weapons School (TOPGUN), before its transfer in 1996 to the western Nevada desert east of the city of Fallon. That's four hundred miles north of Las Vegas, at least in distance. In every other sense of the word, it's about 7,000 light-years from Las Vegas.

To many people, Miramar is still the spiritual home of TOPGUN. It stands ten miles north of San Diego, in 23,000 acres, and its huge 12,000-foot concrete runway is cleaved into Mitscher Field, named for a fellow graduate of the United States Naval Academy (Class of 1920), Admiral Marc Andrew "Pete" Mitscher, a Naval Aviator who became the world's preeminent carrier force commander in WWII.

He was the commander, Task Force 58, and flew his flag from USS *Lexington,* later becoming a four-star admiral and commander-in-chief, Atlantic Fleet.

During the war he spearheaded the US thrust against the heart of the Japanese Empire, including the conquest of Iwo Jima and Okinawa. Admiral Burke called him a "bulldog of a fighter." He came from a tiny little place in Wisconsin. But they buried him in Arlington.

Who could possibly not feel proud to fly off a runway named for such a man? Miramar had a profound effect on me, and on my feelings of patriotism for the United States. I know a lot of people feel exactly the same. When TOPGUN lived at Miramar, they decided to name it Fightertown, and it still is, painted right down the side of the hangars. I believe Admiral Mitscher would have liked that.

I arrived at the beginning of the winter of 1992, and I mention this because at that point, never having flown an F-14, I'd been under the tutelage and guidance of the US Navy for almost ten years, since I first made my way to the preparatory school in Newport. Ten years for the Navy to make absolutely sure of my worthiness for senior command.

I have taken a long time to establish my principal point, but I could devise no other way to illustrate it. I wished to show you, blow by blow, lesson by lesson, year by year, how the Navy does it, how the admirals manage to take these young men and turn them into top-class commanders. And most of all, how utterly thorough our process is.

And I return to the one major flaw we don't have, have never had, and never will have: the weird civilian propensity to take people into the highest levels of corporations and put them in charge of billions of other people's dollars without knowing one way or the other whether they can handle it.

I recently met a former president of a public corporation who told me that his organization had once been looking for a top-class financial director who could pull the place into line. The corporation was hugely successful, but young, a bit immature, with several hundred million dollars swilling about various bank accounts and no computers in the organization.

So they advertised. Very quickly, given the major salary being offered, the apparently ideal man showed up. He was big, amiable, with a formidable track record, having acted as a personal friend and right-hand man to a near-legendary New York industrial giant with enormous flair as an entrepreneur. It was like mentioning you'd been chief financial advisor to Bill Gates.

They hired him. And he proceeded to bombard all the executives, who'd made all this money in the first place, with memorandums. The guy walked around with four briefcases. His secretary almost had a nervous breakdown. He convened meeting after meeting. In that corporation he became a legend in his own lunchtime.

The cascade of money kept rolling in. The new man did all the elementary stuff involving accounts, banking, and delivery systems. He stayed very close to the president, making sure to pander to his every whim. He had an aura about him, made everyone a bit nervous. They bought him a huge new limousine and created the finance department, making him vice president and director.

They then promoted him, and in addition to being VP of finance, he was suddenly in command of a brand-new division, with carte blanche to make something of it, any way he saw fit.

Three years later, despite all the marketing meetings, the air travel, the flights, the potential takeovers, the five-star hotels, the guy had somehow blown it. Despite the maelstrom of memorandums, promotions, and planning, nothing much happened.

The guy was an entrepreneurial catastrophe, unable to make up his mind about the slightest thing. He acted as though there was not enough information in the entire corporation to allow him to make a decision. Or perhaps he was just terrified of being wrong. My new buddy was uncertain.

And when the corporation's stock ultimately crashed, a bit unfairly, he was the only man in the organization to lose everything.

The graph of his career was an upside-down V. And he had to go. But first they decided, a bit late, to check his credentials. Surely this titan of New York industry could not have been so utterly ineffective. What had they done wrong? Had they all missed something?

Answer. Very probably. And the first thing they did, finally, was to check with the aforementioned industrial giant in his gigantic New York corporation. The ex-president, to whom I was speaking, made the call himself.

"Who? Sorry, guys, never heard of him."

Holy shit! Exhaustive inquiries subsequently showed the man had worked there in a very junior position, nothing like right-hand man to the president. That was a mere figment of his imagination. Ultimately he had been a con man all along.

The issue is plain. Large corporations in America identify their leaders way too late. In the US Navy, we're all over them from the moment they join. If the admirals had been in charge of that young and naive corporation, that disaster could never have happened, mostly because we'd never have even read his application for such an exalted position as financial director of a public corporation, listed on the New York Stock Exchange.

I'd say that was the equivalent of a commanding officer of a US nuclear submarine. We don't recruit those from the outside. For that you need to be here from a very early age, coming up steadily, watched and examined by people who really matter. We do not want hotshot corporate guys coming in from somewhere else. We create our own commanders, and nothing else works for us.

Which is why I became a flight instructor, because that process of selection is the creative bedrock of the Navy. They knew I had my own ambitions, but more important was the succession, finding the top men from the new influx.

The people best qualified to achieve that were the leading young pilots, men who had just gone through the process. You will have noticed by now, in my game, personal ambition comes way, way below the requirements of the system.

It comes right down to the thorny issue of succession. In the Navy, everybody's being groomed to move up, right from the start. We have an endless self-healing process and our entire organization is geared to it.

Corporations do not have that mind-set, although, somewhere in the human resources department, they might have a small book explaining roughly what to do if the CEO gets hit by a bus. The truth is, civilian high executives are all jockeying for the stupendously well-paid top job and the self-glorification that goes with it. The whole military ethos of pushing another person, and wanting that person to do well, is entirely foreign to the executives in corporate America.

In the end, they are children of a lesser god, concerned only with personal wealth. They don't always have our ideals, our morals, our adherence to stringent ethics, our relentless training. Most of the time they don't have our savvy.

That's why they make more mistakes. Because they leave their side door wide open to any halfway plausible candidate with a greedy turn of mind and a suspect résumé.

In turn, we don't actually have a side door. Just a wide front entrance, usually with twin cannons and armed guards on both sides. And your business had better be honorable, because, on behalf of the American people, we will find you out. You can bet both your stock options and next year's bonus on that.

Aside from the issue of sideways recruitment, there is another terrible factor in civilian corporations that does not, cannot, exist in the military: appeasement. I refer of course to the centuries-old art of sucking up to the boss, fighting for personal popularity at the highest level, the slick and smarmy process of being liked by the top men.

How many times a day, especially on Wall Street, do young traders and brokers ease down when it's necessary to bail out of a situation masterminded by the president, or someone close to him? I'll tell you. About a zillion. I have personally met, known, and worked with very clever junior guys in financial firms whose sole creed is to do nothing that might upset the big man on campus.

It's a fatal situation. But to attempt to dissuade them in the interests of their corporation, and, inevitably, other people's money, would be like trying to teach a pig to speak. You'd succeed only in irritating the pig.

Getting a big financial decision right, that's one thing. That's just business. Upsetting the man who has sole power of hire-and-fire over you, the man who can snap his fingers and place you on the welfare lines, well . . . that's entirely different. It is why, at all times, that CEO must be appeased by everyone in the company. That's a corporate fault line just a few ticks short of the San Andreas. It's a silent killer, insidious, sneaking up on you. The truths that dare not be uttered.

It's the corporate system that's wrong, the concentration of so much power in too few hands. In the Navy, or any of the other armed services, that system does not exist. There is no one person who can throw that much weight around because everyone knows what's happening. To fire a lieutenant commander who had been in dark blue for all of his working life would take about twenty different people. Maybe more. And several of them would be in opposition.

In the Navy, we appease no one because there is no necessity to do so. From the earliest age, we work in teams, all pulling the same way. We're self-policing, and we hold ourselves responsible. Our deepest culture emphasizes there is no hiding place. You do your absolute best, and if there's a screwup, you will come forward, flanked by the rest of your team, and admit the problem.

The 2008 Wall Street crash would have been stopped by mid-2006 if we had been in charge. Of that I am absolutely certain. We might have required a couple of destroyers to sink the shiploads of lies being promulgated by people who should have known much better, and were damned lucky not to have been jailed for their dishonesty.

I DROVE THE MUSTANG from Kingsville to San Diego, towing a U-Haul trailer that contained my motorbike. It was an extremely reflective journey for me, because it meant the US Navy had finally accepted that I was a proper person to pilot an F-14 Tomcat in combat.

I still recall the dramatic change in landscape all along the 1,500-mile journey from the Gulf Coast of south Texas, right across the desert to the Laguna Mountains, the snowcapped ramparts of which stand guard over San Diego.

It was a hell of a climb over the 4,000-foot-high peaks, and I remember sensing the chill in the air. The ascent to the top pass somehow reminded me of my own upward progress from the eastern shore of Maryland to this western outpost of US combat flying.

"Symbolic" is the word. Climbing my last mountain before the free-flowing downhill run to my destiny. Or as the Navy put it, "Report Mitscher Field, NAS Miramar, 10 miles north of San Diego. F-14 Squadron. Soonest."

Soonest! I was always soonest. But when I drove onto the base I immediately became caught up in the folklore of the place. Out in front of me were the Tomcats, parked in long lines, dozens of them, their noses aligned perfectly.

At last I was going to fly a Navy aircraft that was not white and orange. These were gray, the color of combat, and I instantly checked in and got suited up, cap and wings, and I walked outside to see them.

I did not bother to meet anyone. I just walked out to look at those fabled aircraft. The first thing that struck me was the sheer size of them. These were big fighters, brawny, with broad shoulders and massive landing struts. I imagined the impact one of these things would have when, one day, I rammed the landing wheels into the deck of a carrier. But the double nose wheel was huge, and the hefty, widely spaced, single main landing wheels were especially designed to withstand those harsh carrier takeoffs and landings.

The Tomcat had the biggest tires I'd ever seen on a strike fighter. On the vertical tail was the famous emblem of the F-14, the leering tomcat, Stetson angled jauntily, six-gun handy. I knew when I began serious training there would be real rockets, not just the formidable Phoenix under those wings, but also Sparrows and Sidewinders. With an M61 Vulcan Gatling machine gun (676 standard rounds) on the left side.

I stared at this supersonic brute of a Navy fighter, this thirty-three-ton, 1,500-mph master of the skies, our primary maritime air superiority combat aircraft, which once launched six missiles in thirty seconds—five resulting in direct hits—at targets up to one hundred miles away.

Of course I'd seen an F-14 close up before, but it had never looked quite this sinister, and all I needed to do was three months of pressured study, just so I could strip it down and rebuild it in my lunch hour. Then they'd be lowering that folding ladder especially for me to climb aboard the strike fighter of my dreams.

Of everybody's dream actually. The F-14 is by far the most popular fighter ever built. It's like some Robin Hood of the airways: feared by the bad, loved by the good. There's nothing quite like it. There never has been. For Naval Aviators, the Tomcat was love at first sight. It could outmaneuver every kind of Soviet fighter in any dogfight, right from the start in the 1970s. Son of a bitch could turn on a dime.

One Navy captain said it was the fastest Ferrari and the best Porsche all in one. You could fly it anywhere you wanted, straight up or straight down. The Tomcat took off climbing at 45,000 feet per minute, to a ceiling of 50,000 feet. It could outrun almost any guided missile.

It was the largest, heaviest strike fighter aircraft ever to fly, mostly because it carried the supremely powerful Hughes AWG-9 radar and a big missile load. The F-14 rarely suffered major mechanical problems, built as it was around a superstrong titanium box, like a goddamned spaceship, launching at zero to 160 mph in two seconds.

One captain called it the best drag racer in the world. This was a droll description of an advanced $30 million high-endurance long-range interceptor, built especially for the Navy by Grumman, but with almost exclusive flight and combat input from the scientists who wear dark blue.

I guess that's what we loved about the Tomcat. It was ours. It was the Navy's hunter killer. Nobody else's. And it said so, right there on the fuselage: "Navy." I got so many chills looking at that baby out there on Admiral Mitscher's airfield, I darn near needed an overcoat, despite the eighty-degree warmth of the West Coast.

Finally tearing myself away from it, I walked out to the two-mile-long runway and stared down it, facing west into the lowering sun. Way in the distance, dead straight along our takeoff path, I could see the peak of

Mount Soledad, 824 feet above ground level. I guessed we'd see the Pacific Ocean, maybe four miles away, as we cleared its summit. I could also see some kind of a high white memorial cross, right on the top, in front of the setting sun.

I stood there for a few minutes and then made my way back. I stayed at the officers' quarters in the base for a few nights and then moved out to an apartment in the canyons near La Jolla. Ahead of me was a year of flight training in the Tomcats. Paradise, or what?

The weeks passed swiftly, and on March 18, 1992, I made my first flight in an F-14. By now I knew all about the war memorial on Mount Soledad. It was the Veterans Memorial, a twenty-nine-foot-tall Latin cross on its fourteen-foot base, been there for nearly forty years since the Korean War ended, to honor the pilots who died.

A tradition had built up around it. Pilots taking off from Miramar make a slight, high-speed jink to the right, rolling out and then leveling out. It was our way, I was informed, of dipping our wings to God and, as the sun goes down, showing our everlasting respect for the dead. *Age shall not weary them, nor the years condemn. At the going down of the sun.*

Every Miramar pilot performs this three hundred mph ritual, including the TOPGUN guys. Especially the TOPGUN guys. For they operate every day of their working lives out there on the very frontiers of death.

I remember how much it was in my mind when after the months of training and briefing were over, I was finally cleared to make my first flight in an F-14, March 18, 1992—the result of hours and hours spent in the F-14 simulator, dozens of hours more than anyone else had ever spent. I was in that thing practicing for three or four hours every day. The guys in charge of it became my best buddies, and I was often last man out when they closed down for the night.

As for the other end of the day, that was my specialty. I was in there alone sometimes at six a.m., long before the first classes arrived. I had special arrangements with the simulator team: they would alert me whenever it was vacant, sometimes only for a half-hour. But if I could, I would be up and in there, getting the techniques, feeling the aircraft, honing my reactions.

If anyone on this base or in my flight class was going to be selected to make a real live flight in an F-14 Tomcat, it was going to be me. Not that

I'd had the obsession for longer than fourteen years, three months, six days, and thirty-eight minutes. But who the hell's counting?

On that bright morning, I noted the light California westerly breeze as I walked out to the aircraft wearing my G-suit, flying boots, and harness, carrying my helmet. I was accompanied by my instructor, Lieutenant "Chili" Eberhart. We walked lockstep together, me with an overwhelming sense of joy, he with probably a similarly powerful sense of dread. There are no flight controls in the rear seat of a Tomcat. Chili understood his life was in my hands.

We walked down the line of F-14s. Standing right in front of one of them was the plane captain, a young enlisted guy of about twenty, whose task it was to look after that aircraft, gas, oil, cleaning the cockpit and canopy, etc. He popped straight to attention and saluted me formally: "Sir, aircraft one-o-four preflight and ready."

I shook his hand and then began the somewhat touchy-feely process of inspection, which every fighter pilot goes through before climbing the ladder to the high cockpit. With my flashlight ready, I began the first day of what would be years of ritual inspections.

We don't need coaching for this; it's instinct, but it's also mystical. I know it's weird, and I don't care what anyone says. We all do the same with absolutely no prior instruction, moving around this supersonic, fire-breathing monster, automatically caressing it, running our hands lightly over the fuselage, always touching it, as we probe deep inside the intakes, and then checking for the tiniest chink on the compressor blades.

All the way around the aircraft we now moved, my left hand touching first titanium, then steel, then aluminum. Even when I kicked the huge tires for luck, one hand was always lightly running over the surface. The industrial-sized landing hook was clipped up, and there was the launch bar, the iron gripper that locked us onto the catapult.

Down at the back of the Tomcat, I checked the giant tunnels that housed the afterburners. There'd been a recent flight, and the heat was still there. It smelled of burning and gasoline. It's always kind of rough-and-tough back there. Not like a pristine USAF jet aircraft. Christ, if those guys saw this, they'd be back here squirting Simple Green all over the place. No one on this base needs reminding: this is a strictly functional oil-streaked US carrier strike fighter, the toughest game in military flying.

And I'm a Naval Aviator inspecting my F-14 Tomcat strike fighter aircraft, which I'm about to fly. This was the hard-man of the offense, in the most important business there was. When the inspection was over, I was not happy. I was way beyond that. I was abso-blooming-lutely delirious with anticipation and joy.

I climbed the ladder, stepping into the cockpit like a veteran, adhering to the Naval Aviator's golden rule never to plant a boot on the ejection seat as I slid into the confined space allotted to the driver. That was not just to make sure the seat stayed clean. It was a mark of the deepest respect for the aircraft. Weird? You would not even think that, not if you did what we all do for a living.

Beyond the bulletproof glass of the open canopy, they're driving up the huffer, the mini–jet engine that's required to kick-start this great bruiser of a strike fighter. I signaled the guys to plug me in, and I tightened my earplugs, because the scream of that little tractor was awful, as it hurled my own turbine up to 20 percent of its power.

That's what it takes. This aircraft is so big and heavy it can't carry one more ounce of equipment. It has no self-starting mechanism. Someone has to get it going from the outside. The scream of the jet blast echoed over the base, and I could feel my compressor blades spinning hard. I watched the needles (dials), and at 20 percent I turned the left throttle, which threw the gas in, and there was a jolting *booomph!* as it exploded, sending a puff of white smoke blasting out from the rear. The canopy was still open in case there was a fire and I needed to get out in a hurry.

The port-side engine was running, and I signaled for the guys to unplug the huffer. Now I concentrated on the other side, making a cross-bleed start to kick it off, the power of one engine firing up the other. The noise was deafening, literally. Without the earplugs and headset inside the helmet it would have destroyed my eardrums. It's not just loud, it's evil loud; it was a scream from inside the devil's torture box. I could not wait to close that canopy.

This was a very complicated aircraft, and I tested its state-of-the-art intake system. I tested the ramps, the radar, the aeronautics displays, the hydraulics, the radio, the radar altimeter, the tactical displays, all of the flight controls. It took about fifteen minutes, maybe a little more.

Okay, I was happy (ecstatic, that is). And I signaled to my plane captain, shoving both thumbs sideways, left and right: *Chocks away!* I made one move forward, just a half-turn of the wheels, so he could inspect the tires on the one patch we could not see while the aircraft was stationary. Again I moved forward, and I gave the aircraft a little wiggle, just to make sure everything was working.

This attention to every infinitesimal detail, I realize, must sound as if we're all on the borders of neurosis or paranoia. It's hard to elaborate further, but I will just mention one truth: a Naval Aviator driving one of these things and talking calmly to the tower can be dead in approximately three seconds, maybe only two, if the slightest thing goes wrong, especially landing.

The one thing we all aim for is a landing, because the alternative is really dull. I guess that's why we're fairly thorough.

The plane captain looked up and saluted me, and I returned the salute, driving forward and making my turn down past the hangars with the strike fighters lined up outside. The sparse and critical dialogue began: Lieutenant Chili, my RIO today, opened the radio comms, and they started speaking as if they were on Valium, very calm, very controlled. Never loud.

"Miramar Ground. Gunfighter one-o-four. Taxi a single Tomcat from hangar four with Information India."

"Gunfighter one-o-four, Miramar Ground, taxi runway two-four."

"Gunfighter one-o-four."

We taxied down and approached the runway, and Chili flipped to the tower.

"Gunfighter one-o-four. Takeoff, runway two-four."

"Gunfighter one-o-four. Tower. Winds two-fifty at ten. Clear for takeoff runway two-four right."

I let go the brakes and went to full throttle. I had full flaps, and we were just bumbling down the runway, this massive strike fighter, horizontal tail tilted forward, "digging for air," fighting to generate liftoff.

Thank Christ this runway was two miles long. I eased the stick back and quite suddenly that Tomcat lifted off with unimaginable power. I aimed straight for the top of the mountain, as I had done for most of my naval career.

Up ahead was the white cross that commemorated so many Naval Aviators in whose flying boots I now followed. Airspeed was almost three hundred mph as we rushed toward the memorial, and then I did as I had been told, not just out of respect, but because I really had officially joined the brotherhood. As I would do every single time I took off down that long runway, I jinked the F-14 right, and I dipped my wings to God.

We hung a left and raced to the coastline and out over the water, seven miles west and then south. Back after forty minutes and my first Tomcat flight was over. From now on, I just needed to get better and better and better. Not that anyone would be watching, of course. Except for everyone in the entire pantheon of Naval Aviation at the most important NAS in the country.

HARD FLIGHT TRAINING took place all that spring, summer, and fall. We were diving at targets, dropping live free-fall 500- to 2,000-pound steel weapons. We took our first dogfighting lessons in a proper war machine. There was real combat against the F-16 Fighting Falcons and F/A-18 Hornets, jinking this way and that, closing, banking away at high speed.

The months passed very quickly, until the day they told us we were flying out to USS *Abraham Lincoln,* the last word in US flattops, commissioned for active duty only three years earlier and currently making a slow racetrack pattern eighty miles offshore from San Diego.

We flew out in formation and made our landings on the flight deck. From a distance she looked much the same as the old *Lexington,* but as I came in closer I could feel a truly majestic quality about this enormous Nimitz-class carrier, nearly the size of the Empire State Building lying on its side.

Every takeoff and landing from a flight deck provides a heightened sense of adventure, a kind of death-or-glory sensation for the guys in the cockpit. I, however, had a truly ass-gripping experience on my first night takeoff. And I'll never forget it.

The yellow-shirt guided me down to the daisy line in the normal way. No problem. I was next in the queue, sitting in that uniquely spooky carrier flight deck light while they fixed Cat 2 to my launch bar. The signals were all good. We were all set. JBD in place, and the shooter, arm outstretched, touched the deck. *Bam!* The hydraulic piston slingshotted us on our way, zero to 160 mph in two seconds.

But after a mere ten feet, my RIO, Lieutenant Ian "Chunx" Anderson, sensed something was wrong, badly wrong. And he suddenly bellowed at the top of his lungs, "*Burner! Burner! Burner!*" We were too slow, way too slow, and he knew there was a real issue right here.

In about one-hundredth of a second, I hit the afterburner throttles, and we both felt the acceleration, hurling us along the catapult track, straight toward the bow, below which was the seething Pacific Ocean.

I nearly died of shock. *C'mon, baby, C'MON!* Behind me I heard the RIO again: "*Go! Go! Go!*" I knew we still weren't fast enough. We rocketed off the bow and sagged down, lower than usual, too far, too far. The bright lights from the afterburners were lighting up the wave tops. *Holy shit!* I could see those tops clearly, and that was too low. I could see the fucking whitecaps.

The radar altimeter screamed into life, right in my ear: *deedal, deedal, deedal.* I glanced out left and we were only thirty feet above the wave tops, the carrier towering above us.

The RIO was going to pull the ejection seat handle, I was sure of that, explode us out of the cockpit. I braced myself for the impact, one we might not survive, or at best get out with a couple of broken arms. I guessed, correctly, that the rescue teams on the flight deck were already charging for the helos.

Right then those mighty Pratt & Whitney TF30 engines, howling to within an inch of their sainted lives, pulled us up and out of it.

Chunx, my buddy and RIO, had saved our lives. If he had not yelled for the burners, we'd have hit the water. As things were, he just reported to the tower, in his most laconic voice:

"One-o-seven airborne."

"One-o-seven, interval left ten o'clock. Three miles, Tomcat."

"One-o-seven."

Supercalm or not, it was the first time I ever really thought I could kill myself out here—even if I did everything right. I sensed the problem had been on the catapult. Those two seconds, right before they flung us skyward, was the one time I had no direct control, the one time I was entirely in someone else's hands.

But that's the Navy. We rely on one another. And it's the same for us all, as we pull forward together. Always, for the greater good.

## CHAPTER 6

# The Devil's Waiting Room

The US Navy spends years sorting out the pecking order among Naval Aviators. From the very first moment a student announces he wants to fly rather than sail, the instructors hurl roadblock after roadblock into his flight path.

And the longer he stays, the harder it becomes and the more is expected of him. In the end he needs to be one of the few left standing after the grim dust of failure has finally cleared away.

The final three disciplines are by far the toughest. Can he get a strike fighter into the air from a catapult launch without having a blue fit? Can he land it on the pitching stern of an aircraft carrier without losing his nerve? And can he take off and then land *on* the deck of a carrier—at night?

That's the killer. Night landing. That's the one that sorts out the Naval Aviators from the guys in short pants. And nothing can prepare you for it. It's the ultimate test of willpower, skill, and iron nerve. Fall short and you will definitely fail your grades and very probably die, either beneath the waves or in a fireball.

You need to be very certain of your vocation. Because it's a hell of a way to go. It takes only a couple of seconds for a young, nervous strike fighter pilot to depart this mortal coil.

In Naval Aviation we talk of life and death quite often, because that's what it is. But the apparition of the night landing is never far away. And I don't care how many times you've done it, you cannot escape the dread of that leap into the unknown as you come screaming down that pitch-black glide path. The very thought of it still sends my heart rate up.

I'M FLYING SOUTHWEST about eight miles off the port beam of the USS *Abraham Lincoln,* which is patrolling some eighty miles off the San Diego base. We have five levels of darkness, the best one being bright moonlight. We call that the "commander's moon," since those gods of the flight deck seem to have truly mystical luck in always flying their compulsory grades in such conditions.

The lowest grade—pitch black, no stars, no moon, sun missing, no ships, nothing—is approximately what I'm in right now. Only darker. Beyond my Tomcat's canopy, there is absolutely zero visibility, not even an imaginary shadow. I'm flying in total blackness, no landmarks, no guiding stars. Beautiful.

I could see but one thing, engraved into my mind's eye, the terrifying images they had shown us right before we took off: footage of three of the most terrible night crashes among junior aviators. One aircraft smashed into the stern of the carrier in a fireball that swept across the deck. Another crashed into the stern of the ship and dropped into the ocean, again in a fireball. The third came in lurching left, hooked its wing under the arresting wire, and slewed straight over the portside of the ship.

The crashes were spectacularly different. But the aviators had one thing in common: they were all dead within three seconds.

I'm heading for the Marshal Stack. That's the rigidly grouped aircraft waiting to move forward, first to find and then to land on the carrier. I'm not sure how many are in before me, but I'm following someone, and I know another strike fighter is right behind me.

When I arrive we'll all be flying a racetrack pattern, separated by altitude, not distance. We'll fly two minutes straight, make our left turn, and then fly two minutes more in the opposite direction. One thousand feet above me there's another Tomcat, 1,000 feet below there's an F/A-18 Hornet.

We're in radio contact with "Abe," and I hear our orders:

"One-o-seven, Marshal. Take angels seven . . . push time forty-five."

My RIO replies in that poetic, lucid, and elaborate mode of speech in which we all specialize. That's the reply they want, the only one there is, assuming nothing diabolical has happened.

"One-o-seven."

We've been ordered to 7,000 feet, making three hundred knots through the sky, "push time" forty-five. That means leave the stack forty-five minutes past the hour. It's twenty-two miles to the carrier. By the way, that does not mean 298 knots or forty-five minutes and thirty seconds. This is absolute precision flying, timed to the split second. This is not an ideal place to fuck it up, trust me.

Everyone in the Marshal Stack is doing exactly the same thing, watching the instruments, checking airspeed and altitude, timing the straight runs and the left-hand turns, unable to see anything beyond the cockpit. The radio exchanges with the carrier are sparse, and the voices are calm to the point of casual. Everyone involved in Navy flying spends his entire life trying to calm everyone else down. That radio's an electronic therapist.

"One-o-seven, Marshal, check altitude."

That's rather than, "Holy shit! One-o-seven, you're going too goddamned slow—hit the throttles, for Christ's sake, before you lose altitude, and hit the poor little F/A-18 below!"

At both ends of the line everyone's conveying total confidence, dead calm, no panic or even anxiety. Finally we're cleared to leave the stack, and to keep descending on the nine-mile run down to the point of our hard right turn. At three hundred knots that's less than two minutes.

I'm watching the instruments all along this twelve-mile arc. Otherwise I'm flying blind, like everyone else. The dials are recording my descent, and I'm continuing to lose altitude: 2,500 feet . . . 2,000 feet . . . 1,500 feet, then 1,200. That's how far above the Pacific I'm flying when they update the bearing for the run into the carrier, another ten miles, three minutes. And remember, Big Abe is still moving away from me. Things are changing. I still can't see her.

They call in the final bearing, and I bank left, my eyes flashing back and forth from dead ahead to the instrument panel. One degree wrong right here could be catastrophic. I turn the lights down in the cockpit to the lowest possible setting, and I'm steadily cutting our airspeed down to 140 knots, based on fuel.

"One-o-seven, dirty up" (that's landing wheels down, wing flaps down).
"One-o-seven."

I reach for the levers, left hand, and I slap the gear down and lower the flaps. I feel the jolt as those massive tires slowly drop and lock into place.

Again they transmit from the carrier: "Lock-on six miles. Call your needles."

Right now my glide path into the carrier is like a long, invisible diagonal line, starting high above and behind the aircraft. It's a hypotenuse, really, the longest side of a right-angled triangle, and it lances down, way out in front of my cockpit and onto the flight deck. My instruments will tell me when I intercept that line. That's when I make the adjustments for my final approach.

My heart is pounding. Up ahead I can just make out the dimmed lights of the carrier's flight deck, where every point of illumination is lowered to heighten the starkness of the bright center-deck strobe lights, flashing in a line . . . a calm, cool line, nothing fast.

1-2-3-4-5, slowish, straight up the middle of the landing area. Out here even the lights are forbidden to look excited.

At two miles, we've got the ball. That's short for "meatball"—Naval Aviator slang for the landing system on all US aircraft carriers. A small stack of five state-of-the-art light boxes situated on the port side of the carrier, designed to beam an accurate, powerful shaft of light at incoming pilots.

If it's straight out of the middle box everything's cool. Higher or lower, there's a flight adjustment to make. If the light's out of the top box, it's "Clara," and that means you're too high, so damned high you can't see a damned thing. And you're about to miss the friggin' wire. And remember, at night you always feel you're too high.

Just ahead, the F/A-18 that was below me in the Marshal Stack is "on the ball." That's more Naval Aviator slang for "he's attempting his landing."

"Three-o-four, Hornet Ball, four-point-seven. Stevens."

"Roger Ball, Hornet . . . twenty-six knots."

Right now I need to shut up, especially as I can hear the LSO talking to him . . . and that twenty-six knots is important. It's windy. I need to know that.

And then the LSO gives him a soft command: "a little power" . . . and a sterner . . . "Power!"

He's misjudged the wind. I have to remember that. Keep my power up. This is nothing like landing on the runway. I still need to give the F/A-18 pilot my respect by shutting up completely, unless something diabolical happens.

Finally he lands, and I see his lights disappear in front of me. Someone keys the radio and I hear in the background someone yelling: "Gear down, hook down, gear/lens set. Five-four-zero, Tomcat . . . *Foul deck!*"

"*Foul deck!*"

They call for a correction: "One-o-seven, one mile, on and slightly left." (We're on glideslope, but slightly left of center line.)

"One-o-seven."

Then comes the moment of truth: "One-o-seven, on and on, three quarters of a mile, call the ball."

"One-o-seven, Tomcat Ball, five-point-nine. Lay."

Way down there on the stern of the massive ship, the LSO calls back in a voice so calm, so casual, I think the bastard's falling asleep. *FUCK ME!*

"Roger Ball, Tomcat . . . twenty-five knots" (that's breeze over the stern).

Right now the RIO's calling it, calling out the numbers, charting our rate of descent, feet per minute:

"700 . . . 700 . . . 650 . . . 700 . . . 700 . . . 750 . . . 800 . . . 750 . . . 700."

But the hell with anyone else, we're screaming through the night sky, and I'm doing a million things. I'm checking the airspeed, I'm checking the nose attitude, I'm checking the rate of descent, I'm lined up, I've got the center line, and my heart's almost at bursting point.

The big three rules race through my mind, over and over: meatball . . . line-up . . . angle of attack. More Naval Aviator slang—*meatball:* check glide slope; *line-up:* check center line; *angle of attack:* check airspeed.

I can't stop saying them, while I'm constantly checking all three, plus rate of descent: seven hundred feet per minute; nose attitude, ten times a second. A Naval Aviator is the only fighter pilot on earth who can do that.

I don't care how good anyone thinks they are, no one can do that many things that fast. No one else can cope with that breathtaking combination of intellect, anticipation, and competence. All conducted while operating under the specter of instant death should you screw it up.

The sheer intensity is mind-blowing. No one else can do it. Only us. I still wake up in the middle of the night reliving those moments, the last seconds before landing that big Tomcat on the carrier's flight deck in the middle of the goddamned moonless night.

And out of nowhere, the LSO comes on: "A little power . . ."

(To myself: *All right, all right, I'm a little slow. I know that, asshole, shut up for chrissakes. I'm already doing it. Leave me alone.* Even though I must obey his commands. One day he may save my life.)

*Meatball . . . line-up . . . angle of attack.*

I'm making the inside/outside transition now. That's the time when every pilot stops concentrating 100 percent on the dials in front of him, because he can't see a darned thing, and begins to shift his gaze outside, back and forth to the ghostly, soft amber lights of the carrier up ahead.

When you first see it and locate the ball, and focus on the center-line lights, the change is very swift. Instead of spending only 2 percent looking out and 98 percent watching the needles, you're suddenly half-and-half and then 75/25, consciously making the switch, checking that the dials reflect precisely what you're seeing. That's the transition.

We're taught to accept nothing, to check everything against everything: *Meatball . . . line-up . . . angle of attack.*

I'm cross-checking with the altimeter, cross-checking the HDI (compass), airspeed, fuel, and engines, running the numbers, watching the stern of the carrier.

The best instrument pilot is always the best at landing, and that comes down to applied mathematics, except speed is essential. Accuracy is a given. Otherwise you might not live to tell the tale. My overwhelming strength has always been math. That was my major at the Academy, and I've always been able to flash those numbers through my brain. And boy, were they ever flashing as we came howling through the dark toward the stern of the carrier.

The tension is so great, politeness goes straight out the window.

I still can't really see the landing area, just the friendly flashing strobe light up the middle. Everything's correct, but there's no way this is going to work. The thoughts rush through my mind. I can't even see where the wheels will hit. That fireball on the stern flashes across my brain. *Jesus Christ! Steady, Jeff.*

Through the LSO's radio I hear someone yell, "Ramp!" and I'm on target, holding on to the stick, white knuckled. This has to be impossible.

*Meatball . . . line-up . . . angle of attack.*

I check the nose in the last fleeting hundredth of a second, and I ram open the throttles, and there's a stupendous *bang!* as my wheels hit the flight deck. I feel the hook grab the wire, and the stop is so sudden I doubt whether my harness can hold me. I'm going to fly straight through the cockpit canopy.

But the harness holds. I restart my heart. Like everyone else on the flight deck. In front of me is the yellow-shirt, signaling me to pull back the power, calm down, and just follow him as he walks backward, steering me to my allotted place. I'll admit it, I was trembling from head to foot.

Of course, there was no urgency. We have all of five seconds to get the hell out of the way of the next incoming Tomcat, with a real close buddy of mine at the controls. Suddenly the yellow-shirt crosses his forearms right in front of me, the signal to stop.

I know that through the din outside, the spotter has stopped yelling, *"Foul deck!"* That the magnificent, unbelievably dangerous ballet of the Naval Aviators will continue through the night, with everyone relying on everyone else. Life cheating death. No mistakes. Like always.

It's a choreographed testimony to our endless mantra: *Perfection is attainable. And don't ever forget that, kid. Or you'll be on a one-way ticket back to Maineville, Ohio.*

No one said anything. I had just completed the crowning achievement of my life so far. I'd put the mighty F-14 on the deck of an aircraft carrier in the middle of the goddamned night. And that was considered strictly routine.

Of course everyone understood that first night landing had been a terrific feat of piloting skill and nerve. But hell, they'd been training me for it for years. What else would anyone expect? But it had nothing to do with congratulations, not a shred of "Well done, Jeff." For the high command of the flight deck it was just another confirmation that the system worked. *We selected him, taught him, trained him, and now he's done what we expected. What's the big deal?*

In their eyes I had done nothing exceptional. I suppose in my soul, I knew that. Every Naval Aviator could do what I'd just done. I hadn't excelled or set myself apart. But I had gained something that could never be taken away. On that dark night, out in the Pacific Ocean, I had joined one of the elite brotherhoods in all of the United States Armed Forces.

I was a fighter pilot, and I'd just proved my right to be here. And no one cared. And right now I didn't care if they cared or not. My life's ambition had just been nailed down, in this roaring, screaming, fuel-smelling, danger-zone corner of paradise.

*Meatball . . . line-up . . . angle of attack.* They'll probably hear that being murmured from inside my coffin.

*One-o-seven.*


I COMPLETED MY takeoff/landing program on the USS *Abraham Lincoln,* and we all flew back to Miramar the following morning. We made a long circle over the ocean, out to the west of the base, and came in from the north, touching down on the great two-mile runway of Mitscher Field.

I remember the uplifting feeling as I brought my F-14 Tomcat down through the crystalline skies, high over the white cross, and onto that fabled 12,000-foot strip of concrete. My confidence was high now. I'd pulled off the ultimate challenge of all Naval Aviators and put the biggest strike fighter ever built right down on the flight deck of an aircraft carrier in the middle of the night.

I no longer had that nagging doubt in the back of my mind. The dread that I might fall short at the very last hurdle. Except it wasn't a hurdle. That night landing represented a full-scale barricade that has smashed the hopes and dreams of many a young aviator before me.

I actually knew I had passed the test long before we took off on our return flight to Miramar. The charming and eloquent call—"Lieutenant Lay, you're a qual"—was mere hours away.

But as a result of my activities out on the *Lincoln,* I finally felt I really belonged here at the spiritual home of TOPGUN. Somehow there were a thousand aspects of the place that once had seemed nothing to do with me but now seemed to include me.

For a while I stared out of the window of the officers' quarters and contemplated what precisely was going on out there—the obvious dismantling of the Navy air wings, the parked aircraft, the decommissioned Tomcats, the aircraft being systematically pulled apart for spares, guys walking around kind of sadly. No real joie de vivre.

It was late in 1992, and even I, the newest of the aviators being trained up for the twenty-first century, was suddenly aware of the abandonment of President Reagan's dream. The following morning taxiing out to the runway in my regular Tomcat, I took a long look, for the first time, at the desolation around me.

Once it really had been nothing to do with me, because I sensed I was just a visitor. No longer. Lieutenant Lay, F-14 fighter pilot, was a part of this place. The history was more poignant. The ghosts were somehow closer, and I suppose like a Miramar veteran, I understood what they were doing, and what the United States was losing.

Out there on the hardtop in front of the hangars were all the scars and stains of the fighting force that had once called this place home. You could see boot prints stamped into the hot surface after the jets had come in to land. Those boot prints would be there forever. There were soot marks from the fighters, oil stains, black spots from Tomcats past. There were still wheel marks, plain to see.

But perhaps above all were the silent signs of the immortal Navy fighter squadrons that had sought refuge here after tangling with, and usually obliterating, a foreign foe. A fading insignia, a still visible vertical tail design, a painted word here and there, and the echoes of the footfalls, sounds that only fighter pilots could ever hear. Even if he had only been a "qual" for about a half hour.

Over there was the hangar of VF-1, the historic Wolfpack, founded in 1922, to be deactivated in 1993 as the Navy cuts began to bite. No more the big red wolf's head heralding this first of the F-14 fighter squadrons, whose aviators saw heroic service right through WWII, Vietnam, and Desert Storm. The Pack once went a record 22,000 flight hours without one single accident. Now they'd disappear into the forest.

Signs of VF-51, the Screaming Eagles, were still there, although they'd be shuttered by 1995. The Eagles were the oldest fighter squadron in the Pacific Fleet, Neil Armstrong's old outfit, and scourge of the MiG fighters in the Vietnam War. Everyone was scared to death of those fast jets with the eagle painted against the yellow star on its vertical tail, especially the

Russians, whose big, cumbersome TU-26 Backfire bombers and TU-95 Bears were so regularly intercepted.

Also in that hangar lived the VF-111 Sundowners, that most famous of the Pacific Fleet fighter squadrons. Their legendary insignia showed a couple of Wildcats shooting down the Rising Sun. That banner of aerial warfare was hard-earned.

The Sundowners took out fifty-five enemy aircraft in combat over Guadalcanal between April and July 1943. And then, between October 1944 and February 1945, in strike and air combat flying from USS *Hornet,* they downed 102 more enemy aircraft and blew up dozens more on the ground. They'd be gone soon. To be "disestablished" in 1995. What a perfectly hideous word for a fighting force in which valor was such a common virtue.

In the second hangar, to be disestablished in 1996, was the old home of the VF-24 Renegades, who flew those Tomcats in endless combat for nearly twenty-one years. The VF-211 Checkmates lived there for thirty-five years, with seven deployments to Vietnam, where they earned the nickname "the MiG Killers."

The VF-114 Aardvarks resided along here but would be closed down on April 30, 1993, a date recalled in infamy among aviators, even by the standards of those glum years of the mid-'90s, when almost half of the F-14 community, after Desert Storm, was closed in the post–Cold War reductions.

The Aardvarks were in many ways the aristocrats of fighter squadrons, officially recognized several times as the number-one aerial gunners in the Pacific branch of the US Navy, Tomcat specialists. They too would be gone. Just staring down that line of hangars and seeing aircraft that would fly no more was like gazing along Death Row after the hangman had passed this way.

The huge letters painted on the concrete walls of the weapons storage facility still proclaimed WELCOME TO FIGHTERTOWN USA. There was still a glorious edge to the mere sight of it. But this was a place with a damaged soul, a place where a battle had been lost but never fought.

It was a place where phantom flying aces could laugh with not all of their laughter. But they could still weep for a missing squadron, cut from the skies by accountants and bean counters. People who could not, would not, indeed would never understand precisely what it meant to have been a member of the Wolfpack, the Screaming Eagles, the Sundowners, or the Renegades—the lost squadrons of Miramar.

We could scarcely cast them from our minds because they were still there, at least the remnants of them were still there, lined up, decommissioned, out of action, standing on the tarmac among the boot prints of long-departed US Naval Aviators. As reminders go, that one was pretty stark, because we were all qualified now, and like it or not, we had become guardians of those sacred traditions.

Not that we had much time to dwell upon Navy history. Our lives, as we headed toward the end of the F-14 course, were nothing but a daily increase of workload. We were flying and training day in and day out, right through Thanksgiving and Christmas. And in February it all came to an end.

Class results were published for the F-14 squadron, and once more I finished number one. That was not pure brilliance. It involved brutal hard work, long hours, and total application. A big plus in my favor was that I loved to fly more than anyone else in the squadron. Actually I might have loved it more than anyone else in the world. So I organized a lot of practice time. Results probably reflected this. Anyway, there I was, top of the pile and ready for anything this world might throw at me.

Almost immediately we were told the Checkmates would be deploying to the Persian Gulf, embarked in the 100,000-ton USS *Nimitz,* named for America's last fleet admiral, of course, and one of the largest warships in the world.

This meant I would be leaving Miramar for an extended tour of duty on the other side of the planet, flying missions in Iraq, up into the no-fly zone against Saddam Hussein's increasing goddamned insolent air forces. Matter of fact, I hugely looked forward to the challenge, but I sensed a kind of sorrow at leaving Miramar because I loved the place, I loved the West Coast, and I loved everything that naval air station stood for.

Throughout my entire ten-year career in the US Navy I had been conscious of loyalties that never diminished and grew with each passing year. Looking back I still treasured every one of my four years at Annapolis, and my heart was wrapped in the colors of the Blue and Gold. And so it will be for the rest of my life.

I felt the same about Miramar, where they had taught me to fly the Tomcat. I would defend this place with my life. The same applied to my F-14 squadron, the VF-211 Checkmates. I was not just a part of a terrific group of guys who could fly that great brute of an aircraft. I was joined to the aviators who had gone before me, and worn the patch with the red-and-white checkered pattern, same as the one on the vertical tail of my strike fighter. I was a part of that elite club, which answered the bugle call every time it was sounded, and came out fighting, ripping across the jungles and deltas of Vietnam, hitting their targets, opening fire on those Russian MiGs, whoever the hell was driving them.

I imagined them often, with the music of the Valkyries thundering in the background, as they streaked across the treetops, terrifying the life out of the enemy. I know they lived in another time, another age, and their machines were not quite as fast or as deadly as ours.

But they were not far behind, and I like to think that I and my buddies would have done exactly the same had we been in their boots. Just as they would have stepped up fearlessly if the Pentagon had ordered them to go deal with Saddam. We were, after all, VF-211 Checkmates, to the last man. And that's a bond forged in naval steel.

I WONDER IF THAT SENSE of undying loyalty lies at the root of so many of America's corporate problems. Or, at least, the lack of it. Because the truth is, loyalty, on the scale I am describing, is just about unknown in big business, where, whatever they say, it's essentially every man for himself.

I doubt there is a more perfect example than that of Lehman Brothers, which represents the largest corporate bankruptcy in the history of the universe. Lehman stood for more than just whacking great profits, with which the top men unfailingly lined their pockets.

It had a rich and glittering tradition of building mighty American businesses, enormous operations that had stood the test of time—until personal greed became the only thing that mattered. Any overdue loyalty to the past was trampled in the stampede for the bread, at any and all cost.

The top floor of Lehman could scarcely spell the word "loyalty," never mind act on it. They ruthlessly cast it aside because they cared nothing for what had gone before.

Both the US Navy and the military demonstrate every day of the year what a drastically short-sighted vision that is. The Navy, in which I served, seeks to remind us every step of the way that the past remains the custodian of the future, not the other way around. We act as we do because of the lessons learned in battles fought, sometimes long ago. Somehow the past rears its head whenever times are especially hard, and we are forever reminded of how the greatest men in our history behaved, and what they would have expected of us.

Remember, too, the warning of General MacArthur to the cadets of West Point, the one that dealt with a possible catastrophic failure on their part. Their problem would not be the enemy, but rather the ten million ghosts, all in olive drab, rising up from their white crosses and thundering with one voice, "Duty, Honor, Country." For the general, loyalty to the Corps was everlasting.

Lehman Brothers, as a corporation, was the epitome of a family business, four generations spanning 120 years to 1969 when the peerless Bobbie Lehman died. During this time, they raised money or invested their own in the retail giants Gimbel Brothers, F. W. Woolworth, and Macy's. They helped back the airlines American, National, TWA, and Pan-American. Campbell Soup Company, Jewel Tea Company, and B. F. Goodrich all owed their beginnings to Lehman.

Bobbie Lehman drove RCA forward in its quest to transmit moving pictures and create television. He also backed the Hollywood film studios RKO, Paramount, and 20th Century Fox. He raised money for the Trans-Canada Pipeline and Murphy Oil. He helped start Halliburton and the exploration pioneers Kerr-McGee.

If ever there was a tradition worth preserving, it was that of Lehman Brothers. But it required a loyalty to their past, just as the United States military unfailingly adheres to theirs. Bobbie Lehman's mantra was simple, "I bet on people." The US Navy does precisely the same.

The Lehman management, however, forgot all about that straightforward and uncomplicated business model. Instead they cast caution to the four winds and bet on the most tenuous of all investments, subprime mortgages, which only a madman could think would not end in disaster.

They borrowed money in a way that brought a brand-new dimension to the word "reckless." Billions and billions of dollars, rolling the loans over, borrowing from Peter to pay Paul, dozens of thirty-day loans backed with more thirty-day loans.

They plunged into the market for CDSs, another wild gamble, which if it ever went wrong plainly would bring down half of Wall Street. They gleefully joined in the rush for overpriced property portfolios, in the headlong dash for leveraged buyouts, a procedure so obviously crooked it would have taken a US Navy Board of Inquiry about seven seconds to ban it forever.

They came up with a slew of acronyms that would have blinded Einstein: RMBS, CLO, SIVs, LBO, MBS, and CDO. Contained in that insane version of the new Wall Street alphabet is all the evil and obfuscated deviousness that caused the world financial collapse at the back end of 2008.

It all stood for debt, gigantic debt, mass borrowing, endless leverage, and serious levels of buying on margin. No one understood the counterparty risks, and they lost sight of the keystones that held up this juggernaut fueled by billions of dollars in lines of credit.

No organization was more implicit in this march to catastrophe than Lehman Brothers, a venerable and storied Wall Street investment bank, which, for a few brief, bewildering years, was prepared to accept the $450,000-a-year bus driver at face value.

All of this was caused principally because Lehman's top management had zero regard for the history and traditions of the firm itself. No loyalty to its past. You've heard of betting the ranch? They bet the entire gilt-edged investment bank, as if it were a roulette chip.

Bobbie Lehman would not, as they say, have spun in his grave. Bobbie Lehman would not have believed what he saw. And if he'd stood, wraith-like, for a thousand years in the palatial office of the last chairman of the board of directors of Lehman Brothers Holdings Inc., he still would not have believed what he saw.

It should be remembered that the Lehman brothers were very much interlopers when they arrived on the New York financial stage from Alabama after the Civil War. But the giants of New York finance noted the dedicated way the brothers tried to raise money and finance projects in their home state. As the years passed, their reputation for integrity and fair dealing impressed even the most rarefied of the banking families, like the Astors and the Morgans.

The Lehman family was Jewish, originally from Bavaria, and things were not always easy for them. But well within the boundaries of the first half of the twentieth century they had established themselves as aristocrats of Lower Manhattan, trusted and relied upon by the biggest of New York's financiers.

By necessity, it was a dynasty built on honor and truthfulness, which is why it prospered for so long.

By 2007, the bank had assets of something between $15 billion and $20 billion. But as they steamed toward the iceberg they were leveraged more than forty times. A minor matter that ended up at around $619 billion.

In fairness, some very senior bankers inside Lehman were yelling for the helmsman to turn the wheel, somewhere, anywhere, port or starboard, but to change course and reduce speed from the maniacal all-ahead at which they customarily traveled.

Every serious account of the Lehman downfall graphically describes the remoteness of the senior management: the rarefied domain of the thirty-first floor, where the chairman and CEO, together with close confidantes, ruled supreme. This separation from the bridge to the engine room, not to mention the comms, was clearly fatal. The two senior officers could not possibly have had their antennae to the moving situation if they scarcely spoke to the managers who really mattered.

Despite their lofty attempts to emulate the lifestyle of Bobbie Lehman, polo player, wine aficionado (French Bordeaux only), racehorse owner, and constant friend of the mighty, they were men of a different caste. Bobbie Lehman loved people, high society, and the picking of winners. He dined at all the correct New York tables, and he always kept his ear to the ground, recruiting important financiers to the Lehman boardroom, including the banker and car rental mogul John Hertz.

The Lehman management of the 1980s was inclined to be made up of numbers men, betting on balance sheets, spreadsheets, and financial forecasts. They were happy to take enormous risks, using borrowed money, on deals that, in their minds, had nothing to do with people. Just money.

This policy would have horrified that doyen of investment bankers, Bobbie Lehman, who preferred deals and arrangements that depended solely on the quality of the people. All the Lehman leaders needed during those money-making bonanza years that surrounded the turn of the millennium were a few pages out of the Bobbie Lehman playbook.

If they just could have brought a modicum of loyalty to the grand old firm, and to everything it had stood for, and learned down all the years, that pre–Civil War banking house would still be standing.

As it happened, they ignored every red flag and red light. They charged forward, picking up their huge bonuses, hoping to God the markets would keep going up. During this time they grew very rich, and they continued to do so for a long time. Until the day the markets turned, at which point the Lehman roof fell in and landed squarely on the boardroom table.

And what might have prevented it? Well, certainly military management. Because we would have called into question any deviation from the tried and tested ways of the past. If someone had wanted, for instance, to kick the memory of Admiral Nimitz into the ocean and disregard the brilliance with which he conducted the Battle of Midway almost seventy years ago, that would not have been allowed.

The US Navy's world-leading specialty is assessing and managing risk. We have a system that takes this subject more seriously than any other organization in the world. Basically we have enough risks on a daily basis to top up the Grand Canyon. Extra risk is not encouraged, and we dedicate hours to briefing time eliminating it.

If you tried to sell a Navy inquiry board on the merit of CDSs (credit default swaps), I swear to God the admirals would have laughed. Because that was the knock-down, drag-out joke of the whole crash of '08. It formed the bedrock of the gambling frenzy that had seized Wall Street:

*Is that Lehman Brothers? This is Untold Wealth Pension Fund. Will you insure me for a billion dollars against General Motors going bust?*

*Sure. It'll cost you $80 million a year.*

*No problem. We're holding a billion dollars in GM bonds, which pay a 13 percent coupon.*

At which point Lehman accepted the premium and immediately phoned Goldman Sachs, or whomever, and "laid off" the bet, like a somewhat amateurish bookmaker, shifting 90 percent of the risk in return for handing over $72 million of the premium.

Remember, however, if GM went bust, Lehman was still holding 100 percent of the risk if Goldman or some other bank couldn't pay. However, the $8 million annual profit for doing absolutely nothing proved irresistible. And Lehman had about 1,000 of them. Beautiful.

But what if GM really did go south? What then? Well, broadly Lehman would find themselves hanging out to dry for billions and billions of dollars they did not have. It's the classic dive across the railroad for a $20 bill with a 100 mph express train thundering toward you.

*What do you think, Admiral? How do you like the deal?*

*Have you lost your mind? If that deal goes wrong, Lehman would be ruined—158 years of history and excellence vanished. And that would represent unacceptable losses. Pass. But thank you for your time. Next!*

No one "passed" in Lehman Brothers or, for that matter, in a host of other big Wall Street investment houses. They all just dived for the instant profits, racked up the balance sheet, and grabbed the Christmas bonus, always seven figures, often eight and counting.

But on the other side of the ledger sat the downside, the staggering obligations, if they ever had to pay out on the credit default swaps.

It was the most amazing situation, because there was no firm ownership involved. None of these firms owned vast amounts of stocks in the corporations they were writing insurance for. No one owned anything. These were just massive private bets between parties. The only cash involved was from the coupon being paid by the original corporation. The rest was just a carve-up. A carve-up with a colossal downside.

But the premiums being paid annually represented the sunny side of the banking game. Free money rolling in. Just so long as nothing diabolical happened.

These men showed a complete lack of care for everything great New York banks like Lehman Brothers stood for. They demonstrated a disregard for the past that was, in a way, chilling. There was no sense of duty toward the institution, no duty of care toward those who would follow them. Nothing. Except for this hard-eyed rush for personal wealth, and the hell with everything else.

It is impossible to believe that the top strata of Lehman management was not aware that the bank could fail if they pressed on with their modern-day policy of borrowing on a stupendous scale, and then gambling it on projects that were at best risky, and at worst suicidal.

Remember, it was not just the ephemeral credit default swaps that brought them down. Nor indeed the acutely dishonest subprime mortgage–backed bonds that they hawked to other banks all over the world. There was also the issue of commercial property, buying it with borrowed funds somewhere beyond the top of the market. Let's say the stratospheric pinnacle. Voices in the boardrooms of Wall Street were surely warning of the risk of plunging into a bloated bubble of a market, both commercial and residential.

But no one wanted to hear that. And these massively overpriced buildings were entered on the property portfolios, all over the Street, at face value. There were buildings bought for three times their value before the market went down. As it surely would, and very definitely did.

The problems often came back to the price of investment bank stock. Everyone was paid a part of their annual bonus in corporate stock, which could not be cashed immediately. And everyone lived in a kind of unspoken terror that the price would go down.

But it was impossible to start writing down property values without looking as if the roof were falling in. And so they left those prices right where they were on the ledger, knowing full well the numbers were rubbish. I was aware then, and I have never changed my mind about the intrinsic dishonesty of Wall Street. They can't help it.

Is there anyone alive who does not think that senior officers in the US military could have made a far better job of it? A darned good start might have been to eliminate the lies, to issue a few words of caution and warning, and declaring openly that a risk was just too great to gamble the entire corporation, over and over again. Which they did.

My subject here is loyalty to the institution. And with that loyalty should come a standard of behavior to reflect upon the great men of the past—an automatic requirement. The military, especially the Navy, drums this into its cadets and midshipmen on a daily basis. At the Academy an unspoken code hangs over the place, and it involves the great commanders for whom the halls and the buildings were named.

The code is simple: Would Admiral Halsey have approved of this? Would Admiral Burke have advised this? How would Admiral Rickover have dealt with this problem? The questions are never asked out loud. But they are always there. The presence of those legends, so stridently commemorated at Annapolis, stands four-square in the subconscious of the men who run the Academy today.

They are long departed, but still they provide strong guiding hands in the conduct of the US Navy and its officers. Unseen, unspoken, but well remembered: perhaps that's the most powerful influence there is.

What a pity "Admiral" Bobbie Lehman was not given similar credence at 745 Seventh Avenue after the turn of the twenty-first century. Because if he had been, an element of sleaze would have been removed from his family corporation. I refer to the most suspect of financial dealings that was somehow permitted by the keen-eyed watchdogs of Wall Street. (I do, of course, jest. The watchdogs were on loan from the local school for the blind.)

I refer now to the leveraged buyout (LBO), a crude and ruthless form of Wall Street shenanigans that should have been made illegal. It works in a straightforward way: you borrow the money from a bank and buy out a smaller corporation.

Once in command, you persuade the corporation's bankers to lend it the purchase price. You use that to pay back the bank that made the original loan. You now own the new corporation for nothing, even though it now carries a colossal debt it never had before. If it goes bust, so what? It's a corporate problem, not yours, and you ransack the remaining assets before it goes.

Sweet. And about as crooked as anything ought to be allowed to be. It happened to quietly organized family businesses and to big national outfits. Lehman was involved in a New York swoop on the Hertz Corporation, which, thanks to Lehman, Merrill Lynch bought out from the Ford Motor Company for $15 billion, the second-largest LBO in history.

Merrill Lynch was their wingman, and the two were complicit in the scheme as they shoved the debt for buying the company straight onto the balance sheet of the Hertz Corporation. Then they repaid it with the company's own cash flow! Huh?

There has to be a moral issue there somewhere. But at the time LBOs were the height of fashion. Lehman Brothers financed a $3 billion buyout of the Florida-based Claire's stores, 3,000 of them, selling necklaces, handbags, and headbands.

This time they partnered with Bear Stearns and Credit Suisse, providing the lion's share of the finance. Again the result was enormously questionable, because this family-owned corporation in October 2006 had no debt and $250 million in the bank. By the time the Wall Street guys had finished with them, they had a $2.4 billion bankruptcy-threatening debt, thirteen times annual earnings.

This corporate banditry was rampant. Between June 2006 and June 2007, nine of the ten largest LBO deals in history were carried out. And Lehman Brothers was right out in front, in this charge for cheap glory. If they weren't bankrupting themselves, they were trying to bankrupt someone else. Debt was their god, right before profits and bonuses.

It is inconceivable to me that if the military had been in charge, this would have been allowed to happen. By any standards, there's something offensive about it, and I state this because none of the corporations involved in the LBOs actually made anything or contributed in any way to the well-being of the nation.

They just gambled other people's money to make money for their own shareholders. There was, of course, an area of very intense cleverness behind it, but cleverness outlined by that much native cunning and total disregard for morality is a bitterly unattractive quality.

It is my belief that the high command of either the US Navy or the Army would have banned these practices of making healthy corporations buy themselves and then lurch into gigantic debt, just to benefit a bunch of Wall Street chancers.

Naturally, in the end, it all went south, because the debt the investment banks had plunged into was just too much. And their lines of credit were running out. By the end of 2007, for instance, Lehman Brothers was leveraged forty-four times their own value. The situations at Merrill Lynch and Goldman Sachs were not a hell of a lot better. Bear Stearns was marching resolutely toward disaster and government bailout. Interest payments were just too enormous to be serviced.

As the admirals might have put it, "unacceptable losses." And they would not have permitted those Wall Street corporations to take that route. First because it was too risky, too likely to go wrong, and too amoral. And second, because of an old-fashioned loyalty to the founders and the traditions of those firms.

Not Admiral "Bull" Halsey, or Bobbie Lehman, or certainly John D. Hertz would have in any way approved of the reckless conduct of the Wall Street investment houses.

FOR MY OWN PART, I was awaiting the call to duty when the Checkmates were ordered to embark *Nimitz* and head west across the Pacific Ocean. In February '93, we flew the Tomcats out to her and landed them, one by one, on the flight deck.

It was a long journey from the West Coast of the United States, and I remember being amazed at the size of the swells rolling past us in that enormous ocean. We were out there for weeks, shouldering our way through those smooth, mountainous waves, which occasionally treated the 100,000-ton US aircraft carrier like the Nantucket ferry.

We were accompanied by several US warships and I remember seeing them occasionally disappear behind those great Pacific rollers. And that was from my viewpoint on the high flight deck of the *Nimitz*. Matter of fact, that was probably the most exciting part of the six-week journey that took us through the Strait of Malacca, across the Indian Ocean, and up to the Strait of Hormuz.

Once we were on station in the Gulf, it was a long boring deployment. By this time Saddam was already breaking the rules left, right, and center, but we were under orders not to fire on him without permission. And that took so long to obtain, our enemy was mostly long gone before we received it. So we operated like everyone else in those tiresome, frustrating years of the 1990s, flying up to the no-fly zone, taking photographs, occasionally getting shot at, and then flying back to Mother *Nimitz*.

Our achievements were very hard to assess. I suppose we might have frightened a few Arabs. The mere size of that Tomcat was enough to scare the life out of most people. It was like a flying tennis court hurtling above the desert, and all we wanted was a chance to use it.

Still, I guess the practice was useful. And we all accomplished many, many carrier landings and takeoffs. Generally speaking, we were bored but swaggering, fed up that nothing much was happening, but conscious we were all getting better, more confident, young masters of the toughest game in all the military.

It was hotter than hell, and we were wasting a ton of government money, beating up the aircraft, day after day, and already taking spares from one aircraft to keep another one flying. I have to confess, I had never imagined that we, America's elite Tip of the Spear, would be saddled with cuts that turned us into local policemen, with constant problems in the servicing and repair hangars.

But slowly we came to realize that we had marched into the US Navy under one president, and now we were serving under another. One cared passionately about all of us; the new one appeared not to. It was a bit of a shock, really, as if we had been removed from the sunny side of the street and shunted into the shadows.

So we just got on with it and looked forward to the long journey home, back to Fightertown, far away across the Pacific. Because there, in the not too distant future, one of us Checkmates would be going to TOPGUN. And with my number-one F-14 ranking, I stood in pole position.

## CHAPTER 7

# TOPGUN
# Navy Fighter Weapons School

I spotted him at about a thousand paces. He was headed for the stratosphere, high command, and whatever the hell else his heart desired. You could see it in his quick, impatient walk, in his instant grasp of the most complex problem.

He was a scientist by inclination, a Naval Aviator by profession, and he was my first true fighter squadron commanding officer—a high honor graduate in aerospace engineering from the Georgia Institute of Technology, that bastion of outer-space studies, located right in the middle of Atlanta.

I guess that was his vocation, but it could not have been necessary. My old CO would have breezed right past the space shuttle on his way to high office, because he was the best, the supreme combat fighter tactician of his era.

Readers, I give you Commander James Alexander "Sandy" Winnefeld, at the time CO of VF-211, the Fighting Checkmates, former TOPGUN instructor, workaholic, the Navy's highly disciplined answer to George Steinbrenner, recruiter of airborne rock stars, and the best teacher I ever had. He went by the nickname of "Jaws." God knows why. He was only thirty-seven years old when I first served under him.

It's not that I'm a renowned talent spotter, but no one could miss the upward march of Jaws. He served as senior aide to the Chairman of the Joint Chiefs of Staff, Colin Powell, during the first Gulf War. In later years, long after our paths had diverged, he became a four-star admiral, naturally, commander, United States Sixth Fleet, commander of North American Aerospace Defense Command (NORAD) and US Northern Command, and finally vice chairman of the Joint Chiefs of Staff. At Miramar we all called him, formally, "Skipper."

Curiously, his most astonishing achievement was not in receiving some great command honor but, rather, high praise from the highest authority, for an action that saw him lionized from one end of the Pentagon to the other. On the afternoon of September 11, 2001, the Skipper, by now commanding officer of the aircraft carrier *Enterprise*, was heading home from a six-month tour in the Gulf, steaming quietly southeastward, somewhere in the northern Indian Ocean.

It was early evening locally but around nine a.m. in New York; he and the crew were watching the international news on television. Anyone paying attention saw United Airlines Flight 175 strike the south tower of the World Trade Center. Captain Winnefeld, without as much as a communiqué, a request for permission, or any authorization, ordered the rudder over 180 degrees, for the helmsman to return to the Gulf forthwith.

The enormous aircraft carrier, with a heavy air strike force embarked, made its long, sea-splitting about-turn and came steaming into the Arabian Sea, all-ahead, every department on high alert, preparing for combat.

By the next morning they were within strike range of Afghanistan, on station, right where they wanted to be. Captain Winnefeld understood what had happened, understood who was responsible, and aimed his strike forces directly at bin Laden's terrorist camps high in the Hindu Kush.

He also understood his president, George W. Bush, and he had a pretty good handle on Secretary of Defense Donald Rumsfeld. In the following three weeks, the *Enterprise* air wing flew seven hundred missions in Afghanistan and pounded the place with heavy ordnance. Captain Winnefeld had put the US carrier strike force in prime position probably a week before any other US warship could have gotten there.

It demonstrated initiative of the highest order, which is probably why the high left side of his current dress uniform looks like the inside of a kaleidoscope.

No one was in any way surprised at his actions. Certainly not I. The Checkmate CO was the consummate Naval Aviator and probably the most hardworking man on the base, usually the first into work in the morning, always the last to leave. This was quite often at nine p.m. since he was unable to tear himself away from any subject that was consuming his formidable intellect.

Naturally this did not always sit well with his team, many of whom were tired after flying the big jets throughout the day. But there was, of course, a small group who were devoted to him and his flair for teaching. We could all fly combat missions, but Commander Winnefeld was a true tactician of air warfare.

He actually invented an entire combat tactic. With typical dash, he named it "The Chainsaw" and it represented a high-speed assault on an enemy, from which survival was virtually impossible.

As soon as I met him, I wanted to learn from him, although I quickly understood this meant a general separation from the nightlife of San Diego, which was a terrific city, populated by leggy California blondes and great music.

Jaws was a virtual fountain of knowledge, and he was absolutely willing to share it with anyone prepared to work all the hours God made and to listen, absorb the lessons, and be as driven as he was. I'll say it flat-out: I had many superb teachers and mentors in the US Navy, but Commander Winnefeld taught me to be a fighter pilot.

With all his hard-charging instincts, the Skipper could never be accused of overriding personal ambition. That was not the key to his success. The truth was he only wanted to be the best. As commanding officer of the Fighting Checkmates he was, like it or not, the best aerial combat aviator around.

He wanted his squadron to be the best. He wanted everyone in it to be the best. He wanted everyone else to know the Fighting Checkmates were the best. His ambitions were not a state secret.

He was one heck of a recruiter, an airborne edition of the late New York Yankees chief George Steinbrenner, filling his team with outstanding people. They were very often young aviators with quite high profiles. Under the Skipper, the VF-211 Fighting Checkmates were a team of god-damned rock stars. They were the New York Yankees of the skies.

And he loved to show us off, particularly to the Air Force. In the two years I spent under his tutelage with the Fighting Checkmates, we flew three times up to Nellis Air Force Base, near Las Vegas, for intensive training exercises with the boys in light blue. Nellis represented the heartbeat of the US Air Force. It's a vast 11,000-acre flying complex, home to the USAF Warfare Center, and to more Air Force squadrons than any other base in the United States.

It's wild country up there, miles and miles of desert, an aviator's paradise. I remember we had the best time because they pitched the Naval Aviators against the best the US Air Force could throw at us. Modesty forbids me to relive our triumphs, but we did okay against the acknowledged professionals of the flying community.

Personally, I absorbed all the teaching of Commander Winnefeld, all the tactics and manuals he could level at me. He was unmissable, a maestro of air warfare, and there's not a Checkmate anywhere who served under him who would wish the CO anything but sincere good wishes.

Of course there were people on the base who considered his searing ambitions for his squadron just a step too far. And personally, he wasn't everyone's cup of tea. Men like that usually aren't.

But for anyone prepared to take the very best of him, as the US Navy most certainly is, you're going to end up with one hell of a naval officer; a man whose overwhelming combat talents are surpassed only by his absolute willingness to impart that knowledge to anyone prepared to listen.

Commander Winnefeld picked me out very early as an aviator he could work with. There were five or six of us who were quite prepared to work as hard as he did, and to stay on the base half the night discussing and refining air combat tactics.

Remember, he was a TOPGUN instructor, and in Fightertown that was big: the elite of the elite. I remember the excitement that literally crackled around the squadron when we learned we had been awarded a slot in TOPGUN. Only one, but it meant that one of the leading Fighting Checkmates would be making the move to the earthly paradise of fighter pilots. And every last one of them wanted that honor.

TOPGUN at that time was located at Miramar, their home for the past twenty-five years. They had their own building, their own hangar, and their own fighter aircraft. They were located down near the end of the line of hangars, and no one went near them, not wanting to disturb the resident immortals of the base.

When you fly strike fighter aircraft for a living, you are part of an international network. There are magazines, military and civilian, television documentaries, *that* movie with Tom Cruise, and occasionally books. Everyone in combat-flying nations all over the world has a very fair idea what the others were achieving.

Of course, secrecy is paramount, which is why we currently choose the remotest, loneliest corner of the desert state of Nevada in which to operate. Nonetheless, somehow word gets around. The Naval Aviators know what everyone is up to, and in turn they know a limited amount about us. And yet, the fact remains: TOPGUN's Strike Fighter Tactics Instructor program (SFTI) remains the standard by which all others are judged. It is TOPGUN to which every other nation's air forces aspire. TOPGUN represents the world standard in air superiority.

When I was stationed at Miramar, that was the permanent home of TOPGUN, had been ever since it was founded on March 30, 1969. When they finally moved north in 1996, up to their new headquarters in Fallon, Nevada, two years after I left, one commanding officer stated it was like moving the White House to Los Angeles.

At Miramar, everyone knew what a superlative outfit the old US Navy Fighter Weapons School, its original name, had always been, and very much still was. To be selected to join them for a few months was the single highest honor anyone could earn as a Naval Aviator.

It was about a mile from our own Fighting Checkmates headquarters. You couldn't see it from our briefing room window, but its powerful presence was always there. No more than a mile. A mile, and about 10,000 light-years.

In addition to being the world's number-one combat flight training institution, TOPGUN stands as a living testimony to those basic naval procedures that so often outclass civilian corporations. It was founded on a failure of management back in the 1960s, and its very existence immediately solved a gigantic problem.

It all happened in Vietnam, during Operation Rolling Thunder, the US bombing offensive in which, thanks to a grotesque failure of our air-to-air missiles, 938 aircraft were lost during the course of more than 150,000 sorties. The USAF conducted a lengthy inquiry into this aerial carnage and concluded that the losses were primarily due to unobserved MiG attacks from the rear. To them, this represented a technological problem.

The Navy differed and conducted their own inquiry, in which they arrived at the overwhelming conclusion that the losses were principally due to inadequate crew training in air combat maneuvering skills. Their report strongly recommended establishing an Advanced Fighter Weapons School, "to revive fighter expertise throughout the Fleet."

The principal objective was to define and develop dogfighting techniques, predominantly against Russian MiGs. Thus was TOPGUN born, and thus the US Navy established this center of excellence in fighter doctrine, tactics, and training: a place where young Naval Aviators would learn to fly supersonic warplanes, harder, faster, and more skillfully than any other airborne force on earth.

And no one in the entire living history of combat flight, not since Baron Manfred von Richthofen downed eighty enemy aircraft in the First World War, had any aviator wanted to join an elite fighting force as badly as I wanted TOPGUN.

From the moment we heard that one of our number was going in the fall, just across the way, I guess we all wanted it equally badly. Each of us, in his own personal way, strove to be chosen.

All of us studied, all of us burned the midnight oil, absorbing the lessons Commander Winnefeld had drummed into us, each of us trying to excel. Each of us trying to incorporate the lessons into our everyday flight training and dogfighting techniques. Matter of fact, we all suspected we were pretty hot stuff.

Which made the competitive edge almost unbearable. We knew that win, lose, or draw, we were still a team, still on the same side, still all good friends, and we all wanted the best for one another. We also understood that whoever was selected, he somehow represented the others.

Each of us was the living, breathing example of Checkmate excellence. There was no escaping the fact that Commander Winnefeld had put together a terrific group of aviators. We were recognized throughout the base. We were an accomplished group.

The truth was, any one of the Checkmate's Big Six would probably have finished number one in any other squadron. The Skipper made very few mistakes, and none when it came to selecting his flight personnel.

The day drew nearer. And even Jaws was on edge, as he and several other senior officers wrestled with the problem of who should be selected. He announced there would be an AOM, an all officers' meeting, in the Ready Room, and to this he invited all of us, plus his assistants for the day, his executive officer, four department heads, and one other senior officer. All six of them were TOPGUN graduates.

None of us had the first idea who would be chosen but I think each man secretly thought it would be him. There was little between us in terms of combat ability. And I have to admit that when, midmorning, I was suddenly summoned to the CO's office, I was seized with trepidation that Jaws was going to break it to me gently that I hadn't made it.

I walked into his office and Commander Winnefeld asked me to sit. And then he said very quietly, "Jeff, I have decided to award you the TOPGUN slot on behalf of the squadron. I thought you might like awhile to prepare for this, because the announcement will be made formally at the meeting later today."

He also told me that my regular RIO, Lieutenant Brian Sweeney, "Moose" to everyone on the base, was going with me. I nearly died of happiness. Not just because he was a top-class naval officer, but because he was also my good buddy. We'd had a lot of laughs together.

He was a little bit shorter than I am, probably six feet, two inches, and built like a bull moose. He was bigger than most aviators, and quite a lot bigger than life. He was funny as hell, a former nose tackle at the University of Notre Dame, which didn't work out. Then four years on the varsity football squad at Boston University. He was a sensational mechanic, and he could strip down a car in his spare time. And then put it back together.

Moose came from Worcester, Massachusetts. He was an Irishman through and through, and loved a pint of Guinness and what he called in Gaelic "the craig" (pronounced *crack*), which meant the fun and joy of life as the evening wears on. Now we were going to TOPGUN together. What a day this was.

Back in the meeting I sat quietly while the CO made the announcement. I could see the disappointment in the eyes of my buddies, and I was both happy and sad for us all. One by one they came and took me by the hand, offering their congratulations and words of encouragement. I'd earned the honor, no one doubted that, and the guys respected the decision, as they respected our commander.

Moose and I now faced a one-month work-up period, which is one of the most intensive training programs in Naval Aviation. Merely preparing to go to TOPGUN was the hardest flying either of us had ever done. It's called SPINUP, and it involved hours of air training, whipping that Tomcat around the skies, practicing bombing, dogfighting, air-to-air missiles, and high-speed maneuvering.

The truth was, Moose and I already could have kicked the ass of any Commie bastard who fancied his chances. No sweat. But that standard was not TOPGUN. *That* was an entirely different matter.

This was a time, late summer 1994, when the cuts to the Navy budget were really biting. It was not just the disestablishing of the fighter squadrons, but there were huge shortages of jet fuel. Guys training for the front line of American combat warfare were being restricted in their practice time.

The restrictions were felt at bases all over the country. And even Miramar, which by any standards represented the farm team for those headed directly for the Tip of the Spear, was being cut back. We did not yet have gas-saving airspeed restrictions. Those were just around the corner. But the bite was on. And everyone was suffering.

Except for Moose and me. Our transition to TOPGUN was regarded as so important we were permitted to fly as often, and as far, as we wished every day of the week. We had no cutbacks whatsoever, which had the effect of causing me anguish and guilt.

My buddies had already taken a personal body blow when I was selected instead of them, and now here I was eating all the bacon, while they had their flight times curtailed at every turn in the road, and they were watching ground crews beginning the heartbreaking process of mothballing our aircraft.

We rigidly adhered to the TOPGUN way: Set the objective. Plan. Brief. Execute. Debrief. Capture the lessons learned. Moose and I worked all hours, step by step becoming the best Commander Winnefeld could make us, before we headed across the base.

After one month we were pretty tired, but finally the Monday morning came when we were headed for TOPGUN, and Moose drove us over there. I can sincerely say that, close as the hangars were, nothing had prepared us for our formal entry into the Navy Fighter Weapons School, to TOPGUN's intimidating new building.

I should record here that Naval Aviators have a certain brand of "attitude," especially rock stars like the leading Fighting Checkmates. Our intention was to seem ultra-cool, kind of casual dress, open collars, sleeves turned back, loose jackets. And we had a universal gait, hanging loose, when we walked anywhere, a bit of a swagger, but an element of, "Hey, man, take it easy, we're fighter pilots, we run the real risks around here."

Well, I guess that was Moose and me, as we parked our Jeep very casually and kind of slouched across the TOPGUN courtyard entrance. That attitude, that touch of arrogance, lasted for approximately one and a half seconds, just sufficient for us both to take in our new surroundings.

And boy, did that ever have an effect. The long, lowish building was stark in granite gray, designed like a set of Naval Aviator's wings. Everything about it was deadly serious, everything absolutely pristine. You could have eaten your lunch off the parking lot paving stones. The outside lights looked as if they'd been borrowed from the Louvre, gleaming, polished, immaculate.

Nothing was out of place. I was so intimidated, I went back and reparked the car because it was not straight. Moose came with me, and we zipped up our flight suits, straightened our collars, really sharpened ourselves up. Then we stood up straight and walked forward to the truly unbelievable entrance.

It consisted of two huge pillars, made of glinting glass blocks, shining like crystal. On each one was engraved a relief design of a TOPGUN pilot's "kill," which amounted, of course, to many, many Russian MiG fighter aircraft, each one bearing the name and rank of the Naval Aviator who had knocked it out of the sky. We later learned that one of the great TOPGUN incentives was to earn the right to have your name up there on one of those pillars, a chance at last to join the legends.

This was, without question, one of the two most breathtaking buildings I had ever been in, the United States Naval Academy Chapel being the other. Where one was nothing short of holy, and begged the respect of lowered voices, the TOPGUN foyer was nothing short of a US battlefield headquarters, a place of severity, obedience, and the observance of strict rules, principles, and practices.

This was not a slouching, hang-loose operation. In fact, it occurred to me that if Moose and I had swaggered in here with some kind of a sloppy appearance, we'd probably have faced a court-martial. TOPGUN did not do sloppy.

Two very obvious instructors walked in front of us. No two pairs of pants were ever pressed that sharply. No starched work shirts were ever so immaculately worn, Navy-tucked-back at the waistband, not a wrinkle or a crease. Their shoes were polished to a high sheen, and they walked with straight backs, speaking quietly.

Unlike the rest of us, they wore on their shirts just the TOPGUN patch, no other insignia, and a tan leather badge with their names etched in gold letters. Nothing else. They were former TOPGUN pilots, air combat aces, now teachers. Setting the standards, as always.

Right in front of all four of us was an enormous red and black metallic TOPGUN patch, fixed to the wall, and dominating the entire area, presumably in case someone forgot precisely where he was. Fat chance. The place exuded greatness. I mean that. There was an aura, just like the Naval Academy Chapel with its glorious stained-glass windows, and the sure knowledge that Commodore John Paul Jones rested below in the crypt.

There was no death-or-glory about TOPGUN's high-tech educational center. This was a place of deadly commitment, a high temple of modern warfare. There was not the slightest atmosphere of the cavalier. Only the unique, precise environs of scholarship, like walking into MIT right out of fourth grade. Moose and I felt unaccountably scruffy. We just stood there, knowing we would never feel quite this casual ever again.

We were really taken aback by the appearance of those two instructors. But in the ensuing days we learned, largely to our amazement, just what was involved in *becoming* a TOPGUN instructor. For a start, no one is qualified to teach more than one narrow subject.

There are no classes for air-to-air missiles, only for each specific missile, say, the widely used AIM-9 Sidewinder series, manufactured by Raytheon. The instructors must do whatever is required to become acknowledged experts on their own subject. If necessary the Navy will fly them privately to the missile manufacturer, right to the factory, to spend as much time as necessary.

They must watch the production line, to understand every last detail of the weapon: its speed of approach, its warhead, its guidance system. When a TOPGUN instructor speaks on his assigned subject, you are listening to a world-class expert. Nothing less.

In the classroom everything is perfect. There are whiteboards on the wall, spotlessly cleaned. Every letter on every notice is immaculately shaped, looking as if it came off a typewriter rather than the hand of an instructor. They are even taught to wipe off the whiteboards, standing firm, no ass-wiggling, because that's disrespectful, it's undignified, and too sloppy, civilian, to be tolerated in the US Navy. The teaching in TOPGUN is meticulous to a degree unknown in civilian life. That might seem a little over the top. But then, so is their record in combat.

Perfection is attainable. TOPGUN brilliance starts right there in that classroom. It applies to weapons deployment, missile construction, and every aspect of combat air warfare. There is nothing like it anywhere. It's all about precision: *Set the objective. Plan. Brief. Execute. Debrief. Capture the lessons learned.*

The Navy does not accept an instructor just because he has gone through the learning process. Once they all think he is a master of his chosen subject, they subject him to what is known as the "Murder Board." There he is faced with the most relentless tribunal ever devised by man.

The candidate stands before his peers: other pilots, air combat aces, who have, in their time, faced the enemy and his missiles. For one week they bounce that candidate up and down hour after hour, seeking, probing, testing, trying to trip him, catch him in an evasion or a gap in his knowledge. He better understand the workings and capabilities of that AIM-9M Sidewinder as well as he knows his own address.

The creed is simple. This candidate may be selected to teach some of the finest young Naval Aviators on Planet Earth. We know he's good, he's a TOPGUN pilot, and he's passed every examination we've ever thrown at him. But teaching is slightly different. He needs to be among the best there has ever been before he ever sets foot in a TOPGUN classroom.

We just want to make sure. In our game, there's zero room for mistakes. Some civilians may not quite understand that. Or indeed be prepared to go to the ends of the earth, as we are, in order to eliminate errors.

Of course, while the instructing is going on, the TOPGUN pilots are still flying missions every day, preparing to kick our asses once we get airborne. No expense is spared in this corner of the Navy, no gas cutbacks like the rest of the base. This is cutting-edge. You can screw with everybody else, but no one dares to cross that line in the sand that protects TOPGUN.

When our first instructor walked into the room, none of us had ever seen anyone so perfectly turned out. In addition to the pressed, starched khakis and gleaming shoes, there was a total absence of anything that could be construed as ostentatious: no watch, no sunglasses, no gold pens.

And so it began, a weeks-long campaign to give us a PhD in subjects we thought we knew, meticulous details on every aspect of our learning: deployment, tactics, emergency procedures, every kind of weapon we might fire, drop, or encounter.

They drummed it into us until those weapons became a part of our lives, until we were our own experts on how they fired, why they fired, what they could be fired at, what speed, what payload. And then, above all, about the enemy's missiles: what they looked like, how we should identify them, how to assess the danger, and what harm a certain missile could do us.

They taught us everything we could possibly know about that weapon, everything we could ever hope to learn. They taught us above and beyond the goddamned manufacturer's operating manual. They didn't even trust that.

*Set the objective. Plan. Brief. Execute. Debrief. Capture the lessons learned.* Everything started right there in that classroom. It was as if we'd never even studied an F-14 cockpit until those instructors got through with us and showed us how to memorize every dial, every number, every glowing light, every chime, and the position of every display.

Every sentence they uttered was advanced. They never even mentioned stuff we already knew. Their objective was to hammer away with stuff we could not have known. I've never been to most teaching seminars, but I cannot believe anyone on this earth could have been that thorough, that determined, to leave nothing to chance.

IN THE PAST FEW YEARS I have often asked myself a question to which there really could be only one answer. If those instructors had marched into the land of the NINJA and demanded answers from the subprime mortgage salesmen, from the brokerage houses, from the bond packagers, and the ratings agencies, could that crash of 2008 possibly have happened?

The answer must be an echoing, supersonic no—as deep and resounding as the thunder of Zeus. Because any inquisition by those instructors would have revealed the soft foundations of those derivative sales programs as surely and as brutally as a barrage of Tomcat missiles hitting a desert target.

Wall Street in the middle years of the first decade of the twenty-first century was a furtive place, even though there were people inside those banks who knew what the hell was going on, simply because everything was too good to be true.

The profits were somehow too easy, and an awful lot of people, especially in the upper echelons of those firms, were keeping their heads well down. There were no searching inquiries going on. People in risk management were being sidelined. No one wanted to hear their fears and observations.

The most notorious example of this took place deep inside Lehman Brothers, and it involved a lady widely regarded as Wall Street's Diva of High Risk. She was Dr. Madelyn Antoncic, holder of a PhD in economics from New York University's world-renowned Stern School of Business. Before Lehman she had worked at the Federal Reserve Bank of New York and ran the risk-management division at Goldman Sachs.

She built the market-risk operation at Barclays Bank PLC and then became its treasurer. Her specialty was mortgage securities risk analysis. In 2006 she was voted one of the one hundred most influential people in US finance. Her watchwords in those middle years were "caution," "pullback," and "study it more."

Which was probably why the chairman told her on several occasions to leave the room while deals were being discussed, and once to "shut up."

Finally she was demoted into a peripheral government relations position. Lehman did not appreciate Dr. Antoncic's particular brand of caution.

That could not have happened if the Navy had been running that bank. Traditionally we do not get rid of our acknowledged experts. We pay very careful attention to them. And if anyone thinks they can dodge around them and ignore their advice, well . . . good luck.

We don't put up with that kind of behavior. Ever. We'd have court-martialed the Lehman chairman for what he did. No ifs, ands, or buts. Matter of fact, we'd probably have court-martialed him about a dozen times prior to his leading the old firm into the most spectacular bankruptcy in history.

We're talking about two entirely different cultures, the two most widely separated ends of the spectrum being the devil-may-care, hard-gambling, borrow-and-be-damned management of Lehman Brothers—and then the cautious integrity of the professionals of the US Navy.

If anyone missed it, the men in dark blue are still around, and they are still the best there has ever been. At the Tip of the Spear stands TOPGUN, the feared front-line US muscle and the most careful, painstaking air combat organization on earth.

I REMEMBER THE DAY they told Moose and me that we had been selected for our first mission. There it was, in that impeccable hand lettering on the TOPGUN flight schedule. We're not supposed to give in to personal pride of achievement. But by golly, I felt great.

Moose just kept smiling and shaking his head in disbelief, because there was just no mistaking the day had arrived. We were going up in the F-14 Tomcat to do battle in the skies above Southern California, against two of the finest Naval Aviators in the world: TOPGUN's crème de la crème, the fabled pilot/RIO combination of "Spuds" and "Flex." Everyone called them that.

I'll be honest: One part of me was muttering bravely, "Guess I'll have to kick some ass." Another part was squeaking, "Holy shit ! Not those two. Right here we could get our own asses severely kicked."

But that was the decision of the instructors. And, as usual in the US Navy, there was nowhere to hide. We had to get right into it and risk the embarrassment of defeat. Happily the missiles were not loaded.

Purely for the record, these TOPGUN missions are conducted between two aircraft operating as close as humanly possible to a real dogfight. The speed is real, the missiles are fixed, and the techniques are honed and precise. When one of the aircraft is in position to blow the other out of the sky, it's confirmed by a radar beam.

Thankfully everyone's still alive at the end of it. The training is extraordinary, with TOPGUN rookies like Moose and me being pitched in against the very best. If that does not teach you something, you ought to be in another profession. It's all a part of the Naval Aviator's tradition, the lessons of combat and warfare handed down from one generation to the next, making all the tactical improvements along the way.

Moose and I had spent that previous month perfecting our limited knowledge in the SPINUP program, and we had left behind a bunch of Checkmate aces, guys who were just as good as us. The intense practice had been extremely helpful and when we first entered TOPGUN, we both were at the top of our game.

However, those long days and evenings in the classroom had instilled in us an undeniable suspicion that we could very swiftly find ourselves well out of our depth when they sent us into combat training. We understood the tactics, and I knew how to whip that Tomcat around the skies. Moose was as good an RIO as I'd ever met. But the TOPGUN maestros had been practicing in the air while we'd been studying. In my view, the odds against us were tightening. I kept up my brave face. If it was in any way possible, I planned to kick ass. Yessir. And obviously I understood the basic rule of aerial combat: to get behind your opponent. Then he's at your mercy.

The techniques have not changed that much since the Battle of Britain in 1940 when Air Chief Marshal Hugh Dowding's Spitfires and Hurricanes knocked close to 1,887 of Hermann Goering's Luftwaffe aircraft out of the sky above the green fields of southern England.

I don't think it's quite the same in the Air Force, or the Army, or even in the Navy's surface fleet. But it most certainly is among Naval Aviators. We feel a bond between the fighter pilots of the past and the present. Perhaps that's just because our form of warfare is so much younger than the rest, but I can say with certainty that when Moose and I saw our names up there on the TOPGUN flight schedule, we both sensed we had arrived among the elite. It was a huge deal for both of us.

I never slept for even a half hour that night. And we were both up early to attend the briefing, when Spuds and Flex outlined the program for the morning. As always it was utterly meticulous, and I remember we all walked out together, past the crystal pillars with the names of the immortals, and on to the line of TOPGUN aircraft, one of which was especially designated for Moose and me.

In my mind I had one overriding thought—never on this mission, not for one split second, must I become defensive, because when that happens you're dead. Because you have to get into position to pull the power, slow down, and cool your engines. Otherwise he'll fire a heat-seeker and kill you right off.

The forthcoming dogfight would last several minutes at high speed, and the TOPGUN tactics we'd learned were crowding in on me—it's all about turning room. There's a "bubble" five hundred feet across, into which neither of us may trespass, principally to avoid a fatal midair collision.

But when we slam into our opening combat turn, screaming-hard and fast, the Tomcat heeled over, flat to the boards, with massive G-forces contorting our faces, the idea is to get inside the other aircraft's tight circle, get behind the son of a bitch, and let him have it. Boy, was I ever ready for this.

One of the fighter pilot's sacred phrases kept running through my head: *Turning room belongs to the man who takes it—that's when we separate the elite from the capable.*

Still there was this strange brotherhood among the Naval Aviators. Both Spuds and Flex wanted us to do well. They were rooting for us, in a sense welcoming the new generation of air combat warriors. They knew we'd be trying to "kill" them, and they would probe for mistakes. But if we screwed up, they'd pound us. They might even fail us. In this training, the instructors simulate the enemy, which we affectionately call "the bandit."

We took off down the long runway and dipped our wings over the memorial. Both of us climbed out over the bluest ocean you've ever seen, to 15,000 feet flying at three hundred knots, one mile apart. Nothing sneaky would occur, no stealing extra airspeed. This had to be done right. Spuds came on the radio.

"Speed and angels—left."

I replied, "Speed and angels—right."

We were flying in strict formation now. And 10,000 feet below us was the "hard deck" of 5,000 feet above the ocean. We do not go below that. If we accidentally hit that line, it counts as crashing into the ground at three hundred mph.

I waited for Spuds to call the shots. I knew the last line of his command would be, "Fight's on." When he made the first sound of that word, the f-f-f-f for "fight," I would go for my life, straight into action striving for the inside position, fighting to get inside his turn. If I could steal a split second, that might be critical. The Tomcat flies three hundred yards every two seconds, a mile in twelve seconds.

We were all set: I was right, he was left. Spuds came back on the line, very calm: "Three-two-one. Fight's on . . . Fight's on."

He never even got the first "fight" out, before I slammed the stick over, hurling the F-14 violently into action, ramming open the throttles, over-rotating, rolling hard to the left, desperately trying to get inside him.

I snapped that aircraft around so hard, Moose's head whacked against the canopy. I was trying to lose altitude, trying to sustain airspeed. Basically I was trying to show old Spuds a thing or two, and I was doing it. I came down ten or fifteen degrees, pulling like a son of a bitch.

I glanced out at Spuds and he was pulling hard too, and he rotated his nose even lower than mine. The G-forces were huge. It felt like I was trying to lift five hundred pounds. It was inflating my oxygen mask, and it was sliding down my face. I was sweating like a bastard.

I could see Spuds now, and he was just a tad in front, and goddammit, he was inside my turn. He'd beaten me to it, and I couldn't believe it. The aircraft merged and he comes up on the radio, very calm, as always.

"Left to left."

And then he rolled back, and we passed, cockpit to cockpit, at 315 knots, five hundred feet apart. He was right inside my turn. I could remember no one doing that to me lately.

"This guy's giving us nothing," said Moose, superfluously.

Spuds turned across my tail and I flew across him—each of us flashing through the other's jet wash, causing both aircraft to jump and bump. I momentarily lost sight of him, but I knew we had described two perfect circles. If we'd had red dye in our engines, from the ground there would have been a flawless figure eight in the sky.

For nearly ten seconds I still couldn't see him, and my mask was almost being pulled off by the G-forces. Then he came ripping back into sight, right over my left shoulder. I was only able to see him because there were about six Gs pulling my eyelid out sideways, and I could see just a bit more.

For two and a half miles we howled through the sky, each of us muscling these things in tight circles, two big beautiful jets, wings spread wide fighting to get back into the next merge, which would be almost identical to the last, except we'd both lost altitude in the dogfight and were flying 3,000 feet lower.

Spuds crossed my tail. He sold some airspeed to get some nose advantage, normally a mistake. And now I had a slightly superior position. I moved hard to turn across his tail, and he suddenly pulled a fast one, pitching his aircraft up. I was trying to follow the book, but he was changing the game, and now he rolled his wings level and streaked straight up, climbing, climbing high into the stratosphere.

What the hell was he doing? I was staring at him because he'd made a mistake—and everything about old Spuds was suggesting the violence of the merge had ceased, and he was easing her throttles back. But I was still down there, bewildered, watching him climb ever higher. Where the hell was he going?

And then suddenly he was at the top of his flight path, and he pulled a maneuver I'd never even seen before—a maneuver no one in my squadron could even think about. He made a totally unorthodox pirouette, as if someone were holding the nose of his Tomcat and allowed him to fly around it. And suddenly, *Jesus Christ!* He was coming straight down at us. I'd never seen anything like that. First he was up and left . . . then climbing . . . then his nose was coming around seven o'clock.

Moose yelled, "Break left!"

And I started spilling flares, hurling out decoys, anything to deflect his "missiles." We merged again, and next thing I know, I could see him right above me: this sensational aircraft, silver glinting in the hot sun, streaks of oil and soot along the fuselage, the big twin orange glows of the afterburners. He seemed to have stopped dead in the sky directly above my cockpit.

I could see the glint off his canopy. I glimpsed his helmet. I sensed his lopsided grin, the outlaw-sweet smile of the hunter-killer. It's impossible to be in a more commanding position. The vast airspace directly behind me was his for the taking.

"Break left!" bellowed Moose.

But I couldn't. I had no airspeed. Spuds made this big, beautiful, lazy roll in the sky, very quiet like the Angel of Death. Then he moved up behind me and very calmly gunned me down. The executioner had struck. I felt a chill of fear run right through me. If this had been any more real, I'd have heaved the ejection seat handle right off its socket.

"Guns kill, F-14, 7,000 feet, left-hand turn. Knock it off . . . knock it off."

Spuds might have been ordering a cheeseburger, never mind winning a high-speed modern dogfight, with two of the most lethal strike fighters ever built closing in at six hundred mph over the Pacific Ocean.

"We're all done. Roll wings level, speed three hundred knots, heading one-five-zero."

At that point, Moose and I started to make our notes of the fight, drawing the compulsory picture. I was trying to make accurate circles and descriptions, and I was trying to fly the aircraft, and Spuds was ordering us back to 15,000 feet, and I couldn't tell whether we were coming or going.

Four more times we went at it, and I guess we might have gotten a couple of draws. But twice more Spuds and Flex did it to us. They were more experienced, too quick and too clever. But all four of us hoped for the same thing: that one day we'd be as good as they were.

It was eleven a.m. when we landed, right behind Spuds, our flight lead. The mission had lasted for one hour, the time always restricted by the amount of jet fuel used up by these F-14 gas-guzzling tigers of the skies. Almost immediately we moved into the debrief, during which the entire exercise is ruthlessly dissected in a way only TOPGUN could possibly devise.

It took five hours. Five demanding hours, in which the instructors pored over every last touch on the throttle. They found questions and criticisms in places I didn't even know existed.

They played the entire engagement over and over: everything said on the radio, every move, every maneuver. The debrief is a very impersonal process, and you may as well check your ego at the door, because they are going to take this mission apart. And I have to admit right away that the actual flying was a humbling experience. In those sixty minutes trying to lay up with Spuds and Flex I became ten times better as a fighter pilot than when I started.

I did not think it was possible to notice the sheer volume of activity going on up there. Someone considered we were late with the decoy flares, when the position was hopeless. The engines were not soon enough back to idle. "You did a good job with the power, but you need to get the throttles back quicker."

Spuds said we'd missed a chance by not capturing enough turning room. He'd allowed me the space, but I did not use it well enough against him. Also I was not in perfect air. We were too slow here, too fast there. We were flying at 320 knots when it should have been 300 exactly. Somewhere up there, Spuds had made a deliberate mistake, and he and Flex noticed we did not take sufficient advantage, failed to punish them. They went on about that for about forty-five minutes.

They confirmed that no one in this training school was going to babysit anyone. You go up there and perform, then they bring you down and point up every semi-screwup that took place. They do not expect ever to have to tell you again. You must get it the first time. And correct it on all future combat exercises.

You simply cannot make the same mistake twice, otherwise you are going to seriously irritate a lot of people. No one at this level in the Navy puts up with anyone who cannot learn their lessons. It's not tolerated.

Word would get around very swiftly that a couple of guys were not cutting it at TOPGUN. Any time I screwed it up, I would be letting down Moose, letting down Commander Winnefeld, letting down the Fighting Checkmates. I had to deliver on behalf of our squadron. My errors would make everyone look bad. In this outfit, you better stay right on top of your game.

As the weeks wore on, the demands became tougher and tougher. The debriefs went on until late in the evening. All of us were worried. No one had enough sleep. We had to get up early to fly every single day. The missions increased in complexity, because soon they put us up against the far more nimble F-16 Fighting Falcon, built by Lockheed Martin. Imagine

Spuds and Flex in those fast, lightweight fighter aircraft, screaming rings around us, every advantage in their favor.

But that's a possible real-life war situation. In aerial combat, there's no claiming this isn't fair, no running away. We stand up and fight. We have the best guys on earth to show us how to harness the awesome power of the Tomcat and blow those F-16s, those cocky little sons of bitches, right out of the sky.

Remember that F-16 is a far lighter aircraft, weighing only 19,000 pounds—against the Tomcat's 42,000 pounds. The F-16's wingspan is thirty-two feet against the Tomcat's sixty-four feet (spread). It's only forty-nine feet long, against the sixty-two-foot, nine-inch Tomcat.

The F-16 does not have the sheer industrial strength of Grumman's F-14, and working on carriers would beat the hell out of the little Falcon. Putting down on a flight deck at sea would rip its landing gear right out of the sockets. But in action they have several advantages, aside from being hard to see. First of all, they are extra-fast supersonic fighters capable of flying at Mach 2.

Their flight ceiling is 50,000 feet, and the pilot's seat is angled at thirty degrees to reduce G-forces. It has an exceptional cockpit view and operates with a comfortable side stick on the right armrest, instead of the usual center stick. Her throttle is set left, and she's powered by a mighty GE afterburning turbofan jet. She packs a fair wallop too, Vulcan cannon, with Sidewinder and AMRAAM missiles.

However, she never has been the big powerful jet fighter of TOPGUN legend. The Falcon is a cheaper aircraft in every way, and she's been a huge export aircraft for Lockheed, sold all over the world. They built 4,500 of them.

Compare that to the Navy's enormously expensive, heavy-framed Rolls-Royce of strike fighters, the F-14 Tomcat, upon which no expense was spared. She was built for a real man's task: to bring down heavy-duty Soviet bombers, way out there over the horizon. Only seven hundred Tomcats were ever built. No US strike fighter was ever so beloved.

And now we were headed back up to 15,000 feet to try to protect the Tomcat's reputation against the slick, lightweight F-16, piloted by the best TOPGUN instructors, including, quite often, Spuds and Flex. It was like the Super Bowl every day, against an unbeaten opponent, high-speed maneuvers, jinking, banking, aiming, opening the throttles, shutting them down, cooling, blasting, hiding, attacking, shouting, and cursing.

Every day we fought it out. Sometimes they pitched us in against four F-16s, then they'd try four of us up against sixteen F-16s, then perhaps two against six, then two against ten. On and on, and they were always looking to us to win. Because they were preparing us to go overseas and fight on behalf of the United States of America, perhaps to Iraq, where they might launch forty MiGs against two of our F-14s.

The attitude of the instructors was simple: *You're worried about these one-sided dogfights? Get over it. Just get out there and start whacking some-one . . . because the day's not far off when you'll be doing it for real. And we do not tolerate defeat.*

We were being force-fed victory. We had to keep getting better, especially at utilizing the superb radar system installed in the Tomcat. There was no stopping, no warm-ups, no practice, no days off. Every precious drop of fuel we could lay hands on was used to improve our skills. We trained until we dropped. And we really learned our trade, preparing for combat.

Every one of us ended up believing we were unstoppable. We were not just trying to earn a TOPGUN patch and then leave. We were trying to *be* TOPGUN. The general rule was that each mission would be harder than it was yesterday. Our duty was to finish each day ten times better than we were yesterday.

I am quite certain that by comparison, we made every other teaching institution in the country look bone idle. And, as it had been since that first day at Annapolis, the watchword was *still* "teamwork." The phrases never varied. They were still carved on granite slabs: *There's no "I" in "team." And there's sure as hell no "I" in "TOPGUN."*

In early November, we were preparing for our graduation exercise, which would be a kind of supercharged compression of all that we had learned. Our instructors were revving us all up—as if that were possible—to a fighting pitch. They battered away at our psyche, confirming what we already knew: that no one must fail this course. Because that would have been a failure of us all.

Any one of us would have been heartbroken if someone did not reach the finish line successfully. It would be like one of your buddies being shot down. One fails, we all fail. At least that's how we thought. Because this is the carrier strike force of the US Navy. We need everything and everyone we can get.

We're the most important team there is. We cannot stand losses. Every day we're out there driving one another mad, essentially risking our lives to ensure that never happens. And one day they're going to send us out to face the enemy. That's what this is for.

I remember late one night, a few of us were taking a half-hour break before going to bed. We were just watching a sports program, and some huge defensive lineman, earning probably $5 million a week, was talking about a forthcoming football game and said, "Man, we're soldiers, and we're going out to fight a war."

One of the instructors just stood up and muttered, "Yeah, right. Why don't you wrap it up, you overpaid little creep. You don't even know you're born." No one laughed. No one spoke. But every one of us knew precisely what he meant, and why he had said it.

One of our first one-day preparatory exercises for TOPGUN graduation took place in California, way out at the sprawling Naval Air Weapons Station in China Lake, nearly 140 miles northwest of Los Angeles. This is a vast desert landscape, the Navy's largest land facility. It's situated east of the Sierra Nevada, southwest of Death Valley. China Lake stands in 19,000 square miles of restricted airspace, but Naval Aviators can really get the old ass in gear up there. It's a specialized area for air-to-air and air-to-ground attack missiles.

In one way it's an aviator's paradise, a high desert sierra, but it's surrounded by mountains, and for our particular training day they were firing missiles at us. It's hard to learn effective battlefield evading tactics and instant reprisals if you don't practice.

Every mission we flew up there, we were very, very low to the ground, screaming in, sometimes at supersonic speeds, with missiles locked-on against us. All we had to do was avoid them. We undertook advanced dogfighting tactics, flying fast at low level, hiding from the instructors who came hurtling around the mountain peaks in hot pursuit.

They made it as fast, as dangerous, and as real as it can get. Any one of us could have wrapped one of those Tomcats around the haunted face of one of those great mountain escarpments with considerable ease. Except they knew we wouldn't. They knew how well we'd been taught.

The other place we trained was on the Marine Corps Air Station Yuma, in Arizona, way down on the Mexican border. Again, this is a flat desert wilderness with a mountainous background and the sensational Barry Goldwater Bombing Range, where Naval Aviators can wind those Tomcats up to supersonic speeds and fly legally over vast stretches of land.

It's as well-organized a practice ground as there is in the United States. They even have electronically scored surface attack ranges, where we come racing in at low level, honing our skills at bombing, rockets, and strafing. They have mock-up ground-attack ordnance, vehicles, aircraft, and tanks we can hit and obliterate, which is the best possible training for our strike and close air support roles.

I remember Moose and me racing across that desert, at around 1,000 mph, fifty feet above the ground, raging along that Mexican border, fighting for our lives, with Spuds and Flex screaming in on us from the mountains, guns blazing. Our inert bombs were the same weight as the real thing, and we had targets to hit. But most of all we had instructors to evade; the bastards were diving at us, trying to register a "kill" at high speed. My forearms were aching as I wrestled that Tomcat back and forth, accelerating, cutting back, climbing, diving, anything to get away.

"Break left!"

"Bandits two-three-zero!"

"Throttle-back . . . he's on our four o'clock."

"Jesus Christ!"

And then suddenly four more F-16s are coming at us from over the Mohawk Mountains, flying hard at 3,000 feet. We're only making 1,000 mph.

"Break right, Jeff . . . Break right!"

If you can't get sharpened up at Yuma, you're doomed to the life of the obdurate dull-wit.

We, on the other hand, had an exam to pass before they would give us the key to the Naval Aviators' holy of holies. It wasn't even a proper key. In fact it was just a small scrap of embroidered material, round in shape. Black and red in color. The name on it was "Navy Fighter Weapons School"—but to all of us, those twenty-four letters spelled only "TOPGUN." I willingly risked my life every single day, just to see it one day on the left sleeve of my flight suit. I asked for nothing else.

I HOPE I'VE DEMONSTRATED that the Navy Fighter Weapons School was nothing if not thorough. The teaching, the training, the practice, theory and practical, represents the most searching test of nerve, skill, and character that any aviator could ever undergo. Remember, Naval Aviators who come to TOPGUN have already proven themselves over and over in Navy fighter squadrons.

I can't say the senior commanders always make the exact right choices, but they pride themselves on few mistakes, and their track record for getting it right is just about without equal. I'd say that even before TOPGUN candidates are awarded their patch, they would be more than a match for the combat pilots of any other nation in the world. Except maybe for Israel. Their fighter pilots are nearly as good as ours, which, since they are almost totally surrounded by angry, scowling enemies, is probably a good idea.

It's the thoroughness we always remember. It's the lack of thoroughness that causes so much heartache in the civilian investing community. I mean stockbrokers, hedge funds, even pension funds—the pure civilian instinct to have a gamble, often with other people's money. Most of them do not do their homework like the TOPGUN senior staff.

Why, I ask, were so many billions of dollars lost in the crash? The answer is, on the face of it, perfectly simple. Because hardly anyone took a long and detailed look at the facts behind those subprime mortgages and those leveraged buyouts, not to mention those reckless little killers, the CDSs.

Except for one man, who notably described them all as "financial weapons of mass of destruction" as early as 2003, five years before disaster struck. The name was Warren Buffett, the sage of Omaha, the peerless investor who is reputed to read nothing except corporate 10Ks—the compulsory annual reports of publicly traded US companies. He, of course, lost not one nickel for his investors in the 2008 financial catastrophe. The reason is contained in just one word: thoroughness.

His systems of analysis are legendary. He likes corporations that are real, selling stuff that people want and will want again, such as paint, carpets, fabric, furniture, Harley-Davidson motorbikes, and Coca-Cola. He knows more about those corporations than anyone else on the planet. He checks their debt, checks their management, then their senior execs, probing into their background, trying to assess whether they have the right to hold their current positions.

He wants to know who failed in the past, when and where? Did the man learn? Should he be entrusted with our money, or anyone else's? Warren Buffett will go to the ends of this nation to find out just who is capable of managing what. He knew the derivatives represented a house of cards. And he knew there would be an almighty collapse.

Over the years, on an upward mistakes scale of 1 to 10, he's probably not yet on the chart. His thoroughness is one of the great investing parables of our time. And that's not the only similarity he shares with the Navy Fighter Weapons School. Down all the years, he has put together a team to whom he will one day hand over the reins. In his own way, he has taught them everything he knows, coached and trained them. His legacy will live on at Berkshire Hathaway.

The man from Omaha is a kind of latter-day Spuds, always willing to impart his vast knowledge to the younger generation. He's as devoted to his team as they are to him. And it's only 1,609 miles from Omaha to Miramar. Mr. Buffett would have made a darned good TOPGUN instructor.

## CHAPTER 8

# Even the Nevada Mountains Trembled

Heroes are people who struggle against great odds to win great victories. I guess we'd all be heroes if we knew how. They remind us of our dreams, and of our destinies, and the US Navy knows precisely how to unlock the hidden pathways that lead to glory.

From the portals of the Academy all the way to the remotest Naval Aviator's flight deck, we acknowledge and pay tribute to the Navy's private fellowship of heroes, in halls, statues, and, too often, memorials. Some may be unknown to the public, but they are not unknown to us. Their names, to us, represent folklore, US Navy folklore, and their legend often was paid for in blood.

Such a man was Lieutenant Commander Bruce Van Voorhis. They named the airfield for him at Naval Air Station Fallon in Nevada. I mention him because that's where we were headed, flying every TOPGUN fighter aircraft there for our final full-scale barnstorming battle against the instructors in November 1994.

The name of Lieutenant Commander Van Voorhis was the first one I thought about as I brought my Tomcat in to land after the six hundred–mile journey north from Miramar. He was also the last, as I took off for home from Van Voorhis Field, at the end of the combat missions. Tell the truth, I thought about him quite a few times in between.

Lieutenant Commander Van Voorhis had been a personal hero of mine, ever since they taught me about him in the naval history classes at the Academy. They loved guys like him, towering heroes, Class of 1929. The story of his entry into naval legend is apt to silence every student, especially plebes.

On July 6, 1943, he took off from a US Navy airstrip in the Solomon Islands and embarked on a perilous seven hundred–mile journey, in varying winds and poor visibility. His objective was to attack Japanese installations at the eastern end of Caroline Island, and there he fought a lone and relentless battle under fierce Japanese anti-aircraft fire and overwhelming aerial opposition.

Forced lower and lower by pursuing Japanese aircraft, he coolly persisted in his mission of destruction. Abandoning all chance of a safe return, he executed six bold ground-level attacks to demolish the enemy's vital radio station, their ground installations, anti-aircraft guns, and crews, with bombs and machine-gun fire. He also blew one enemy fighter out of the sky and destroyed three more on the water.

Finally the US lieutenant commander from the Pacific coast of Washington state was caught in the blast from one of his own bombs and crashed into the lagoon near Hare Island, thus sacrificing himself in a single-handed fight against almost insuperable odds.

They awarded him a posthumous Medal of Honor after that, for conspicuous gallantry and intrepidity at the risk of his own life, above and beyond the call of duty. Bruce Van Voorhis was commander Bombing Squadron 102. His citation included the words "Daring, courage, and resoluteness of purpose, enhanced the finest traditions of US Naval Service."

They do not lightly name airfields after Naval Aviators, especially places like NAS Fallon, which today is home to TOPGUN, and is officially regarded as sacred ground to the carrier air wings. Its reputation as the ace training station for strike warfare has, if anything, grown over the years. But when we went there for that last exercise before graduation in 1994, it was very much second to Miramar in the TOPGUN pecking order.

The whole complex comprised 6.5 million acres of western Nevada, fifty miles east of Reno. There are four separate training areas: Bravos 16,

17, 19, and 20, which form an integrated air defense system and the focal point for all Navy fighter pilots.

We land and take off from Van Voorhis Field, and its very name is designed to remind us of "the finest traditions of US Naval Service." And, of course, of a long-lost Naval Aviator, who fought a lone battle half a world away but will never be forgotten. Not by us, his successors, and, should the bugle sound, I hope his disciples.

Nations have gone to war with less air power than we took up to Fallon. We flew four F-14s and eight of our McDonnell Douglas F/A-18 Hornets—that's a supersonic, all-weather, dogfight specialist and ground-attack bomber. We fly them off carriers, and in their sharp metallic blue livery, they are the chosen aircraft for the Blue Angels aerial demonstration group.

They take some criticism for lacking the range, toughness, and payload of the F-14, but they're a formidable opponent, fast, maneuverable, and heavily armed with a six-barrel Vulcan machine gun, air-to-air and air-to-ground rockets and missiles. In addition, our instructors flew an entire squadron of F-16s north to the Fallon air station.

When battle commenced, it would be, I suppose, a fair fight, but I'd never have swapped my personal Tomcat for anything else. We were scheduled to fight two missions against the instructors, and I was selected to lead one of them.

On the face of it, everything was stacked against us, because our opposition was based at Fallon. They had all the aircraft they needed, all the fuel, with instant ground-crew and mechanical support. They could all sit around watching television until they were summoned into the air. We, on the other hand, had to take off, gain the appropriate altitude, and stay up there for the duration, trying to conserve fuel and munitions, because we could not lay hands on resupplies.

If we got tired, that was too bad. If they got tired they could just launch new, rested personnel with newly serviced aircraft. By this time, however, we thought, probably wrongly, we were better than them.

On that bright November morning, Moose and I walked outside, with the sun rising beyond the runways. It was a spectacular desert day, no wind, and we made our way to the hangars quietly, each of us preoccupied with his own thoughts. But there was one we both shared: by the end of this day, we'll either be dead in a 1,000 mph air crash with our 1,000-pound live bombs on board, or anointed members of TOPGUN, a deep and abiding honor that could not be taken away.

I conducted the briefing in the hangar and decreed that the twelve of us would fly in three groups of four. We studied our maps, which were redrawn as if the mountainous Nevada desert was situated in the wilderness somewhere south of the Euphrates River. Pity the fighter pilots ranged against us weren't tribesmen wearing crash helmets in old Russian aircraft, rather than the TOPGUN maestros in that lightning-fast little F-16 Fighting Falcon.

Our designated "safe zone" was above the peaks of the Clan Alpine Mountains, around one hundred miles east of the base, over the Stillwater Mountains and close to the Dixie Valley area, where the land is pretty flat. There were, however, some high summits, a few of them 9,000 feet—a perfect spot for the bandits first to vanish and then come screaming into the attack against us, somehow behind the radar, as they cruised along the escarpments, out of sight and essentially out of range.

My eyes in the sky would be the Fallon ground control crew, with their fantastically powerful radar, keeping us posted, alerting us to the arrival of the enemy. I guess I'd just have to trust them. Our mission name was Warlock—a male sorcerer. Moose and I were "Warlock one-one."

About those bombs we were carrying. Among the twelve of us we'd each have two dual-fused Mark 83s, 1,000 pounders, plus a few Mark 84s, and the lighter 500-pound Mark 82s. All made by the missile specialists at Raytheon. And all live, which is apt to concentrate the mind. Our targets were designated deep in a long, wide valley, marked out plainly, and named in clear naval parlance DMPI (that's desired mean point of impact). Piece of cake, right? We're only traveling supersonic fifty feet above the ground, at 1,000 mph, or approximately a mile in under four seconds.

The instructors' task was to stop us. To attack from every which way, to drive us away, prevent our onslaught on the desert floor. However, they would not want to take us head-on, because the heavily armed Tomcat could take them out. A heavily armed Tomcat could take anything out.

Our problems were also heightened by our lack of knowledge about our opponents. We simply did not know how many of them were coming at us. No one was telling us either. All we knew was their armada, based on the gigantic Fallon air base, was unlimited. They could launch any amount of bandits at us, and if that didn't work, they could just send up more.

For us, however, everything was finite: our twelve aircraft, our fuel and munitions. What we had was what we needed for the fight and the attack. If we ran out, tough. If the instructors decided to finish us off, I guess we'd lose the exercise.

But that's naval air warfare. Flying from a carrier involves all the same problems. Out over the Iraqi no-fly zone we're hundreds of miles from the carrier flight deck. We're always trying to conserve fuel, always cutting back our airspeed, and above all, trying not to waste missiles and bombs. When TOPGUN opens fire, something gets hit.

We flew out over the Stillwater Mountain range, reached the vast Humboldt Salt Marsh, and took a long right-hand swing to the Clan Alpine range, to an area somewhere between the great peaks of Mount Grant and Mount Augusta, both almost 9,000 feet high.

By now we had established a "bullseye" point—that's a spot on the ground from which we call the bearing, range, and altitude of the enemy approach. Sometimes it's where we will target bombs, sometimes not. But when that number is called out, we know precisely where the F-16 squadrons are positioned.

I ordered a line of battle, with the F-14s flying a three-mile-wide formation, each one a mile apart. The eight F/A-18 Hornets were similarly spaced, which made our group twelve miles across.

No one wanted us to be kept waiting for long because of the fuel situation, and then, quite suddenly, I heard the critical signal from ground control:

"Big Eye . . . Big Eye! . . . Bandits launching. Navy Fallon."

This was it. Here they come. The base swiftly informed us there were more and more of them, launching from Fallon, F-16s streaming into the sky and heading east. With Moose right behind me, scouring the radar, I opened up the radio and called:

"Fight's on . . . fight's on! Big Eye, picture."

Instantly ground control was back on the line announcing an approximate strategic picture—that's the azimuth, the angular distance along the horizon between a point of reference, usually the observer's bearing, and another object. According to the Fallon operators it was azimuth forty miles, the approximate width of the incoming attack.

"Big Eye, picture. Three groups. Northern group, Bullseye three-two-five . . . twenty-five . . . fifteen thousand. Heavy."

Translated, that meant the first group of Fighting Falcons, probably led by the devilish air ace Spuds, was to the north, on bearing three-two-five, slightly west of due north. They were range twenty-five miles from bullseye, flying at 15,000 feet. And there were a lot of them.

I replied in our traditional poetic and grateful style:

"Warlock one-one."

Then in quick succession came:

"Middle group, Bullseye two-five-five . . . ten . . . twenty thousand. Heavy—southern group, Bullseye one-eight-five . . . twenty . . . fifteen thousand. Heavy."

"Warlock one-one."

I estimated the northern group was about seventy-five miles from us, but we still had no idea how many. We just had to wait until ground control told us, which they would as soon as they picked them up. We just kept thundering forward in this heavily armed, twelve-mile-wide attack group.

Not for the first time, the brilliant Moose got them first. But the controllers were not far behind, and I heard:

"Big Eye. Bandits. Bullseye three-three-zero . . . twenty-eight . . . fifteen thousand."

"Warlock one-one."

And now we were closing in at colossal speed. Moose spotted them at sixty-five miles; there were six Falcons in the northern group, and these were the bad guys, our TOPGUN instructors.

"Warlock one-one. Contact. Northern group."

And then the radar picked up the F-16 missiles.

"Big Eye declares Bullseye three-three-zero . . . twenty-eight . . . fifteen thousand. Hostile."

That was permission to open fire, and I instructed Moose to hook the southern man in the northern group. He locked on the guidance system to our AIM-54C Phoenix missile, the F-14's heavyweight long-range weapon, the eighteen-foot, 1,000-pound monster missile, capable of carrying a 500-pound depleted uranium warhead. This thing could knock down the Lehman skyscraper, as if they needed any help.

I immediately called in "Fox Three" when I was preparing to launch—that's just a brevity code. And at fifty miles I took the first shot, pulled the trigger, and unleashed our "buffalo," more Navy slang for the biggest, baddest guided missile in the world, our fire-and-forget jet killer. There's only a 10 percent chance it will miss, if the target evades and the missile runs out of fuel in pursuit. This one did not do so, and I nailed down our first "kill."

"Warlock one-one . . . Fox Three, southern man, northern group."

Right then all hell broke out. Moose was watching the F-16s breaking out in all directions, trying to confuse the life out of us. But two can play at that stuff. I made an immediate command decision relayed to the other eleven in my group—a command to break our formation, split up the twelve-mile wall.

No one was talking except me. We were still heading for the valley where we targeted our bombs. But the three bandit groups were climbing, heading for the hills, scattering in different directions, and I was going after them with the three other Tomcats.

But it was my task to issue every command to all of the others: my trigger-happy buddies, the Tomcat pilots with the "buffaloes," and the Hornet drivers with the AMRAAMs (the Advanced Medium Range Air-to-Air Missiles), twelve-foot-long, deadly accurate, 335-pound little brothers for a much smaller strike fighter.

"Warlock one-three . . . target northern man, northern group, twenty-two thousand."

"Warlock two-one . . . target southern group."

"Warlock three-one . . . target middle group."

The replies came back, short and sharp, as they prepared to open fire with those lethal AMRAAMs:

"Warlock one-three . . . Fox Three, northern man, northern group, twenty-two thousand."

I rammed open the throttles and aimed the Tomcat high over the Hornets, which in turn dived under us in every direction. Right then the enemy began to launch ground missiles, firing up at us from all over the desert.

These things were just surface-launched AMRAAMs, known in the brotherhood as SLAMRAAMs, and just as dangerous. In this case they were mere laser beams, but you don't want to get whacked by one of them, or you're out of the fight. Jesus Christ, as if I didn't have enough trouble.

I was at supersonic speed right now, and the signals were coming in fast and hard.

"Warlock two-one . . . Fox Three, southern man, southern group, fifteen thousand."

"Warlock three-one . . . Fox Three, northern man, middle group, twenty thousand."

"Warlock two-four . . . Fox Three, northern man, southern group, fifteen thousand."

Thousands of feet above the Nevada desert it was like the Battle of Britain: prepare to fire again, another Phoenix.

"Warlock one-one . . . Fox Three, middle man, northern group, eighteen thousand."

I heard one of the Hornet pilots coming in:

"Warlock two-two shows southern man, southern group, DRAG." That's target stabilized at 120 to 180 degrees, running away from us.

I replied: "Warlock one-one . . . Pitbull, southern man, northern group, fifteen thousand." (That's informative, meaning the AIM-54 is at high PRF active range—pulse repetition frequency—not bound by radar limitations. We got him. He's history.)

Then: "Warlock one-three . . . Pitbull, northern man, northern group, fourteen thousand."

Moments later: "Warlock three-one shows middle group now DRAG."

"Bullseye zero-nine-nine . . . five miles . . . ten thousand."

They were flying lower, and they were running away from us. We nailed all six in the northern group, missed everyone in the middle group, and nailed two of the four in the southern group.

But they weren't finished with us yet. Big Eye was on the line again.

"Group launch Navy Fallon. Bullseye two-three-zero, low, headed west."

That was away from us. I guess we scared 'em. But it was still a new launched attack, and it was being flown by guys who'd just been sitting around, waiting to join in. They had full gas tanks, full complements of missiles. Eager little sons of bitches. But my Warlocks were ready for anything.

We cut back our throttles, trying to conserve fuel, and everyone searched for the new squadron from Fallon. But they were way out of range, somewhere west of the air base.

I guess they were making a long sweep, to come in on us from the flanks of the valley, across the mountains. But we could not tell which side. I ordered everyone to press home our attack, to increase airspeed right now, and go for our lives straight at our target valley. They probably knew we'd already been successful, and I doubted they'd be crazy enough to take us head-on.

So I lined up the four Tomcats in the lead and essentially charged for victory, straight toward the Bravo 17 drop area, straight at the eastern entrance to the designated valley, engines howling, nerves tight.

For a split second I thought they might have decided to leave us alone, maybe not wanting the semi-humiliation of getting hit by the graduating class. But suddenly Moose spotted them on the screen. Goddammit, they were first into the area, waiting for us, flying wide along the escarpments, setting what must be, by any standards, a well-planned ambush.

My F/A-18 Hornets were occupying our middle position, with the Tomcats slightly higher. We were burning. All twelve of us came raging into the long valley at supersonic speed. The noise in there must have split the eardrums of anyone on the ground.

The Nevada desert shook, the thunder of the sound barrier causing the very mountains to tremble as we flashed low level across the sky, and every one of us pounded home our big Mark 80 series bombs, veering away as the shuddering explosions altered the shape of the valley floor.

But those TOPGUN instructors were not done with us yet. They came diving in at us from every direction, suddenly appearing like howling ghosts over the mountains, guns smoking, missiles flying. Suddenly we were fighting for our lives, trying to find a way to escape back to the eastern end of the valley, from whence we came.

It wasn't real; no one was going to die unless they crashed at these very high speeds. But for us, the laser beams of our opponents lit up the desert sky, and Moose was seeing them, issuing orders trying to evade, while I concentrated both on opening fire and trying to conserve the ordnance we had left.

They made it as difficult for us as any enemy could dream of, but dog-fight after dogfight, we finally turned tail for home. I had one final set-to with one of those F-16s, and I thought I got him. But he was very quick, cunning, and aggressive. I'm darned sure it was Spuds, probably laughing his head off.

Thinking back, as we flew home, watching our fuel gauges all the way, I have to conclude the instructors gave us nothing. All week they'd been telling us they wanted us to be great, but they surely could not have tried harder to defeat us.

That evening we debriefed for between eight and nine hours. I thought it would never end as they shredded the entire exercise, criticizing, nit-picking, finding faults, noting mistakes that were made by more than one of the graduating class. Too fast, too slow, poor reaction, missile delay, fox three this, pitbull that, bullseye the other.

Somewhat grudgingly, it seemed, they admitted we'd done pretty well. But it was all an act. They knew we'd been fantastic. They knew we were about to step through the portals of TOPGUN and that we would do so because we had earned it, not to mention deserved it.

The actual question of victory or defeat never came up. But as I left, Spuds came up to me and asked, "Okay, Lieutenant, who do you think won?"

Without hesitation I replied, "We did, of course. Warlock one-one!"

And old Spuds smiled the calm smile of a TOPGUN Naval Aviator. I couldn't miss it, because it was the smile of a battle commander who knew, beyond all doubt, that the front-line of the United States strike force, the Tip of the Spear, was in safe hands.

WE FLEW THE JETS back to Miramar the following day, coming in to land before a light southwesterly breeze off the Pacific. I think we all knew we would be awarded our TOPGUN patches. But it was some-thing no one made a big deal about. Perhaps they'd all known before we started that we'd be successful, based on our previous records. There was no ceremony, no glory moment. Just a private meeting with the CO, who pointed out that the TOPGUN badge, though revered and coveted by aviators all over the world, signified a privilege and a responsibility for all who wore it.

I know of no other modern military organization in all the world that embraces precisely the same ethos as TOPGUN, that selfless daredevil creed where men are willing, on a daily basis, to put their lives and sacred honor on the line for the benefit of others. In fact you'd have to go back in history nine hundred years to find anything comparable, to a near-mystical military brotherhood of world-class fighters, whose motto begins, "Not to us, Lord, not to us the glory."

I refer to the Knights Templar, the Poor Fellow-Soldiers of Christ and the Temple of Solomon, who in the time of the Crusades were the most feared combat force in the world, the most skillful, the most courageous, and the best trained and armed. And the most secretive. Their mystique still remains, right down to cornerstones of popular culture like *The Da Vinci Code* and *Indiana Jones.*

The secrets and customs have never been exposed, although there's been a lot of guesswork. TOPGUN is very similar. No one knows what happens among that elite and select society. Only that no one mentions themselves or their personal prowess. It's a code to which we rigidly adhere. And I like to think, a bit wryly, our hard-earned patch, which does not even bear our name, compares perfectly to the great seal of the Knights Templar, which is still preserved after seven centuries.

I made my way back to my squadron, the Fighting Checkmates, with my lifelong ambition achieved with the minimum of acclaim. As, I suppose, was only to be expected from an organization that reviles all desires for personal fame and treasures only the teams, the teams, and the teams. The way it should always be.

Even the exam results in TOPGUN are kept secret. Of course, we know how we've done, but we do not mention it—especially the guys who've finished first or second. No one cares who's the very best; the entire edifice of TOPGUN is based on the brotherhood.

Nothing, in a sense, had changed. Except that among my fellow Checkmate fighter pilots, I alone wore the patch, that unobtrusive mark of achievement. And that has a special private glory of its own.

I was immensely proud of my squadron, and they welcomed me back with a promotion—to pilot training officer, the job every young Naval

Aviator wants. It involves the teaching of TOPGUN tactics, by the freshest minds, men who have just returned from the holy of holies.

It was at that time perfect for me, because I was an extremely dedicated teacher. I had been ever since they sent me down to Kingsville, Texas, to be an instructor five years previously, in August 1989. I got a real kick out of teaching the kids and an unmistakable sense of satisfaction. Also I experienced the firm, natural desire of the true Naval Aviator to make my students as good as I was.

There was for me a terrific sense of achievement in watching a student of mine pull out of a dogfight with his opponent on the ropes and head for home. I never could help it. I used to lean back and tell myself, "I taught him that. I helped to make him that good a fighter pilot."

I think all instructors need those moments to appreciate their work as only they can. I always got a special charge out of it. It's true what the older instructors once told me: the greatest thrill there is in US Naval Aviation is to coach and train a kid to be a better fighter pilot than you.

It was of course all amazingly serious, and the responsibilities weighed down upon us. But in groups of young(ish) men, there is always an undercurrent of laughter, and I guess that's part of it. No one could do what we managed for a living and not seize the moments for fun.

In the Checkmates, ours often centered around one of the most unreliable automobiles on the base. It was a Cadillac and I guess it was close to twenty years old. Moose bought it for $200 as a kind of Fighting Checkmate runaround, our official transportation in a sense. We named her Sweet Mavis, painted her red, and had the fire department cut off the roof to create a slightly downmarket convertible, with the red-and-white squared Checkmate pattern on the hood to match the squadron's fleet of F-14s. Mavis also sported a pair of bullhorns, real Texas longhorns, which Moose somehow fixed to the area right above the hood ornament. Anything we hit had a better chance of being gored than flattened.

We used to take that car all the way up to Las Vegas, where the hotel doormen parked her without a flicker of annoyance. It was after all likely that the doorman's official top hat cost more than Sweet Mavis. She nearly always broke down on the way home across the desert to Miramar, but Moose could always get her going.

Of course, she finally could stand no more. We'd treated her like a Sahara camel for so long, rattling her way through the heat and the sand,

and the day came when we knew Sweet Mavis was dying. We held a meeting and decided she could not be asked to suffer the indignity of the scrap heap, nor could she be handed over to a possibly unworthy new owner.

So we elected to tow her out into the desert, to one of the Arizona bombing ranges, where I would conduct the final ceremony. The following morning target practice had an air of the unorthodox. I brought the old Tomcat in, low and fast, and fired four Mark 82 Snake Eye bombs directly into the cockpit of Sweet Mavis. She blew to smithereens with spectacular force, dying in combat, the way a true Checkmate warrior should.

I spent almost the whole of 1995 teaching, and they were marvelous times. Wednesday nights at Miramar were the best, and we all gathered at the Officers' Club, the heart of the Miramar social system. I had a buddy there, Lieutenant Logan Allen III, a big guy with a bushy mustache from Oklahoma—terrific pilot.

Like me, he was really frustrated by the cutbacks to the fighter squadrons, and we were somehow thrown together by proxy, even though he was a VF-31 Tomcatter, and I was a Checkmate. Friendships are a strange thing, and you would not immediately have put Logan and me together as buddies. But we shared a common belief, and a common passion for flying, plus an overdeveloped sense of patriotism. He was a couple of months behind me, but he ended up going to TOPGUN, as I was always sure he would.

Finally, in November of that year, at the age of thirty-one, I received a new posting—back to the Gulf in my old carrier, the USS *Nimitz*. Thanksgiving on the rough and desolate Pacific, Christmas and New Year's in the heat, back up to the no-fly zone, where I was told the friggin' Lion of Babylon was being a bigger pain in the ass than ever.

When I left Miramar for that deployment, I did not understand it would be for the last time. I would never again return to the TOPGUN base on the West Coast, where I had made the leap from adequate into the halls of the elite. I'm glad I didn't know. It would have been very sad.

As things were, I moved cheerfully back into the famous carrier, and when we finally arrived in those old familiar Arabian waters, there was a real feeling of déjà vu. The temperature was still fiercely hot. There were persistent rumors about Saddam's air forces venturing into the no-fly zone, and the White House cuts to the Navy were beginning to bite harder than ever.

This was the first time we would experience serious fuel shortages. Our flying time was being curtailed almost weekly. The guys were fed up, bored, and disheartened. No one could understand what we were doing there if we weren't actually heading into Iraq and punishing Saddam for breaking his UN resolutions.

It was also the first time we had the distinct impression that civilians were running the show. We could not quite believe it, but we had to accept that the entire concept of command, at least among the aviators, was slipping away from us. No one moved a strike fighter without specific White House permission. And that, in every sense, was not what we had signed up for.

Little did we know the situation would grow worse and worse, as famous US fighter squadrons were disbanded, and the US government continued to play Left against Right, stalling and evading, knocking the heart out of its own front line.

As things happened, I was recalled to the United States early to take up a position as F-14 instructor at Naval Air Station Oceana, on the coast of Virginia, east of Norfolk. That's Virginia Beach, home of the East Coast Navy SEALs. It was also home to one of the most famous fighter squadrons in the US Navy, VF-101, the Grim Reapers, and I was assigned to that legendary outfit.

To my great delight, I was reunited with my old Miramar buddy, Logan Allen, still sporting his luxurious mustache, still with his ridiculous call sign, "Lurch," and still about ready to kill the politicians who were doing near-permanent damage to the US Navy's air wings. Logan was such a character, and he just loved flying that F-14 Tomcat, with its distinctive, somewhat chilling tail painting, showing a hooded white skeleton holding the scythe of time and death.

In the middle of the year, after several months of instructing, I was moved yet again, and for the second time in my career I was extremely disappointed. I was having a great time, flying the F-14s and teaching the younger pilots all I had learned. To me it seemed such a worthwhile part of my career and allowed me hours each day to fulfill my schoolboy dreams of flying that fabulous aircraft.

But they decided to bring my personal joy to an abrupt end and send me back to school. Super. I was posted back to the West Coast, this time to the US Navy's School of Aviation Safety on the shores of Monterey Bay,

California. This was the organization largely credited for the colossal strides made in cutting the numbers of noncombat accidents.

And for a while I was so preoccupied with disappointment at leaving the Reapers, I forgot entirely what a critical part that Monterey school had played in the Navy's safety record. I recall checking the place out and finding that in 1953 we were coping with 51.2 accidents per 100,000 flight hours.

In the period from 1999 to 2003, this was down to 1.89 mishaps per 100,000 flight hours. And the school at Monterey had made it a full-time program to end the huge waste of equipment and people, with decades of study involving aerodynamics, aerostructure, psychology, searching investigations, and every branch of safety education and training.

They had selected me to go there and study. And in the undying traditions of the Navy I was required to do my absolute best, and to return to my squadron in the autumn as a senior expert on the safe flying of the strike fighter aircraft I still loved so dearly.

I was there for the whole summer, and I knuckled down to the subject and worked long hours, training myself to understand the possible weak points of the aircraft, how to conduct an investigation, and how to ensure the mistakes never happened again.

The rules and the creeds don't change. It's just that the Navy needs personnel to carry them out to the letter, just as they had drilled into us at the Academy all those years ago. Besides, at Monterey I learned techniques that might one day save someone's life.

I guess it was a weak intake that year, but somehow I finished first in my class. When I returned to my squadron, the Reapers appointed me their aviation safety officer, and so far as I recall, old Logan and I raised a glass to my new promotion.

It's funny, but the phrase "safety officer" has a dreary connotation in civilian life—the kind of job someone is shunted into after a lifetime of not quite making it. In the US Navy, safety officer is a revered position, always held by a leading fighter pilot, probably a TOPGUN graduate. Because he's an officer upon whose judgment the lives of the bravest of young men depend.

I found out the hard way precisely what all of that meant in the late afternoon of Thursday, October 2, 1997. I had finished work for the day and just arrived home when the phone rang with a formal message for the squadron safety officer. It contained the worst news I'd ever had.

An F-14 Tomcat, Fighter Squadron 101, flying from our base, had crashed into the Atlantic, maybe thirty miles beyond the Outer Banks of the North Carolina coast. Good parachutes were reported for both aviators. The RIO, Commander Craig A. Roll, had been pulled uninjured from the ocean by a US Coast Guard HH-60 helicopter. The pilot, Lieutenant Commander Logan Allen III, thirty-three, was missing, "whereabouts unknown."

I don't know why, but I almost went into shock. I just stood there, saying nothing. Then I got a grip on myself, headed to my car, and drove back to the base, the questions surging through my mind: *What the hell had gone wrong? If Craig had ejected, what had happened to Logan? We'd gotten a "good chute" report on both men, and Logan was strapped to the son of a bitch? Where the hell was he? And why had they ejected? What brought down the Tomcat? Are they still searching?*

I was so upset, it's a bit of a blur, but I do remember I was thinking very clearly. I vowed to get to the bottom of this. Logan was a supreme operator at the controls of an F-14, more than 1,000 hours flying it. Something diabolical must have happened.

And if he had ejected and his parachute was open, why couldn't they find him? I hoped against all hope that they would. I told myself we still had a chance, because the Navy would not give up the search all through that most terrible night.

My own thoughts kept ranging endlessly between life and death, and the horror of my old buddy Logan out there in the water, perhaps injured but, if I knew him, still fighting for survival. If he was alive, he'd never give in. *Goddammit, he's got to be alive. Please, please, God, let him be alive.*

I remember staring out the window, distraught, watching the worst sunset of my life. By the following morning, Friday, they still had found nothing, despite three Navy ships searching all night. At dawn a Coast Guard HC-130 Hercules, three search-and-rescue helicopters, two F-14s with infrared spotting equipment, and a Navy E-2C Hawkeye turboprop joined the search.

In the early afternoon they called it off. Logan was gone. From that moment I became obsessed with the mystery of the Grim Reaper's crashed

Tomcat. I headed up an investigation and worked off a three hundred–foot Navy ship that we took out to the last known position of the F-14.

We had almost nothing to go on, and astern we towed a side-scan sonar to cover the ocean floor, three hundred feet beneath our keel, too deep for divers, and very, very dark. We brought a submersible with us, a remote-controlled submarine with robotic arms, cables, cranes, lights, and cameras. As soon as the side scan located the predicted wreckage of the aircraft, we heaved the sub overboard and put it to work.

First thing we found was the canopy, shattered. And then separate, quite far apart, were the engines. Logan's Tomcat had hit the water at six hundred mph. I had learned how to assess crashed airspeed at safety school. Then we began the laborious business of bringing up the parts of the obliterated F-14 from the ocean depths and laying everything out on board our investigation ship.

I was there for days, and we were running out of gas as we made dozens of preliminary examinations. I refused to leave anything to chance. If there was any piece of aircraft lying down there that could shed even the remotest clue to Logan's death, I wanted it landed and stored.

I think a few of the guys were a bit fed up with my thoroughness. I was only slightly more obsessed than Captain Ahab searching for the White Whale.

We found practically everything. The huge vertical tail, the nose, the titanium box beam, the pilot's ejection seat, smashed in half—but no sign of Logan. It had been just a regular, routine training exercise, which had somehow turned into a modern-day *Mary Celeste*. It was just as baffling and equally inexplicable.

We finally packed up and turned back to Norfolk, transporting our cargo piece by piece to a rapidly assembled investigation laboratory in one of the hangars. And it took a while to reach conclusions, but in the end we cracked it.

The engines had been running when the F-14 hit the water. But there had been some kind of breakage way back at the stern of the aircraft. A rod, containing hydraulic and electric wiring, had snapped, and when Logan tried all the correct moves, the Tomcat had rolled back and forth. The more he tried, the more dangerous it became. He could not force the aircraft to climb. When he tried, it dived.

This ought not to have been fatal. Logan and his RIO just had to get out, fast. And Craig Roll did so, ejecting routinely to the right as he left the aircraft. My inquiries showed that the initial explosion scheduled to take place under Logan's seat, the one that lifts the ejection seat up and prepares it for blast two, never happened.

Thus, when the second ejection seat blast happened, the seat was too low in the cockpit. Logan was sucked out as his parachute inflated. He did not have the height for a clean exit, and the seat kind of floundered out and slammed into the tail, which was moving at six hundred mph.

The impact killed Logan instantly. It also snapped the seat in half. I first saw it on the floor of the ocean, lying there, a dark, silent memorial to my buddy. The sinister, deepwater image seared into my mind. It's still there. It reappears in my dreams too often.

I found the key to the accident in the starboard vertical tail. Right there was the exact round indentation of the rear strut of the ejection seat. There was even red paint from the seat clearly visible on the tail. Such was the massive impact, the tail had been ripped back like a piece of paper torn out of a notebook.

The mystery was solved. But it did not make it any easier. If I live to be a thousand, I'll never forget his funeral. To me, it will always be like yesterday, that terrible hour when I stood with his family and his friends at the grave site, next to the empty coffin, tears streaming down my cheeks, unreasonably berating myself for not knowing where he was or how he had died.

The service at the Naval Air Station Oceana Chapel was over, and the last ceremonial event is always the Navy fly-by. Four of the Grim Reaper's F-14s were advancing slowly toward us, flying tight, echelon-right, low level, only three hundred feet above the road down to the church. They flew in the Missing Man Formation, a fitting farewell to a true Naval Aviator who had died at sea.

Everyone's eyes were turned to the skies, and no one moved as the number-two Tomcat suddenly peeled off, and its twin GE F-110 engines thundered as it angled upward with the force of 10,000 Ferraris, wings back, afterburners blazing, a monster howling up into the stratosphere.

The ground in the chapel garden shook as the Tomcat climbed straight up, leaves on the golden autumn trees trembled, and the whole station seemed to come to a complete standstill, at once holy in the morning light at this traditional Navy ritual. The shuddering reverberations almost took my breath away. A sensation of heat seared through me. Was it the 'burners? Impossible. I guess that's something between me and Logan.

And suddenly my tears dried, and all my anxieties drained away, because I believed that somehow my lost buddy was being lifted to heaven. I stood there, long after most people had gone—I think because I sensed a kind of answer. My buddy Logan was at last safe, with his God.

It was many months after the funeral that the complete dossier was completed on the death of Lieutenant Commander Logan Allen, and I stayed with it until the bitter end. When finally we wrapped it up, I remember being left with one thought: if this inquiry had been left to civilians, it never would have been completed in a satisfactory manner.

The difference between us and them is elementary. We are not afraid of the truth. They are, invariably. Because in American corporate life, and especially in political and bureaucratic life, too many people are desperate to prove their own innocence, that the disaster was nothing to do with them. Well, we do not operate like that.

We have just one objective: to find the truth. Our personnel will state anything necessary to shed light on the problem. We never sweep stuff under the table. No, no, no. Let's go figure out precisely what happened. We never start off looking at our own infallibility, and we sure as hell understand we might have gotten it wrong.

We only want the truth, to locate the causes of any disaster that befalls us. And then to state unequivocally what those causes were. In Logan's case we interviewed every one of the pilots who were in the area, we interviewed the ground crews, and it was all very difficult, because everyone was mystified. But no one stopped looking, especially me. And slowly everything was identified.

In the aftermath of the crash, every last one of the F-14s was examined and checked, over and over. We knew by now what had broken and caused the malfunction of the aircraft. In the end, our findings were almost certainly of major assistance in tightening up our operations, making those big strike fighters even less risky for the guys who shove them around the skies.

It's not a word we use all that often. But risk is something we all live with. In fact, you could say we live and breathe it every day of our lives, even though we assume the whole concept of risk is minimized for us, who undertake the riskiest end of the riskiest business in the world.

The truth is, there is no bigger risk than being a military pilot. In the immediate three weeks before Logan died, there were six military air crashes in one horrendous seven-day period that killed several US fliers. It's just the nature of the business: the unbelievable airspeeds, the constant proximity of high explosive and jet fuel, the enormous reliance of one man upon every other colleague. Risk goes with the Naval Aviator's territory. How could it be any other way?

I CONSIDER MYSELF an expert on risk. Some would say I've been a trusted advisor to many high-net-worth families, corporate institutions, and nonprofit organizations. When I was a wealth advisor at Neuberger Berman in Washington, I safely steered my clients clear of every single one of the toxic financial assets Warren Buffett deemed "weapons of mass destruction."

As a member of the board of the Market Technicians Association and director of the Chartered Market Technician Institute, I have trained over four hundred financial professionals in risk control. That's in addition to the hundreds of fighter pilots I taught to avoid death.

Nobody can understand risk like TOPGUN pilots because these are naval officers who live and survive on the razor's edge, knowing that one millisecond of inattention can cost them their lives. That is why when Spuds first put me in my place in the debriefing room, he was absolutely delighted to explain everything in searching detail.

He understood that one day I might be his wingman. That we might end up on a carrier together, maybe fly a mission together. Spuds was motivated by the Navy to teach me, not just to learn it, but to comprehend everything well enough to go forth and pass on the knowledge.

Every time he taught me, he was in a sense handing over the torch, sending me forward, to light another thousand torches. It's a culture that could not possibly be wrong. It's a culture entirely missing from the ethos certainly of Wall Street, and largely from corporate America.

In those places, knowledge is measured in money. All is secret. The bond-trader equivalent of air ace Spuds, in one of the big investment houses, would have tipped me a wink, never explained, and thought he was doing me a favor.

They don't have teamwork in corporate America. They might say they do, but that's mere window dressing. Every single member of those "teams" is out for himself, and information is kept away from others, not shared. It's designed for people to get ahead and move up, leaving their buddies behind.

There's no incentive to help others. There is no benefit to individuals working as a team. Everyone's bonus is independently determined. Individual performance is everything. They both judge people, and pay them, on their personal performance.

The entire culture comes right down to greed. That's not greed on behalf of the corporation. It's greed on behalf of each individual, playing their cards close to the chest, secretly hoarding knowledge, storing it, using it for personal advancement. They're all chasing greed, not perfection.

And as most of us know, greed is the third of the seven deadly sins. It shows up right after lust and gluttony, and right before sloth, wrath, envy, and pride. Its biblical definition is "excessive or reprehensible acquisitiveness."

Since Wall Street's god is the acquisition of personal wealth, I doubt that the third deadly sin really cuts the mustard down there. It's too heavily ingrained. But the greatest use of greed in corporate America, both on Wall Street and in big business, is the way they attempt to overcome risk with greed.

They use it as a mechanism—a kind of muse, to fire up their people to a fever pitch of anticipation, which has the unfortunate effect of blinding them to the risks. Worse yet, it very easily overwhelms their judgment, causing them to focus so intensely on the possible rewards, they barely consider the consequences of failure.

How else can anyone explain that culture of greed that effectively brought down the world's economy in 2008? In the investment banks, entire departments were piling money into one of the most obvious real estate bubbles this nation had ever seen, paying stupendous prices on the basis that the market would keep going up.

Others were waist-deep in debt, buying probably the most suspect mortgage-backed bonds ever issued by any brokerage against homes bought by people who were penniless. Banks were effectively writing insurance policies against major corporations failing. The premiums were terrific, the income sensational.

Then there was the stock market itself, edging ever forward, climbing to new heights. By golly, there was money to be made there, especially if you took the diabolical risk of buying on margin.

Those were the bedrocks of the catastrophe. And it's perfectly obvious that no one bothered to ask the four questions that might have caused some kind of braking mechanism to kick in:

1. What if the real estate market was at a high and probably would suffer a major correction? How much could we lose?
2. What would happen if these subprime mortgage holders started to default because they simply could not pay? What would that cost us?
3. What would happen if major US corporations started to fail and we had to pay out billions of dollars on the wrong side of the insurance trade? Could we afford that?
4. Is the stock market due for a correction? Can it keep going up forever? How badly do we get hurt on our long positions if it crashes?

Plainly it was not corporate policy to ask these questions. Or, if anyone did, not terribly loudly. Because the overwhelming emotion was the third deadly sin. Everyone had their eyes on the prize, the lower orders were firing in reports, spreadsheets, forecasts, possibilities, and God knows what else to bosses who sat gleefully anticipating the rewards.

It's easy to see how this culture manifested itself. Everyone became used to these gigantic successes in the good years, and then began to chance their arm more and more, charging ahead with schemes constructed on beds of straw, not rock.

No one wanted to put forward an investment plan that showed an interesting possibility for profit but carried a big red skull-and-crossbones of a warning, that if it went wrong it would probably bring down the entire organization.

That was not precisely what CEOs and board members wanted to hear. So, I guess, no one said it. They just stuck with the upside. As for the downside, would Dr. Madelyn Antoncic kindly leave the room?

Greed, without fail, conquered risk assessment. That's why the whole disaster happened. Wall Street attempted to overcome risk with more greed. For a few brief and glorious years, risk was darn near outlawed in the United States since the real estate market couldn't fail, all those poverty-line householders would continue paying huge mortgages, the markets would keep going up, like always, and no one was going bust. So keep grabbing those premiums, boys. Cash flow problems? Forget that. Borrow more.

In the US Navy, particularly in aviation, there is no greed. Therefore, it never gets in the way of our judgment of risk. Our risks are so much worse than everyone else's. Just the other day, while I was researching this book, I took a phone call that announced a bad accident on board the Nimitz-class carrier USS *John C. Stennis* (CVN-74).

She was steaming about one hundred miles off the California coast, west of San Diego, when the engine of an F/A-18 Hornet suddenly exploded as they prepared for takeoff. Ten sailors were injured; four of them were flown to the Naval Medical Center in San Diego, the others were treated in the carrier hospital.

The carrier's fire crews swiftly dealt with the blazing fuel, racing as ever into the jaws of danger, risking their own lives to save everyone else from being burned alive if another of those tight-lines of parked aircraft should catch fire.

Thanks to them, there was no extensive damage to the ship. However there was a million dollars' worth of damage to the Hornet, which was based at my old home, Miramar.

Accidents like that always affect me, as they affect anyone who's spent years on operational duty on a carrier flight deck. We all live in fear of fire, and every last one of us is aware of the danger when those strike fighter aircraft are coming and going, which is all the time.

I just hate to think of those brave guys getting burned. We all understand how volatile it can be when the engines are fired up. Remember, that's why we leave the canopies open until the last minute. Just in case something blows.

Risk, to us, is a way of life, and we never discount it, and we never stop thinking about it. That's why Navy fighter squadrons include the most careful daredevils on the planet. Pity there weren't a few Naval Aviators on Wall Street, when the researchers marched in with their lopsided schemes that gazed only at the bonus money.

But on Wall Street you can get into serious trouble for not chasing the upside. Certainly at Lehman Brothers some of the highest financiers in the entire 9,000-strong Manhattan workforce were told they must take more risks. If they were unable to do so, that meant there was almost certainly no place for them at a thriving, risk-orientated outfit like that 158-year-old merchant bank.

Right at the core of all the trouble is that inbuilt force of never sharing things. That iron drive of selfishness lies deep in the heart of all of Wall Street's problems, because no one is encouraged to watch out for the downside. There's no glory in playing it safe. And since the high fliers are all charging for the upside, that sets an example, and indeed the pace for everyone else.

It's not quite a bandwagon. But it's close. When the mortgage department is flying, the real estate guys want to fly with them. And when the big profits are coming from those departments, there's the inevitable onset of arrogance. Because that's where everyone wants to be. No one wants to befriend the person left behind, plaintively calling for caution, because if this goes wrong the roof will fall in.

That careful person becomes an outcast, the pariah whose deepest thoughts not only will irritate the chairman, they will very possibly upset him, and perhaps bring down his wrath upon them all. Wrath is, by the way, the fifth of the deadly sins and something to be avoided in every way.

In the land of the money-making philistine, it is easy to see why, how, and where the culture of greed can manifest itself on an almost permanent basis. That's why corporate America needs strong military guidance and, in the end, to be controlled by the men in dark blue, who have so brilliantly upheld the standards of duty, honor, and country, which have served us all so well down the centuries.

It's not just the raw emotional drives that I'm discussing. The Wall Street architects of the world financial collapse lack something else too: brains. They don't know how to debrief properly, and in the last couple of chapters I've surely demonstrated the vital part this plays in all naval operations, especially TOPGUN.

The year 2008 showed, once and for all, that civilian finance houses go straight to execute, with some half-assed plan, and then fail to sit down and conduct a monumental debriefing session, which will iron out once and for all the flaws, the mistakes, and the lessons.

Ask yourself: How much real debriefing is conducted in corporate America? How often is a lesson learned, and then learned again, and then again? That's one of the major differences: in Naval Aviation, and especially in TOPGUN, we do not learn lessons over and over. We cannot afford that. Because too many of them are written in death, sorrow, and tears. We learn them once, and then we take action, and we'll shift heaven and earth to fix things. We *never* just go out and make the same mistake again.

Business, however, measures its lessons in lost treasure and lost opportunity. And while that's not much fun, it's not as drastically serious as having a strike fighter piling into the stern of an aircraft carrier, killing the pilot and the RIO and anyone else who happened to be in the way. Never mind the ensuing fires raging on the flight deck.

That's the risk with which we all live, many, many times an hour. It comes right down to one brutal truth: risks are only eliminated when everyone starts paying strict attention to their previous mistakes and capturing the lessons learned.

And this means everybody. The first thing that needs to be assessed when a new deal or opportunity is presented to the management committee is the list of things that have gone wrong in the past and can go wrong again. There will always be failures in business, and you will have setbacks. But setbacks are a part of the battle; they're not the defining moment of the war.

Any quasi-idiot can deal with success and accept the accolade. The really difficult part is to have studied the past and to be ready when the problem comes, or the failure surfaces, when the phone rings with the dissatisfied customer, or the bad news that you've lost a contract.

Leadership belongs to the executive who can cope with all this. And it's much more than just being adaptable, and strongly committed. It's the skill to have known all along that this could, and might, happen. Just knowing it's a possibility is a critical element. And if you do not have a searching, ruthless debrief after every mission, then you are doomed to make the same mistakes, again and again.

The most elementary example of this is, in my view, the position and the permanent state of readiness of the Navy fire crews on the carrier's flight deck. They know as well as everyone else that there's probably been several dozen takeoffs and landings in the previous few days and that the LSOs are right on top of it.

The fire guys also know the pilots have been coached and trained to within an inch of their lives. Every man working on that flight deck is a maestro at his particular task. But there could still be an accident, and in Naval Aviation that probably means fire, and fire means death and injury and possibly millions of dollars of damage.

In that explosion off San Diego I mentioned earlier, the fire crew was up and out with their high-pressure extinguishers within seconds. Not minutes. Seconds. Because they were ready. Because all the many lessons of carrier flight operations had been captured, absorbed, and acted upon. Because they all knew this could happen. And they all knew what might happen if they were late, or if they failed to get out there in lightning-fast time: the ship might go up in flames.

They hit the deck running, toward the fire, because of a thousand Navy debriefs and because of a thousand lessons learned—several, of course, the hard way. History has no limits. If it's happened before it probably will occur again. Until corporate America learns to conduct hard, formal naval-style debriefs before embarking on any new forms of investment, they are destined to repeat the elementary blunders that brought down half the world in 2008.

Remember, when the roof collapsed in mid-September 2008, they did not even know how to put out the fires, so to speak. The US government had to step in with a new crew and take care of it for them.

I guess even the government debriefs better than corporations. But no one does it better than the military, and absolutely no one does it as well as the US Navy.

## CHAPTER 9

# Commander, You Will Never Fly Again

O ne of the key points in Naval Aviation is to avoid collisions at all times. Especially those of a high-speed nature. We don't live life occasionally in the fast lane, we operate 24/7 right in the heart of the fast lane, boot to the floor, eyes front. Anything can happen at any time.

This made the weeks between October 1997 and late January 1998 the most stressful times I'd experienced in a highly stressful life. It was a time of collisions, a time of crashes and sorrow, mystery and enlightenment, sadness and joy. October until the dawn of February. They were my high-test months.

I was trying to cope with the loss of Logan, at the same time trying to conduct the naval inquiry into the crash of the F-14, trying to reconcile the two, trying not to let the regrets get in the way, and making progress with neither. In addition, I was due for a promotion, and in the Navy that usually signifies change. I was diligently trying to teach my students, every day trying to live up to the unspoken demands of that round patch high on my left arm.

I refused to acknowledge something else that, right in the middle of all this, was threatening to obstruct my progress. I was not well. However many times I cast it to the back of my mind, on the grounds of its downright impossibility, I still was not well. I was losing weight for a start, but I put this down to the long hours and physical strain of literally hurling a thirty-ton strike fighter through the skies.

We all get knocked about. It's the G-forces as much as anything. But I'd never felt this tired before. I often woke up exhausted. I had some numbness in the fingertips of my left hand.

A few times in the night, starting mid-October, I had awakened with drenching night sweats, sheets soaked, pajamas soaked, bad enough for the entire bed to need changing. I had a chat with one of the Navy doctors, but I guess he thought I looked too goddamned fit. It couldn't be much. I was told to quit working out, running, and driving my beloved 178 mph Honda CBR-1100XX Super Blackbird, the world's fastest production motorcycle.

I don't think I ever reported an occasional minor chest pain. As ever, I put this down to the daily grind of my profession. Until one January morning that minor chest pain receded and someone drove an ice pick right into the middle of my heart. At least, that's what it felt like.

The pain almost overwhelmed me. I grabbed my chest and stopped breathing. I actually went down on one knee. But it eased, and I splashed water on my face. And then it went away. "It's nothing," I told myself. "How could it be? I'm the fittest guy I know. I have a class to take. I must have indigestion, and I cannot frig around like this, wondering if I'm ill. Onward and upward."

Days later, my promotion came through. The US Navy had made me a lieutenant commander. I hastily set about arranging a celebration party, and given the way I kept stealing off with the big prizes, my colleagues and friends were unsparingly generous to me. I arranged a gathering in a local civilian pool hall and ordered in the drinks and food. Everyone was invited.

The very next day, February 2, Groundhog Day in the United States, I was shaving at around six thirty a.m. when I felt a lump in my neck, right above the clavicle. It didn't hurt and it was not in any way scary. It was just there, right under the skin, like the top third of an egg.

Whatever it was, I had no time to deal with it. I was flying twice that day, and I had a brief to attend. So I pulled on my flight suit, fired up the

Honda Blackbird, and roared over to the Grim Reapers' hangar, pondering the twin problems of the day as I drove: the stupid lump in my neck, and whether the immortal Ohio groundhog, Buckeye Chuck, would see his shadow.

I guess it must have been around eleven a.m. when I decided I could take a half hour and have a chat with one of the base doctors. I drove over to the clinic and saw Dr. David Penberthy, the main man, flight surgeon Matt Rings being absent that morning.

"Hey, Doc," I greeted him, "I got a weird little problem," and I showed him the lump on my neck. He spent a little time prodding about, pressing the lump, and saying calming things like it was probably a cyst. No need for alarm. I should point out the Navy doctors have the same kind of demeanor as LSOs operating on the stern of a carrier. Everything's calm, things are not said that might provoke panic. Also they know that none of the aviators ever wants a "down-chit," the little document that stands us down from flying, through illness. There are so many compulsory hours to be completed, we all live in fear of falling behind.

Doc Penberthy was well aware of that. He would only issue me with the down-chit under pressing and obvious circumstances. I told him about the night sweats and the numbness in my fingers, and he made some notes but did not issue the chit. I guessed he was putting the problem down to the Gs. He knew as well as anyone that all pilots get knocked about.

I went out and flew the F-14 with my students, debriefed them, and walked to the Officers' Club for lunch with a couple of my fellow Reapers. I flew again in the afternoon. I still didn't feel great, but nothing felt serious. However, the following morning the lump was still there.

I flew again that day, but at the end of the afternoon I found a note waiting for me: "Doc Rings wants to see you." Matt Rings, whom I knew, seemed more concerned than Doc Penberthy had been.

He asked me about the sweats and the numbness. He checked my neck, chatting calmly. Navy doctors do not have the star of command on their sleeves but they always have our respect, and in turn they respect the aviators, never blowing our cover when we say we're fine, even though we might be slightly ill. There was no down-chit, but the senior doctor asked me what I was doing this afternoon.

I told him, and then he said, "Come and see me before you fly. And when you get down, I want you to go over to the Naval Medical Center in Portsmouth. They're expecting you."

I flashed the facts through my mind: Doc Penberthy had reported my symptoms to Lieutenant Rings. He'd seen me personally, asked several questions, and consulted with someone at the grandest and oldest hospital in the US Navy, our medical flagship. And I was to go there not next week but today, right after work.

And so, I flew my missions, kept my flight suit on, and saddled up the Blackbird for the forty-minute ride from Naval Air Station Oceana, Virginia Beach, to the majestic, columned building on Holcomb Road, Portsmouth, right on the Elizabeth River.

I remember the journey well. It was raining, and I rode right across Virginia Beach, around twenty-five miles, and crossed the bridge into Olde Town Portsmouth, across from the gigantic Norfolk Naval Shipyard.

This is a very modern hospital, and I went through the procedures, signing in, and filling out a long form, and waiting. I was thirty-three years old and I already knew this was unlikely to be a trifling matter. It all felt very lonely, even though I knew I was in the best place in the world for a Naval Aviator.

When I finally saw the doctor, he told me he'd heard from Matt Rings, and thereafter he probed and pressed the lump in my neck and asked me many, many questions. In the end he asked me if I'd ever had an ultrasound. I told him no, and he immediately sent for the machine.

I took off my shirt and he X-rayed the lump. When the readout came he showed it to me, a white egg on a jet-black background.

Right away he made a call and sent me up to the fourth floor, to a new doctor who said he would conduct a fine-needle aspiration biopsy.

"This may be a cyst," he said. "And it may reduce. But it'll hurt a bit."

That was like telling me an F-14 was pretty fast. Hurt! I nearly jumped through the ceiling. The needle looked like a hypodermic for a full-grown bull elephant. And he lanced it into my neck like a Spanish matador. He did it several times, sucking out blood and God knows what else and squirting it into a surgical tray.

I was shaking with the pain, and when it was over I gladly got dressed and made my escape. The next day was more or less normal, and with my promotion party coming up in the evening, I hoped it would stay that way.

No such luck. At two p.m. Matt Rings called and ordered me immediately back to the Naval Medical Center, and once more I saddled up and set off for Portsmouth, checking into the general practice area and filling out another long form. By now I realized this was real trouble, because I knew the "cyst" was still there. I waited for around twenty minutes and the same doctor called for me.

He was wearing his white surgical coat and holding my X-rays. He looked me square in the eye and said, "Commander, you have lymphoma and we need to do a biopsy. You should be here at four thirty in the morning." Right then, he did not quite tell me the whole story. Lymphoma's bad, real bad, but I was worse. I had a cancerous tumor the size of my fist wrapped around my heart, almost encasing it. The lump in my neck was a branch of that tumor. This was not just bad, this was dire.

The doctor, while not wanting to scare me to death, was nonetheless very straight about it, and it took me about a hundredth of a second to grasp that this senior naval medic was talking emergency surgery. I tried to hold on to the stiff-upper-lip demeanor I considered to be the norm for a fighter pilot. But in about three seconds my whole life passed in front of me. I had just received my new orders, which were to report to the fabled VF-213 Black Lions, the outfit that was to fly the very latest Tomcat, the F-14D.

They had requested me by name, Lieutenant Commander Jeffery Lay, TOPGUN graduate, one of the most highly qualified aviators on the base, to train men to fly the most advanced F-14 in the country. This was a very big job, and I was geared for success, revved up to join this legendary squadron, which had flown 11,500 combat missions in Vietnam, been stationed at Miramar for thirty-six years, the heavy hitters who flew into combat with the feared Black Lion emblem on their vertical tail.

It was the most perfect appointment I'd ever had, back to the West Coast for the first promotion I'd ever truly loved instantly, in my favorite place in all the world. And right now, in a matter of seconds, it was over. My entire career flashed before my eyes. My life had hit a wall, and I was about to be handed the down-chit to end them all, the one that sounds the death knell for a Naval Aviator.

No one had ever been diagnosed with as deadly a lymphoma and lived to set foot in a Navy strike fighter again. This was it. I stood there and wept. It was five thirty on the afternoon of Friday, February 6, 1998, and I guess I was in shock. But I actually wept for precisely fourteen seconds. And then I muscled up.

My old familiar surge of determination somehow swept over me. I brushed away my tears with the sleeve of my shirt and told myself, "I'm going to beat this. I'm going to take what they throw at me, and I'm not going to come up short. I will win. That's the way the US Navy brought me up. Whatever it takes, I will win."

I thanked the doctor, told him I'd see him at four thirty, and then drove home to host my promotion party at the pool hall. That was a pretty tough evening. Everyone turned up, and I remember having a long chat with Commander Craig Roll ("Tootsie," of course—what else in a world-famous cathedral of wit like the Grim Reapers?).

He was as upset as I was over Logan's death, so we had much in common. Neither of us knew precisely what had happened, but Craig had ejected safely and Logan had died, and my board of inquiry was still working on a final solution.

I told Craig I had been diagnosed that day with lymphoma, and we both knew that was down-chit *finito*. I would have to leave the squadron.

He just stood there and said, "Oh, my God, Jeff. That's the second-worst thing that's happened this winter." Matt Rings was there, and I guess word traveled very quickly. Lieutenant Commander Lay was finished.

With some difficulty, I saw out the party and left early, without having a celebration drink. I went home, rested awhile, and then pulled on my flight suit for the last time. Shortly before three thirty, I set off on the Blackbird. It was like driving through the set of a horror movie. The night was very dark, and a low fog bank had drifted in south off the Hampton Roads, the US Navy's ocean highway in and out of the Norfolk yards.

I remember that flat freeway, spookily quiet with its creepy sodium lights shining up at me through the fog. And the rhythm of the tires as I sped along: *p-thump . . . p-thump . . . p-thump*. For a guy going to attend his death sentence, it was as close as anyone could get to perfect: a dank place of swirling night shadows and ghosts, the kind of setting you'd expect on the moors, midway through *The Hound of the Baskervilles*.

When I arrived, I removed my flight suit and swapped it for a surgical gown. They took me to a holding area, where I waited for twenty minutes, and spent my time deciding I was very definitely going to kick this thing right in the ass. Whatever the hell it was.

Finally they came for me, and I climbed onto the mobile bed, and they took me to an operating room. The anesthesiologist attached a few wires and tubes, gave me an injection, and told me to start counting backward, from one hundred. I think I made one number and immediately crashed. Looking back, it was the latest variation on the ninety-nine, shut down.

I felt a bit sore afterward, and there was a sizeable dressing on my neck. Being fairly swift of thought, I worked out they'd probably cut that hard-boiled egg right out of there. The surgeon told me the operation had been quite severe and that I should remain in the hospital for a couple of days.

But unaccountably I was seized by a totally unreasonable fear. These were the nicest people, and I knew the doctor really wanted to help me, but I somehow believed that if I spent one night in the US Naval Medical Center, I'd never get out.

I told him I had to go. I had to get home, back to work. I could not just lie around in a hospital bed. In the end, he accepted I was going. They wrote out some instructions, told me when the dressing had to be changed, and allowed me to leave.

Cramming the painkillers into my flight suit pocket, I went out and gunned the old Blackbird back down that flat and creepy highway, through the fog, arriving home as dawn was breaking over Oceana Naval Air Station. It was still quiet, and no one was yet taking off or landing, and I had a curious feeling that I just wanted to stand outside for a while and watch the guys going into action, just to feel a part of it, albeit a remote one now.

I remember the new sunrise climbing out of the Atlantic and casting its pink morning rays on my TOPGUN patch. At least I thought it was. I would have done anything for an omen, and the morning light of God illuminating that little black-and-red circle was, to me, not much less than the great light seen by Saint Paul on the road to Damascus.

Once more the flame of defiance burned within me. Standing there in the new dawn, I was a new commander, struck down ruthlessly by a vicious disease, and I swore to all that was holy I'd beat the hell out of it. The Navy had taught me how; TOPGUN had shown me how it was done.

I went into the house and turned on my computer. I punched in the word "cancer." I resolved to become an expert on the subject. Not just any old expert, but an expert like those TOPGUN instructors: someone who knew every last thing about this terrible illness and its cures, in all their forms.

I spent the morning pounding into the keyboard words I'd never even heard before. I was writing stuff down on a legal pad, laying things out in order, and as ever, I was weighing up the all-important ratio of risk to reward. Especially risk. That's my specialty, despite the irony of having cheated death a thousand times and now having to face my own personal executioner.

I didn't feel much like lunch, and I kept on studying all through that Saturday and long into the night. By the time I forced myself to go to bed, I had one outstanding dread, and that was the standard course of chemotherapy given to cancer patients. It was called MOPP, which to me sounded absurd.

MOPP, I discovered, contained one ingredient I could not have: bleomycin, which, while being a definite killer of the cancer cells over the course of a year, also ruins your lungs, wiping out your ability to diffuse carbon dioxide. That was the kiss of death to a fighter pilot, the one surefire guarantee that he'd made his last flight.

Fat lot of good that was to a lieutenant commander who was slated to report to his next fighter squadron, as a department head, in Miramar in August. I mean, Jesus Christ, you're dealing with a newly promoted Black Lion right here, and I'm too busy to die, and far too busy to be taking stuff that would screw up my lungs.

Still, it did occur to me that if not MOPP, then what? I had to be back in the air by November, otherwise I'd miss compulsory time, and that was very bad indeed. It also occurred to me that I also might be dead, which was grim, but not as bad as missing my flying time.

So I delved into every possible alternative, poring over the lists of alternative cures, delving into a new and revolutionary treatment called the Stanford V Experimental Protocol, which turned out to be more powerful than MOPP but contained much less bleomycin.

To this day, very few people have ever risked Stanford V because it represents twice the drug but might work in half the time. I realized it might also kill me pretty quickly, but it had one overriding merit: if it worked, it would be swift enough to keep me in the flying program. And I weighed the risk against the reward. No contest. Stanford V it would be.

I didn't care how bad it was, and by the small hours of that Sunday morning I was keenly aware that all chemo can kill you. It's just a matter of how fast it can kill the cancer cells, hopefully in time for the doctors to save your life. Basically, MOPP was a safer and probably better bet, but not for a TOPGUN guy, no, sir. Forget all about that bleomycin lung-killer, and face me to the enemy.

I liked the alternative stuff very much. After hours and hours of re-search I accepted the widespread but controversial scientific conclusion that I needed hefty doses of vitamin B17—laetrile, it's called, and you find it in apricot and peach seeds. I also liked the sound of shiitake mushrooms and shark liver oil.

However, I guessed that proper medical doctors would not love this kind of thing, and I resolved to take the alternates in secret and pay for them myself. So I kept at it, reading, noting, making lists, detailing the pros and cons, weighing the risks.

In the end there was much that was unclear, but so many doctors pointed up the importance of attitude, many of them believing a patient's chances were increased threefold if he could find a positive and deter-mined frame of mind with which to fight his battle.

This part was easy for me. I had a great attitude, and I was unwavering in my determination to win at any and all costs, like a TOPGUN pilot. Defeat was out of the question. I was a stranger in a foreign place, a place with different priorities from any I had ever known. There were no dare-devils here, this was a careful land, at once hopeful but nonetheless sor-rowful, where people who had been struck down struggled to survive among quiet, hardworking nurses and doctors.

I did not belong here, and I was damned if I was going to be shot down over enemy territory.

Lost in my research, I pressed on through Monday morning, studying chemotherapy like I studied guided air-to-air missiles, until, at eleven thirty, the phone rang. Matt Rings told me I was to return to the hospital. He wanted me to see a new surgeon, Captain Shen, whom he cheerfully described as "the Tiger Woods of cancer surgery," the Navy's top man.

And so, armed with my new knowledge and steel-edged sense of purpose, I drove over to the old traditional part of the medical center, trying to cast to the back of my mind the fact that my own life was in ruins. The day had taken a turn for the worse. Captain Shen was not available, and they accompanied me to a different surgeon, Commander Steve Hager, who I could tell was getting my test results on the phone from the Bethesda Naval Hospital in Maryland.

Without even looking up, he said, "You're late," which I considered was a pleasant way to treat a condemned man, right up there with "You're a qual," as a recognition of a lifetime of hard work.

I made no reply, just waited, until he spoke again.

"How do you like your news, Commander?" he asked.

"Same as everyone else," I answered. "The truth."

"Okay, Jeff," he said, softening a little. "You have Hodgkin's lymphoma—stage 2B. That's six months of chemotherapy, then two months of radiation. You're getting MOPP."

My first words were, "That's not going to work for me."

He looked at me incredulously and replied, "What do you mean, that's not going to work for you?" His expression was indignant, communicating unmistakably that he was a naval surgeon and I was a know-nothing, sick pilot.

I then spoke formally. "I have orders to my new job as a department head at Miramar. I report in August and begin flight testing and training within three months. I prefer the Stanford V Protocol."

He looked at me coolly and uttered what I considered to be fighting words. "Commander," he said, "you are never going to fly again."

"We'll see about that," I answered. "But I'm not doing MOPP. I've done a lot of research and I cannot risk that much bleomycin."

My new doctor blinked. "MOPP," he said, "gives you odds of 70 percent survival for five years. The odds of Stanford V working are much lower, and the risks are unknown."

I quickly debated a polite way to inform him that he could shove his odds up his ass. But I just said, "You don't know me."

He motioned me to take a seat, and we began a long discussion about the cure I should go for. Steve was not against the Stanford Protocol on principle, but he was plainly very wary of the risks involved in having that much chemo.

However, unlike many frightened cancer patients, I did not subscribe to the idea that I had to do precisely what the doctor said. He's not God. He's just doing his darnedest, like the rest of us. I told him I approved of the drug adriamycin, known in the trade as "the Big Red One," because of its color. It can cause heart damage, but I figured if I died that wouldn't matter much, and "adria" was a virulent killer of cancer cells.

I was also very big on nitrogen mustard, a clearly poisonous substance similar to mustard gas, but containing nitrogen instead of sulfur. I read that it had been known to reverse leukemia and was a very powerful enemy of cancer. The Stanford scientists admired it. And that was good enough for me. But once more I appreciated the irony that the notorious WWI killer of armed forces would now be utilized in my proposed cure.

I'd read that mustard gas was used by the German army at the Second Battle of Ypres, and it literally choked people. The French army fled its horrors, and the stuff caused terrible blisters, which I was prepared to risk.

The bleomycin was a continuing problem, and although I accepted it was a very strong cure for cancer, I could not risk my lungs. Stanford V liked it, but seemed not to regard it as the critical element. We compromised. I would take a little, intravenously, slowly, and my lungs would be carefully monitored at all times.

THE FOURTH STANFORD CHEMO I wanted was vincristine, or VCR, an alkaloid drug produced from the Madagascar periwinkle. It had to be effective, because it was used to treat acute leukemia and various lymphomas. It's kind of tough, causing swelling, dizziness, and danger to the skin from the sun's rays. I could deal with all that. They administer it intravenously.

The fifth one was prednisone, a synthetic steroid hormone produced from cortisone and used to combat autoimmune diseases. The Stanford guys were into this as a precaution, such was the high-test concoction they prescribed to kill the cancer itself.

I think Steve was somewhat unhappy about the strength of the stuff I was planning to subject myself. But in the end we agreed on this experimental combination of drugs. I may even have gone some way toward convincing him that being a fighter pilot was more important to me than life itself.

We settled, mustard gas and all. They began a series of tests designed simply to see whether I could take that much punishment. They injected nuclear medicine into me, radioactive isotopes, which showed I was personally radioactive, a walking nuclear weapon, and this part of my treatment had to be conducted behind a door six feet thick.

But they had to keep injecting, just to make sure it was not going to kill me, to be absolutely certain my heart and lungs could take it. The early prognosis in the first couple of days was good. I had a tough enough heart and lungs to withstand it, even though my heart was slightly enlarged because of the G-forces, and surrounded by the goddamned cancer.

Nonetheless, the doctor said the medical battering I was taking was nothing less than preposterous. He also thought I must be crazy. He never lost that attitude that constantly implied he was the doctor, and who the hell did I think I was, insisting on this harsh, uncompromising treatment against his better judgment? *Don't you want to live? Why risk it?*

No one knew I was already taking my alternative vitamin, trying to cut back the effects of the bleomycin. More important, to me, I was proving I could and would take the punishment, even though a lot of people most certainly could not.

That business of the doctor disapproving my methods did not trouble me overmuch. But somehow I felt his disapproval would naturally spread to everyone else in the medical profession. And that induced a feeling of total and utter loneliness. It would be a rough and maybe life-threatening struggle. And it was a burden I would essentially need to carry all alone.

But one line I had read during my weekend of research kept coming back to me. "With good drugs and a bad attitude you will die. The other way, with a strong and resilient determination, will almost certainly raise you up, and bring you through it." That sustained me, because I knew that when the chips were down, I had enough of the right stuff to somehow find more, that in the end I could find more than anyone had ever found.

I set off on my journey with my teeth gritted. I was not afraid now. My aggression toward the situation had taken me far beyond that. I'd charged straight past the doctor, and I'd charge past anything else that got in my way, including this lymphoma bullshit.

I mean, what was this thing that had dared to interrupt my life? I ask the question now, as I asked it then. The truth was, only I truly understood how I had contracted the disease. I rammed it into the back of my mind, because it had developed on the flight deck of aircraft carriers, and in the cockpit of the F-14s.

Just imagine. That flight deck is assailed by all those AWG-9 radar systems, the most powerful radar ever made. I flew more than anyone, and the radar was six feet in front of me. There was radiation everywhere in the systems, and I was right in the middle of it for most of my working life.

When I wasn't flying, I was always up on the flight deck, taking my turn as the LSO, taking care of my buddies, bringing 'em home, safe and sound as I could manage. I spent half my life on the LSO platform, because whenever I was in the ship, I never missed one landing by any one of my buddies the whole time I was there.

Perhaps if I died, some of them would still hear me out there as they came screaming in:

"One-o-five, Tomcat Ball, five-point-four."

"Roger Ball, Tomcat . . . twenty-five knots."

Perhaps I would find my heaven in that knife-edge paradise where I'd always been most at home. It's funny what you think of when your back's that hard against the wall.

Of course, the fear was that the cancer had spread all over the place, not just remaining in the lymph nodes. But so far the scans had shown no evidence of that. There was, however, one final test that needed to be conducted: the bone marrow biopsy, which would demonstrate whether the cancer had spread to my bone marrow. I was told to return to the medical center for that. As soon as I entered the building, I understood this might not be the most joyous experience of my life.

I reported to the hematology clinic and was dispatched to a seemingly remote part of the building. I remember distinctly how empty it was compared with every other department I'd attended. It was like Times Square with no cars.

They were awaiting my arrival, and two nurses swiftly popped two needles into my backside to numb up the area. That took about five minutes. I was lying facedown on a table when the doctor arrived, and I noticed the doors were all shut. Right next to me was another table covered with medical equipment.

I could see the needle the doctor was about to use, and when he did I sure as hell could feel it. He injected right down to the bone and then squirted the blood into a tray. *Christ!* I thought. *I'm glad that's over.*

*Dream on, Jeff.* Next he picked up a little instrument of torture that looked like an apple-core remover, warning me very calmly that this might hurt a bit, but it was nothing to be concerned about.

*Roger Ball, Tomcat.*

At this point he plunged the apple-core remover right into my back. I was supposed to be numb, but the hell I was. I darn nearly hit the ceiling, and I let out a yell that might have been heard in the Pentagon. He removed the implement and I saw him, right next to me, tap the contents into a dish.

*Thank Christ that's over.* I was just recovering when he did it again. And again and again. I was clenching my fists on the rail of the table. My knuckles looked like pure ivory. Nothing could stop me crying out in agony. It crossed my mind they might be trying to kill me because of my insolence toward the medical profession.

I knew they were trying to help me. I also knew why the area was so empty. Plainly they did not want other patients to see or hear the proceedings, because they would certainly think they were in some kind of medieval torture chamber with a "victim" screaming for mercy. So I guess the entire area was off-limits. Except for me.

I can truthfully say I have never yelled like that in my life. I would be unable to yell like that if I were on the LSO's platform with a strike fighter headed straight for the stern of the ship and instant death. Not even if I could see that I too would die. I've never even heard anyone else yell like that. Holy shit! Looking back even now, that was bad.

I guess it's one thing to stand in a doctor's quiet office and assure him I could take whatever was thrown at me. But it's rather another, when the time comes, to front up and face it.

They expertly dressed my throbbing back. There'd be results in a day. And so, I pulled my flight suit back on and rode the Blackbird back across Virginia Beach to the base.

The following day, the results came in. The biopsy showed I was okay, nothing had spread. I already knew the cancer was around my heart, but not in it. My lungs and my brain were clear, and now I knew it was definitely not in the bone marrow. And that was real good, because that would be leukemia, which, like Hodgkin's lymphoma, is a disease involving the white blood cells, and I really did not need that as well.

That's when my chemo started, mid-February, as soon as I was cleared of leukemia. They told me it would be twelve weeks of the harshest treatment, but the chemo was highly effective. It would destroy the cancer cells. I had read the books, and someone had likened it to Pac-Man, that little son of a bitch in the computer game that charged along the lines, devouring the enemy as it went.

I understood, without it being confirmed, that Pac-Man could slowly kill me. So far as I could tell, it was a race against time. Could it kill the cancer first?

So I zipped on my flight suit, pulled down my goggles, and flicked on the afterburners. *Here goes, Jeff . . . one-o-seven cleared for takeoff . . . Cat 1 . . . Mission Cancer-Destruction, and to hell with the enemy.*

The program was scheduled for twelve weeks, until mid-May. That's three cycles, five sessions each with the chemo being fed into my veins, and right from the start I could feel it pumping into my body, the stuff that would surely kill me if it did not accomplish its mission before I was battered to death.

I started to go downhill pretty fast. The treatment was so harsh on my blood, my immune system was shot to pieces. I was officially diagnosed as neutropenic, one of the most undesirable side effects of chemotherapy, when the neutrophils in the blood are so low your risk of infection skyrockets.

I asked for more prednisone to combat it, but it was no use requesting anything more. Doc Hager couldn't condone anything more. He knew I couldn't take it.

Within four weeks my condition was becoming serious. My hair started to fall out, and Commander Hager said I would have to go into the hospital for several weeks, because this intense attack on the cancer was being as otherwise damaging as he had feared.

I knew it was killing me. In a way I knew I was dying. But I still lived in dread of the hospital, of never coming out again. I flatly refused to check in. I told him why, and he still thought I was crazy. But those hospital wards were, to me, like the gateway to oblivion, and I was never going there.

He told me there was only one drug that might work, but that I'd have to stab myself in the stomach three or four times a day to help my neutropenic system. There was just a suggestion of, "Well, you won't let us do it for you, so I guess you'll have to do it yourself."

It wasn't much fun, but I tackled it, did what I was told and injected the drug that might rescue my immune system. I remember it all so well. I could always feel the stuff flushing through my body, and it felt terrible. But I would not give in.

Something happened that I found obliquely inspiring. One day I was told to report to an entirely different part of the hospital for my treatment. I guessed they were short of staff or something. I found my way to this different building and sat down among my fellow patients. I spoke to a couple of guys who were both very gloomy, highly pessimistic about their chances. Then a young guy came in and he was just about the same, as though the end was nigh. Jesus! I was trying to be chipper among the melancholy section.

Well, that ended my social instincts for the afternoon. I sat silently and waited my turn. When I finally got in for my treatment, I mentioned to the nurse that it seemed everyone was having a real bad day.

She smiled and said, "Lieutenant Commander, I'm sorry, but we separate our patients. Some people have just given up, and we have a policy to keep them away from people like you. Because you have most certainly not given up. We do not want these two very different kinds of people mixing. Because it will do none of them any good. You'll be back among your own group next time."

"Ma'am," I replied, "I'm never going to give up."

And she said quietly, "We all know that."

But, nonetheless, right through that early spring of 1998, I was getting weaker. By the end of March my hair had completely gone, and even my eyebrows had vanished. I was very weak. I had no muscle tone. For much of the time I felt awful. They scanned me every so often, and the cancer was retreating, no doubt about that, but I was too weak to start radiation.

Every day I went to work, never missed. I couldn't fly, but even on the days I had chemo I still went back down to the hangar, which was like purgatory to me, especially when the guys brought the F-14s home after the day's flying. But I never gave up. I would not leave my squadron, I would not leave my buddies, and I would not allow myself to slip behind in the program.

March turned into April, and in the warm Virginia sun I kept right on going, subjecting myself to the brutality of the chemo, five sessions a week. The good news was my heart had returned to normal size, and the chest pains that had been there for so long were gone. The bad news was some of the cancer was still there, and they couldn't zap it with radiation, because they were certain I couldn't take any more.

I stepped up my vitamin B17 intake, which no one knew about because I had a sure and certain feeling they were doing me some real good. It's funny how you know certain things, and I knew the vitamins were helping me overcome the effects of the bleomycin, and I sensed the mushrooms and shark oil were helping me get through every day.

By May I was feeling better, and the drugs had completed the majority of their work. I was almost clear of the cancer, I was still alive, just, and the radiation would hopefully finish off the lymphoma. So now the biggest deal in my life was the radiologist, Commander Mark Sobczak, a very, very smart former Naval Aviator, who was prepared to move heaven and earth to cure me.

He explained how the radiation worked, and I have to admit I was a bit skeptical, since it was the goddamned radiation all over the flight deck and the aircraft that had given me the cancer in the first place. That was not an official diagnosis, but it was mine, and I was sticking to it.

Mark mapped out a detailed plan and walked me through it. It was a personalized form of treatment, geared to slam into the specific areas where my cancer persisted. It was laser-focused radiation, beams aimed right at the bad parts. I guessed correctly it would need to be administered in a room more isolated and protected than the one where they scanned for leukemia.

With laser radiation firing all over the room, it had to be, and I knew to my obvious cost that radiation had to be contained. Guess it didn't matter so much about me. By this time I was probably walking around like a goddamned nuclear reactor. And more radiation was my only chance of survival. *Bring it on, guys. I've gone this far. I'll stay the course.*

In mid-May they finally stopped the chemo injections. The Stanford V Protocol had come through for me. I knew I had almost died. And Steve Hager, who became a damned good friend in the end, confirmed it was what he called "your iron will" that saved me. Without it, with the wrong attitude, I could not have survived. He said he only agreed to that treatment because he believed in me, believed I had the guts for it.

Mark was planning to fry me, in just the right places. I was weak, but I still zoomed back and forth on the Blackbird along the freeway. I entered the domain of the radiologist. The room was barred from the outside by a six-foot-thick door. *Holy shit!* These guys were not joking.

I was lying in total darkness while they fired sixty-second bursts of radiation straight at the cancer. TOPGUN to TOPGUN, right? The sessions lasted for forty minutes, and it was like being in a microwave, one minute one side, and then the other. Then my top, then bottom. They kept it up, week after week.

It should have been scary, lying there in the pitch dark, while someone pumped radiation into my already radiated body. There was nothing to hear except the hum of the machinery. I could only imagine someone was watching, but it was near impossible to cast off the feeling that if I cried out or panicked, no one would ever know.

But every time it was okay. The machinery fell silent, and someone opened the door, swiftly letting in the light, and I was wheeled out into the world, still breathing, still fighting. Still defiant. Whatever it took.

Zipping up my flight suit and revving the Blackbird became a symbol of my hostile refusal to obey. Do you think my doctors would have allowed me to ride my motorcycle back and forth to the base every day? Hell no. They'd have put me in an ambulance if they could have.

But I was striving to be normal, to cast this affliction from my mind. Sometimes I told myself it had never happened. Other times I admitted it had, but that I would beat it. I had never seen myself as a normal patient. *A patient!* Not me. I was Lieutenant Commander Jeff Lay and I'd caught some kind of outlandish disease because of my work as a pilot of strike fighters in the US Navy.

You think I'm a normal guy? Well, I believed I was different. Which was why I drove this 178 mph record-breaking production motorcycle instead of a goddamned wheelchair. They've never even built one of them tough enough to hold me. At least those were the kinds of things I kept telling myself, stuff to boost me up, stuff to keep me fighting, stuff to confirm I would never give in. Never.

I hammered that Honda east, back to the base, and every yard of the way I heard only the sound of the roaring engines of the F-14 Tomcat, and before me I imagined the vastness of the sky, and the touch of the stick, and the pull of the Gs. Someone was always whispering, "Fight's on . . . fight's on!" You can say that again, pal.

By the end of June my radiation course was complete. Mark told me he was highly optimistic. And the signs were pretty good. I had no hair, and I had scars on my neck. But I was feeling much better, and there were no night sweats, chest pains, numbness, or any of my other symptoms, except for a little weight loss, and muscles that had trouble with a coffee cup, never mind an F-14.

In July I reported for a scan and a blood test. When the results came up there was nothing. The cancer had gone completely. Somehow, by all that was holy, I'd whipped it. The Stanford V Protocol had done what it promised, in the time it had promised. It was still only July, five months after my initial diagnosis, five months since I'd declared I would not do MOPP, that I believed it could be done with twice the drugs in half the time.

I guess it was time to announce my innermost hopes and dreams. And I went over to see flight surgeon Matt Rings, who was full of congratulations, until I told him what I'd come for.

"I want it all back," I said. "I want to be restored to flight duty."

He looked pretty surprised, you know, the way people are when you fire something at them right out of left field. For a moment he made no reply. But then he said what I was sure he would say. "Jeff, no Naval Aviator has ever come back from cancer. No pilot has ever made that comeback. The flight manual forbids it."

I knew he was referring to the waiver guide, which lists the precise situation for pilots who have been ill or injured. However, I was not about to bow down to a friggin' manual.

"I want to apply for a waiver," I said. "Cancer is an absolute. You either have it or you don't. And I don't. This stupid manual says I cannot apply for five years. Well, I'm about to stamp all over that. I'm going to apply in one month after being cleared. I'm classified Stage 2B, and there's nothing that says I can't stay in the Navy."

Matt was thoughtful. "You can stay in the Navy, and you can, perhaps, fly. But not a strike fighter or from aircraft carriers. The manual is pretty definite about that. It says no, certainly for anyone who's Stage 2B."

In the politest possible way, I informed him that I did not care if I was 19D. Because there was one thing I knew beyond doubt. Pac-Man had eaten the cancer—no ifs, ands, or buts. I had believed in the impossible. I'd listened when those Navy instructors had told me never to give up.

They'd spent years hurling tests at me, probing to find a weakness. But they could not do so. And now I considered myself the Van Voorhis of cancer survivors. He wouldn't have given up either. And that friggin' manual was not going to succeed in stopping me where all others had failed.

Matt Rings and my immediate bosses began to petition for me, informing the authorities they wanted me back in the flight program. They recommended a special dispensation, and in the end I flew to the Naval Operational Medicine Institute at Pensacola to see the presiding doctor, an Air Force colonel who looked, frankly, astounded when I showed up.

"Why are you here?" he asked. And I told him I wanted a waiver.

"We don't just hand those out, Lieutenant Commander," he said. "Not here."

That just about ruined my day. He said he'd give the matter "due consideration" and that I should see him again the following day. So I retreated somewhat morbidly to the local Irish pub, where, to my enormous delight, I ran straight into Moose, who unhappily had left the Navy a couple of years before with a recurring neck injury. This made it impossible for him to continue as a radar intercept officer. He'd been battered down by a lifetime of football and flying. Everyone had agreed, even the mighty Moose, that he could not tolerate the blast of an ejection seat, should it ever come to that. And the Navy does not take risks.

We had a whole lot of catching up to do, and the evening passed like it always did with Moose, quickly and packed with fun and jokes, mostly at my expense. A couple of pints of Guinness definitely restored my good humor, and we parted with a handshake and a bear hug.

There was no need to swap addresses, because both of us were on the move. You don't need that formality with a blood-brother TOPGUN graduate, like Moose was to me. We'll be in touch for all the days of our lives. He knew it, and I sure as hell knew it. How could it be any other way, after all we had gone through together, me and my ace RIO, the best radar officer I ever met?

The following day a cloud of gloom descended on me once more as I made my way over to that Air Force doctor. I cursed the fact that he was not Navy, because there I always had a fair hearing. I sensed this guy didn't really give a damn whether I flew strike fighters again. And the book said no. The recommendation of the senior flight officers from my squadron cut no ice with him.

He told me again he'd have to think more about my waiver, and whether it could be granted. It was no use arguing with him, because he definitely was not going to hand it to me. From where I stood, it looked like he would have the last word. So I left him with his "little Napoleon" complex and returned to Oceana, where I was receiving more and more support.

However, this thing was not going to get organized very fast. I had to do something. I suppose I've always been a workaholic, having studied under the grinding regime of the peerless Checkmate Commander Winnefeld. I could not stand the feeling of being useless to everyone.

I was getting stronger every day and I asked if I could return to the Academy at Annapolis—only 230 miles north of there—and teach for a couple of semesters. Apparently no one thought this was much of an idea, despite my protests that I'd always loved teaching and instructing.

But that friggin' Air Force colonel was in no hurry, whereas I was, just to make myself useful again. They handed me a job as the operations officer at GIANT KILLER, a single-story building housing around one hundred people, mostly controllers. This was the radar control hub of the enormous Oceana air station, and I was pitched in there as number-three man, under the command of Captain J. B. Connelly.

Now here was a guy who had his own little bit of history. Flying off the US aircraft carrier *John F. Kennedy* (*Big John* to her friends), the young Lieutenant Connelly was part of that President Reagan fighting force that was detailed to keep the newly obstreperous Colonel Gadhafi in check.

Well, the Libyan dictator had just decreed that, unlike other nations, he no longer accepted a twelve-mile limit around his country. He declared that Libya controlled the coastal waters out to one hundred miles, a sizeable area of the Mediterranean Sea. Ronnie did not love that.

To make matters infinitely worse, the colonel kept sending up his fighter aircraft, Russian-made MiG-23s, to swoop around the ocean like he owned the place. One of them finally came pretty close to *Big John*, which turned out to be a very uncool plan. Hurtling in toward the MiG, at the controls of his F-14 Tomcat, young Connelly opened fire and blew the Libyan clean out of the sky, dropping him right into the disputed waters, 7,000 feet below.

Everyone, of course, loved it, especially, I guess, President Reagan, and Captain Connelly has lived in a kind of mischievous glory ever since. I actually enjoyed working with him very much, and he approved my intentions to rev the whole place up a bit, teach the controllers the advanced radar techniques of the TOPGUN pilots, stuff they were never taught, because TOPGUN graduates *never* come over here to work.

It was kind of a wide-ranging brief, because the basic function of GIANT KILLER was radar clearance, tracking aircraft in flight, plus ground control intercept. TOPGUN ground control was very different, and I half turned the place upside down, redesigning the airspace and communicating techniques.

I was just being me, I suppose, striving for perfection, the way I'd been taught, trying to impart all of my knowledge to the radar guys. Trying to keep my mind off my illness, because I was still reporting to the hospital every day to confirm nothing had recurred.

It might have all been quite pleasant, except that every darn time an F-14 took off, I'd hear it, and my eyes would swivel to the window, and I'd silently pray to God that one day, not too far away, that would be me, right there at the controls, preparing to fight a foreign foe on behalf of the United States. But the vision of the USAF's Napoleon of Pensacola stood squarely before me.

I'd heard nothing from him. Every day I rode out to GIANT KILLER, which was on the fringe of the base but not inside the main gates, and that was unbelievably difficult for me. I had to drive the bike right past that entrance, and somehow, to me, it was as if I was not allowed to go inside.

I was a part of it, and yet not included. I think seeing the Tomcats take off and land made it even harder. Where once people looked at me with that certain admiration accorded to anyone in US Naval Aviation who wears the TOPGUN patch, now I noticed people would sometimes avert their eyes, as if somehow I had been disgraced.

I imagine they thought they were looking at a former high flier, brought low by one of the world's cruelest diseases: TOPGUN air ace, grounded for the duration, and no one quite knew how to cope with such a man.

But they all thought wrong. I was still in this fight, and whatever old Napoleon down there in Pensacola was planning, a very powerful army of supporters was beginning to rally to my cause. I'd fought the good fight, absorbed the blows, won battle after battle, and yet the spoils of victory were still being denied me. It seemed pretty unreasonable to me, and, thank God, to a number of other people.

Behind the scenes, a grim little struggle swayed back and forth, doctors versus bureaucrats, Air Force versus Navy. So far as I could see, it was good versus evil. On August 13 a letter arrived from the Bureau of Medicine and Surgery on the desk of the Chief of Naval Personnel in Millington, Tennessee, which flatly turned down my request for a waiver.

On September 7, I sent in a new request, in which I pointed out I'd flown 1,195 hours in an F-14 Tomcat, I was a carrier-based strike fighter pilot, in full physical training, cycling, running, and lifting, and confirming my fitness for duty. Nothing happened.

So Captain Connelly in person went to bat for me and fired off a letter to the Chief of Naval Personnel, requesting again that I be granted a waiver. He assured them I was "a singularly impressive career Naval officer, who consistently performed at levels far in excess of expectations." He said my dedication to naval service was unprecedented.

The captain described my prowess as a strike fighter pilot as "superior." I was a front-runner and the Navy desperately needed such a person. He ended by demanding this irreplaceable naval officer and carrier aviator be returned to full-flight status without delay. In his own hand he scrawled at the bottom, "The fighter community—my community—needs Lieutenant Commander Lay—get him moving."

There followed a week later, a long and detailed plea from the "Tiger Woods of cancer surgery" himself, Dr. Shen, who swore to God I had been restored to completely normal health, in complete remission.

In his considerable opinion, and in the opinion of the Naval Medical Center Portsmouth medical board, I did not even have the symptoms of any illness. Lieutenant Commander Lay, they declared, was fit for full duty. They recommended I be returned to flying forthwith, but remain under medical evaluation.

A letter from flight surgeon Matt Rings, on the same day, to the same bureau, listed every one of my achievements: the best of this, top-ranked at that, selected for highest honors, ranked number one, a safety officer par excellence, outstanding instructor.

Then he confirmed I was in complete remission and that a board had found me fit for full duty. He pointed out my dogged determination to return to flying, and my true love of the US Navy and carrier-based aviation. He recommended an immediate waiver.

With this bombardment of support I now awaited the decision of the all-powerful Air Force doctor at Pensacola. On September 21, it arrived addressed to me, via my commanding officer.

It began by pointing out that I was indeed not physically qualified for all duty involving flying. And after careful review, a waiver of standards was not granted. I might have known it. He was going by the book, the part that stated that any aviator who had been diagnosed with Hodgkin's lymphoma and received that hard and uncompromising treatment could not and would not be returned to flying strike fighter aircraft.

So far as he was concerned, that was an end to it. But God knows why it took him close to two months to decide what he'd already decided the moment he saw me.

The letter also asserted that my aviation career incentive pay would be suspended on March 17 the next year. It was all a terrible shock. I stood there staring at the brutal words that seemed to end my career, and my mind flashed back to the very day when I entered the United States Naval Academy, to the very first and most important historical fact I learned there.

For a split second I was back in the crypt below the chapel, where Commodore John Paul Jones rests, and where his immortal words at the 1779 Battle of Flamborough Head are so graphically illuminated.

Like now, it was a late September day. America was locked in combat with the British. And Captain Jones's fabled shout of defiance rang out across the waters off the east coast of Yorkshire, as his flagship, the *Bonhomme Richard,* stood battered and burning under the guns of the British frigate HMS *Serapis.*

"Will you surrender, sir?" taunted the British captain.

"I have not yet begun to fight!" roared Commodore Jones.

Neither had I. And I know precisely how he felt.

Particularly when he told his gunnery officer, "We may sink, but I'll be damned if I'll strike."

That's the spirit of the US Navy, which he did so much toward founding. I was a part of that tradition. I've stood in my officer's uniform right next to his tomb. And while I understood they still might ban me from flying, I'd be damned if I'd strike my colors.

This USAF doctor would not prevent me from flying an F-14 again. Godammit, he wasn't even in the Navy.

## CHAPTER 10

# Not Federal and No Reserves

I must have read a zillion words on the subject of cancer, and there was one truth that was never far from my mind: you must not, cannot, ever check out. You can't join the many people who quickly start saying their good-byes. Maybe not in outright words. But the thought is within them. I could always tell.

It would have been easy just to sit at home and watch television, or sit around with the squadron and goof off. But that would have been fatal for me, and for anyone else who might give up.

However godawful you might feel, you have to keep working, keep pushing forward. In your mind you have to stand back and dare that son of a bitch Big C to lay you low. In the ensuing years since my treatment was concluded, I've met people I knew had surrendered too early. I knew they could not make it.

But I will always be in the Lance Armstrong school of thought. You have to stand up and fight, like he did. And when you've finally won, it is your duty to pass on the essence of your own struggle to others who may not have that strength of will.

You have to give them that strength. You have to help, as only a survivor can. For the rest of my life I will be willing to do that, for anyone who has contracted the disease. I will take the time with anyone. Because

God granted me that steel, and, ever the instructor, I can pass on that sword of hope and determination. It really works. Trust me.

Which brings me sharply back to my own struggle on Naval Air Station Oceana, with about 7,000 bureaucrats ranged against me, every one of them waving a book of rules. Every one of them saying no.

My task was to communicate my own sense of outrage to the big hitters who knew and I hope respected me. That was a lot easier than I had hoped. My own commanding officer, leader of the Grim Reapers, was right in my corner. He was Commander Brad Goetsch, call sign "Stalker," a TOPGUN pilot and instructor who would later go on to command Naval Air Station Fallon, after the TOPGUN operation moved there as its permanent headquarters.

Commander Goetsch was a terrific guy, and one hell of a friend to me. He wrote an awesome letter on my behalf, darned nearly demanding my reinstatement. And believe me, a letter from him was the kind of shot across the bow that would have made even John Paul Jones pay attention.

And he was by no means alone. Down at the Bureau of Naval Personnel in Tennessee, I had two more supporters who were right in the heart of the struggle. One was Captain Hamlin B. Tallent, a former F-14 RIO and a TOPGUN instructor from the Ozark Mountains, Missouri, call sign "Hamm." This was a very tough character, at one time catapult and arresting gear officer in USS *Kitty Hawk*. He commanded VF-142, the Ghostriders, not to mention CVW-14. That's a guy who comprehends stress in all its forms, and if he says I'm good to go, then I'm ready. I know that his letter to the authorities on my behalf carried a lot of weight. By the way, he swiftly became an admiral.

The other was Captain David J. Mercer, an ace F/A-18 pilot who commanded VFA-131, the Wildcats. He also commanded CVW-8, which slammed into Afghanistan from the flight deck of USS *Enterprise* right after 9/11. Unsurprisingly, "Merc" Mercer also became an admiral, and his letter of enormous support for me was a gesture I'll never forget.

At exactly the same time, my old TOPGUN instructor Lieutenant Commander Tom "Tip" O'Dowd also lined up alongside me and made it clear that he supported my quest to return to flying strike fighters. He was actually the F-14 detailer for the entire base and his support meant a huge amount.

It was strange how suddenly my battle ended. A very powerful Navy captain suddenly stepped into the fray and said he basically *did not care* what the recommendation was. He thanked the Pensacola medical center for their efforts but announced he was overruling their decision. He was not sure whether any of them understood how hard I'd fought for reinstatement, or how much it meant to me, or how badly the US Navy needed aviators like me.

All he knew was I was completely cured, and everyone in the fighter squadrons wanted me back. On November 11, 1998, I received a new communication from the personnel bureau, via Captain Connelly. It stated ominously that I was "aeronautically adapted, but not physically qualified for all duty involving flying." Whatever the hell that meant.

The next sentence lit up my life. It read: "A waiver of standards is granted." With a certain irony, it was Veterans Day in the United States, formerly Armistice Day . . . the eleventh hour of the eleventh day of the eleventh month, 1918, when the guns of WWI finally fell silent. And it was the eightieth anniversary of the moment when the defeated German army, like me, no longer needed the use of mustard gas—different moments for two heavy users. Nice timing, right? History has tidy habits.

I could at last return to the Grim Reapers as a fighter pilot, and in truth I probably deserved another major promotion, having just gone twelve rounds with their patron saint. But all I would get would be a program of tough missions to get me sharp, because I had not flown for nine months.

Almost immediately I volunteered for a couple of stints on an aircraft carrier serving as an LSO, a task I used to be able to accomplish as naturally as drawing breath. I rode out from Norfolk with the ship for the first one, and it took me about ten minutes to understand how comprehensibly I had fallen back, out of the loop.

Of course I still knew what to do, how fast and how high incoming fighter aircraft should be traveling. It was like second nature to me. But the subtleties were missing. In the old days I could judge an increase of one or two knots of breeze in an instant and relay it to the guys preparing to land. But I could not do that anymore.

Where once I could spot a Tomcat making three knots too many through the air, now I was blind to that infinitesimal increase in airspeed. I could spot too high, and I could spot too low, I could even spot a suspect angle of approach. But not with the same pinpoint accuracy on which I had once prided myself.

It was, to be truthful, a goddamned humiliation. I'd get it back. I knew that. But right then I did not have it. You can only demonstrate that fabulous accuracy and instinct when you're right at the top of your game, and I had suddenly become a rookie, regressing from the best to the struggling in nine dark months.

It was not a whole lot different when I finally climbed the ladder into the cockpit of an F-14. Of course the actual operation of the aircraft was like riding a bike. You never forget. But I felt different as I stepped into the cockpit, still careful to avoid stepping onto the seat. Still observant of all those unspoken rules and superstitions, but still a stranger in the place where I belonged. *Sharpen yourself up, Lay . . . A lot of people stuck their necks out to get you here. So remember that patch on your left arm and don't fuck it up.*

I had to requalify as a combat pilot, and no one was going to nurse me through it. I had to organize everything myself, schedules, briefings, and instructors, and then get airborne. That's the Navy way. They treat us as entrepreneurs, as they have right from the starting line at the Academy, allowing us to go precisely as far as we wish, but leaving the drive and the coordination entirely to each individual.

In the Air Force they would have marched me back into the fighter squadrons in a much more regimented and rigid manner, laying out exactly, to the letter, what I should do, when and for how long. I guess that's why they came up with that little hero at Pensacola, the one who tried to ban me from my profession. I bet he sleeps with that friggin' rulebook under the pillow.

Me? I just had to get on with it, moving at my own pace—as fast as possible—until I'd gotten all my ducks in a line. I came up with my own little agenda and flew darned nearly every day, getting the feel of the big strike fighter all over again. I passed all my exams as quickly as possible and declared myself ready to face the enemy anytime.

I knew, of course, the Navy would reward me in the time-honored way, the way they reward us all, by loading on more and more responsibilities and longer work hours. I guess they just want to see who buckles under the pressure. And, when you think about it, that's not such a bad way to select your top commanding officers. Of course, their record of locating and promoting the very best is just shy of sensational.

It beats the hell out of recruiting guys for the top jobs from other organizations, the way corporate America behaves. And I was back on the ladder, metaphorically, as well as the one on the F-14. No sooner was I requalified, when they appointed me a department head in VF-103, the Jolly Rogers, one of the truly great fighter squadrons of the US Navy, the guys who fly with the sinister white-on-black skull-and-crossbones on their vertical tail.

They complimented me more than I can explain by making me an F-14 instructor, confirming what I had always known: given a little practice, I could still fly that Tomcat with the best of them. The Jolly Rogers' call sign, "Victory," had a suitable touch of arrogance about it and they usually referred to themselves as "Fighting 103."

As I had personally been required to go right back to basics to requalify as a fighter pilot, so Fighting 103 was required to undergo the most unbelievable work-up program to prepare for their next deployment, which was a six-month tour in the Gulf, embarked in USS *George Washington*.

The fifty-year-old fighter squadron had years of experience dealing with Saddam Hussein, but we still needed operational flight training, which would last for months and months. We trained here, there, and everywhere, constantly flying out to various aircraft carriers, polishing our regular landings, takeoffs, and night landings, especially night landings.

The Navy understands the importance of everyone staying right on top of their game. That cannot be done without continuous practice. I, above all, could testify how difficult it was to stay in the loop. The Navy would not have cared if the Jolly Rogers existed for 1,000 years, the orders to practice until we dropped still would have been issued.

So we went all over the East Coast honing our skills, often pitching the squadron against the instructors, the bandits, who were all under specific orders to give the Jolly Rogers a seriously hard time.

We trained from Norfolk all the way down to Key West, mostly flying out to the carriers, on what we call "feet wet" operations. It was not just landings we were perfecting, there were complex maneuvers designed to protect the ship at all times. There was a ton of night flying.

By now we considered the United States Armed Forces had Saddam pretty well bottled up, but if the son of a bitch broke cover and started harassing us or the *George Washington,* our job was to ram him right back into his box—a coffin, if necessary.

It was a grueling all-around workup, and most of us felt like we'd fought ten wars in practice. In the spring of 2000, we were at last ready to go. By now I was right back on the front line of my game. I was flying combat missions and dogfights as well as I had ever done, teaching the squadron pilots every technique I ever learned at TOPGUN. But something was happening to the Navy I had joined—President Reagan's Navy, that is.

Aside from watching the historic fighter squadrons disappear before our eyes, "disestablished" all through the 1990s, the cuts to our programs, aircraft, and fuel supplies were obvious to all. We were growing drastically short of spare parts and people, especially expensively trained pilots. We spoke of almost nothing else.

Morale was going south. They were phasing out the F-14 programs, looking ahead to the time when Grumman would build no more. This had the most depressing effect on us. We were coming to the end of an era. Nothing was the same, and we seemed to have flown out of the golden years and were headed into a near permanent despondency. It was not only morale going south. It was everything.

I recounted in some detail in Chapters 1 and 2 precisely how bad it was on this upcoming cruise, how everyone just sensed we were going into a potential war zone and we were not properly equipped. On our way in, we had to stop and undertake some major cross-decking with an outgoing US carrier on its way home to Norfolk.

I remember one afternoon, as tons of supplies were being lifted from her flight deck to ours, seeing yet another helicopter flying in from the mother ship parked out on the horizon. *I just wonder,* I thought, *what's in that helo, what precisely is it carrying that we ought already to have?*

In the final days leading up to our departure, I arrived at an irrevocable decision: I could not stay here. I could not remain in a US Navy that was losing not only its heart and soul, but also its supplies.

They had taught me the highest possible ideals, and now we were short of fuel. They had stressed the importance of teamwork, selflessness, and honor, and we were running out of spare parts for the aircraft. And every day we heard of another epic Navy fighter squadron that would probably be disbanded.

We did not have enough instructors to train the new guys making their way up after the Academy. And we, above all else, need instructors. Every corporation needs instructors. And we're the biggest corporation there is.

I made my decision to leave the US Navy not because I sought greener pastures for myself. I decided to go because I cared too much. It hurt me more than it could possibly have hurt anyone else. I could not bear to watch it, the destruction of the history, the traditions, the supreme management, the philosophy and organization. Not to mention the distant call to arms that would summon each and every one of us to the flag.

When those things are threatened, because a government has ceased to value its supreme asset, that's the time to go. I was not alone. Literally dozens of the best men in the service were starting to call it a day. True devotion is a fragile thing, and it has to be nurtured. But in the White House, we had men who did not understand us, refused to take our advice, and didn't much care whether we stayed or left.

I submitted my resignation from the US Navy before we set sail for the Gulf in the spring of 2000. I was the operations officer of the Jolly Rogers, and that was a huge position. My TOPGUN patch was revered by all of those who did not have one, but that was a diminishing group, there was such a shortage of pilots. My role in teaching the new guys was considered critical.

Nonetheless, I had made up my mind to step down. It was a decision I had thought for years I would never make, and it was very hard for me, worse than I can ever explain. I didn't want to go, but I couldn't stay. I still think about it, though at the time of the resignation I cast it to the back of my mind, because I knew it would be another year before I finally left.

I completed that final cruise and returned to Naval Air Station Oceana. In April 2001, I made my last F-14 flight, engaging in a pretty fierce dogfight with another TOPGUN graduate, Lieutenant Commander Lou Schager, who darn nearly beat me. But not quite. I pulled back, got right in behind him, and gunned him down for old time's sake.

The squadron rallied around, and the guys gave me a terrific farewell dinner, presenting me with a personalized Jolly Rogers plaque and a big, beautiful framed photograph of my last carrier landing at the very second my hook grabbed the wire. I did not have many shining memories of that cruise, but the *George Washington* was a great ship, and I loved my fellow Naval Aviators. It was all very cool, and I'll treasure that picture more than anyone will ever know, mostly because of who gave it to me.

May 1, 2001, was my last day in the squadron. And that was awful. I felt absolutely bereft, desolate. As if my life had been torn in half. The truth was, I knew nothing else. I had been shaped, coached, and molded by the service that wears dark blue: my work ethic, my sense of moral duty, my dedication to fairness, even my courage and my flying skills, my ability to command, to decide, to issue orders. Everything. The US Navy was my life and my existence. But that was another Navy. Not this one.

However, even this one retained the vital core of the old—that sense of duty, honor, and country, and everlasting leadership for all of the correct reasons. During my final years, really throughout the '90s and beyond, the Navy had suffered blow after blow, until it became clear that they served a government that was disinterested in them.

Year after year, their budget was clawed back. While prosperity reigned in the United States, thanks to the financial policies of President Reagan, the Navy was systematically reduced. Still the admirals pressed on, trying to uphold everything the American fleet stood for.

In many ways it was the hardest of times for them all. But they stood firm and tried to uphold their peerless standards of behavior and professionalism. In a sense, this made it harder for me, leaving a ship that had been hit and holed. But no one ever called me a quitter, not even my buddies at my retirement party, which was something of a miracle, knowing their sense of fun and lack of reverence.

The trouble was everyone knew why I was going. I suppose, as a TOPGUN graduate, I was a fairly large presence to be bailing out. I think it saddened them, as it saddened me. Because we all felt the same, and there would be many more evenings like that.

When I drove out through the main gates for the final time, I was utterly sorrowful about everything: about leaving my buddies, leaving my students, leaving the service I loved. Most of all I was sorrowful for myself. A small piece of that sorrow has remained with me to this day. I'll always have it, somewhere in the recesses of my dark blue heart.

But life must go on. I flew back to Ohio to regroup. I did of course have a plan, and I had begun work on it many months ago, studying long hours in my downtime aboard the USS *George Washington*. The subject was finance, and I had always thought my penchant for mathematics would give me a good start. Of course, I tackled it like a TOPGUN graduate would, gathering around me the reference books that would steer me into another world.

I started off with foreign currency, because I'd always been interested and had traded my dollars for other nations' banknotes many, many times. My early studies took me naturally into the realm of the US Federal Reserve system, and I actually tackled one of the most influential books ever written on the subject: William Greider's *Secrets of the Temple: How the Federal Reserve Runs the Country.*

This seven hundred–page monster detailed the interlocking rules of President Reagan and Fed Chairman Paul Volcker. But for me the best section of the book was the part on fractional reserve banking, where banks take deposits and create money out of nothing. It seemed to me like flying a combat mission without your F-14. Because there was nothing there.

Here's how it works. The bank takes from you a deposit of $10. They then loan nine of those dollars to someone else. And out of nowhere, the payments on those dollars become *assets of the bank,* of which they then lend eight dollars to someone else. The cycle continues, and the new payments on those eight dollars also become assets, allowing the bank to lend another seven dollars.

On and on it goes, until the bank may have lent forty-four bucks against your ten dollar deposit. Multiply that by a million, or a billion, and you'll have a sound idea of how they nearly went collectively bust in 2008. You'll also have a clue as to why they want your deposits more than life itself.

And remember, all banks give a "promise" to all of their depositors that they will pay back the deposit any time the customer demands it. However, if the bank has already lent the money four times over to customers who wish to borrow, that's kind of tough, because there are, then, more promises than there is cash in the vault. They've handed it all out and cannot get it back in a hurry.

Word of that can cause an instant run on the bank: the specter that haunts every banker from Wall Street to Timbuktu. In modern banks it is not unusual for "promised" money to be ten times more than there is in actual hard cash still "on deposit." Banks hand it all out to their borrowing customers by this astounding sleight of hand, which creates assets out of precisely nothing.

I stared at those pages in amazement. I pondered the massive liabilities of banks, liabilities that literally dwarfed their own assets. From that moment I began to work on an entirely new dimension to the word "risk" and how it might apply to money. I based my new studies on the very cornerstone of the TOPGUN system, and that's thoroughness, the meticulous attention to every detail.

Since TOPGUN believes implicitly that perfection is attainable and *must* be achieved, it's essential to consider the core of their doctrine. The neutron that holds that core together is the relentless study of history: its triumphs, its failures, its pathways, its components, and its leadership.

If a TOPGUN pilot is fired upon by an enemy missile, he will know, first of all, the nationality of that missile and precisely where it was made. He will know the weight of its warhead. He will know its dimensions, its range, and its speed. He will know whether it's heat-seeking or laser-guided. He will understand its dexterity in the air, whether it can follow him, how susceptible it is to chaff or electronic decoy. He will know how fast he needs to travel to outrun it, how much farther the missile will run before it's out of fuel.

And if the TOPGUN pilot does not understand 100 percent of all of the above, he will not be allowed to set foot in that F-14 until he does. I now needed to be that comprehensibly skilled on the subject of money. That meant history, and lots of it.

Greider's *Secrets of the Temple* offered one of the world's great accounts of money, its origins, its evolvement, and those who have abused its purpose. He taught me, with unflagging certainty, that the precise date when America's dominance of the world's economy ended was August 15, 1971, when President Nixon changed the monetary rules under which nations had traded for twenty-five years since WWII.

On that date, he decreed that the United States would no longer honor the terms of the Bretton Woods agreement pegging foreign currency to the dollar, which was backed by gold. It was a momentous decision that saw Treasury Under-Secretary Paul Volcker on a plane to Europe that very night to try to prevent world panic.

Volcker knew this was "a failure of American leadership, an unwillingness to confront the nation's economic excesses, and to impose self-discipline." The dollar was no longer anchored to that shiny precious substance that did not lose intrinsic value and, unlike paper money, could not be manufactured at will. Gold was priced in dollars, $35 an ounce, but in the two years that followed President Nixon's announcement, the dollar was devalued 11 percent, and gold was priced at $42 an ounce.

The president had made it clear he wanted lower interest rates and more money. And since the Federal Reserve is empowered to print US currency, that's what he got. Quite suddenly the Federal Reserve took on an even more mystical aura, because it held the key to the nation's wealth, possessing, as it did and does, the ability to print and issue the Treasury's banknotes. Each one bears the seal of the United States and the phrase "IN GOD WE TRUST," which does, of course, suggest the approval of an even higher authority than the US Treasury.

Greider pointed out that the Federal Reserve was not, however, a sacred temple. "The seven governors," he wrote, "were not high priests performing mystical rights . . . Yet it was still the modern equivalent of mysterious sanctification, for its officers performed the ancient priestly function: the creation of money."

It was surrounded by the same protective cloak that adorned the temple: secrecy, mystique, and overwhelming authority that was neither visible nor legible to mere mortals.

"Like the temple," wrote Greider," it did not answer to the people, it spoke for them. Its decrees were cast in a mysterious language people could not understand, but its voice, they knew, was powerful and important."

It amounted to the American people completely repressing their knowledge of money. You could put it down to mass ignorance or a "collective blocking out." But it was unexamined by a nation that prided itself on free political debate. And with that mind-set grew the mighty legend of the Federal Reserve.

Yet history was showing me about enormous boom-and-bust cycles. I was striving to understand what precisely it was that gave the Federal

Reserve its infallible reputation, and its directors some divine right, some thought, to "usurp the powers that belonged only to God."

At this point I decided I'd better find out what precisely the Federal Reserve *was*. To establish this I turned to another seminal publication, G. Edward Griffin's *The Creature from Jekyll Island,* in which he demonstrated what he called the biggest financial scam in history, the mirrors, smoke machines, pulleys, cogs, and wheels of the grand illusion called money.

On the very first page of the book, he mentioned something most people have never even considered. The Federal Reserve is most certainly not federal, and it doesn't have any reserves. Griffin does not do a great deal of sugarcoating.

He opened his book with a truly spellbinding account of how the Federal Reserve came into being. Others have told the story. Others have even elaborated. But no one, in my view, gave it quite the gravitas of Griffin's bludgeon of a typewriter. Certainly no one so brilliantly set the scene of subterfuge, cunning, and secrecy present in a clandestine railroad car silently attached to a southbound train and shortly to leave from a cold, snowy New Jersey station at ten o'clock on a freezing November night in 1910.

Inside that plush and ornate car were six men who controlled one-quarter of all the wealth in the United States. The owner of the car was Nelson W. Aldrich, Republican Whip in the Senate, chairman of the National Monetary Commission, business associate of J. P. Morgan, and father-in-law of John D. Rockefeller Jr.

There was Abraham Piatt Andrew, assistant secretary of the US Treasury, and Frank A. Vanderlip, president of the National City Bank of New York and representing both William Rockefeller and the great investment banking house of Kuhn, Loeb & Co.

Also ensconced for the journey was Henry P. Davison, senior partner of J. P. Morgan & Company, and Benjamin Strong, head of J. P. Morgan's Bankers Trust Company. The sixth man was Paul M. Warburg, a Kuhn, Loeb & Co. partner and a representative of the Rothschild banking empire in London and Paris. Warburg, endeared to both firms by birth and then marriage, was also brother to Max Warburg, head of the vast Warburg banking operation in Germany and Holland.

Every possible precaution was made to conceal the identities of the group, Christian names only, total secrecy from all the other passengers riding in the regular carriages up front, and breathtaking security to protect any of the servants from recognizing them.

The eight hundred–mile journey would take them to the little Georgia coastal town of Brunswick, from where they would take a ferry out to one of the outer islands, purchased by J. P. Morgan and his associates expressly for duck hunting. That was Jekyll Island, where one of the most momentous private conferences in US history would take place.

It led to the establishment of the Federal Reserve System. These six men were on a mission, and that was to establish a cartel that would protect them all—the banking dynasties of Morgan, Rockefeller, Rothschild, Warburg, and Kuhn, Loeb—from their sworn common enemy, competition.

Of course the very word "cartel" in the United States at the time was liable to provoke riot conditions among the public, so abhorrent did people find the concept of any brake on free markets, free trade, or the closing out of competition.

But these bankers had no other intention. They were a group of independent businesses planning to join together to reduce competition, and thereby increase profitability. They were planning a shared monopoly over their industry. It was a way of making the public pay higher prices than would occur naturally under free enterprise.

Which is why they did not wish to be seen together, or to make public their intentions. The result was this creation of what amounted to a central bank, working in close cahoots with the government under an astonishing set of laws that would benefit them and their banks for a hundred years.

The Federal Reserve was indeed an organization that dare not speak its proper name: an independent banking cartel, specifically designed to work with the government, and make for its members gigantic profits in a business protected by government guarantees and the taxpayers' money.

It is an all-too-modern scenario, because there is still an utterly unholy alliance between the government and the Fed. Consider this: the government wants more money, so they issue "bonds," which is merely another word for "debt."

Who buys the bonds? The Federal Reserve. What do they buy the bonds with? Money, of course, money they just printed! They even have a special name for it now: "quantitative easing." Very sophisticated, right? So what is it really? It's taxation, masquerading as inflation. Because every time they print a few billion more dollars, it dilutes the value of the dollars that were already there, the ones you own yourself. And they plainly cannot be worth what they once were.

All of these modern complexities trace back to that duck-hunting lodge off the coast of Georgia, where one hundred years ago they laid out the blueprint for the Federal Reserve System. They wanted a name that did not contain the word "bank," and they got it. They needed to disguise the cartel from what it really was: a central bank dedicated to holding down interest rates, to make public borrowing more widespread, because banks mostly make money from interest payments, and the more of these they have the better they like it.

What they also needed was a smoke screen to demonstrate that their wishes were only to protect the public, benefit the economy and the nation, provide funding for industrial projects, and stop periodic panics in the economy.

When all was said and done, it was a master plan to serve their private interests, with the government backing them with taxpayers' dollars every time the banks screwed it up. The Fed is not a bank, it's a union of banks. And a few years after I began my studies, we saw them in action in big black spades, stepping in to do precisely what the hunting-lodge bankers had intended: come up with $700 billion to bail out the banks in the fall of 2008.

The money was duly printed and handed over: $100 billion each for Freddie MacBonehead and Fannie Mayhem, $85 billion for AIG, the gigantic insurer that would have gone bust without it, $25 billion for Citigroup, $15 billion for Bank of America. A few months later BofA received an additional $20 billion, plus a government guarantee of $118 billion to gather up the historic but nearly bankrupt brokerage house Merrill Lynch. Every last dollar was down to the American taxpayer.

Of course, in 2000 I could not have known this. But I knuckled down to the financial history of the United States, and it took me only a couple of hours to realize the Federal Reserve had presided over the crashes of 1921 and '29, the Great Depression of 1929–1939, shocking recessions in 1945, 1958, 1969–1970, 1973–1975, and 1981–1982, followed by the stock

market's "Black Monday" in 1987. In addition, there had been 1,000 percent inflation.

Now, I was relatively new to all this, despite a lifetime perusing the
stock markets. It was pretty obvious even to me that whatever the hell the
Federal Reserve was actually doing, it was not achieving anything even
close to its stated aims. I think it was bang on the money concerning its
nonstated aims, which was massive government-guaranteed banking
profits for its members.

I do believe they all wished and hoped for full employment, high pro-
ductivity, and low inflation. But when push comes to shove, they are in-
capable of delivering those things, and as a cartel, they will always act in
their own interests, rather than those of the public. In case you had not
noticed, that's the normal way of all cartels.

Edward Griffin thought one of the shrewdest commentators on this
very suspect situation was the late Emperor of the French, Napoleon
Bonaparte. When he returned from the wars, his stated aim was to get his
country and his people out of debt and out of the control of bankers. He
banned loans for current expenditure, whether civil or military. He felt
no government should depend on bankers for its money.

Somewhat poetically, he declared, "Money has no motherland; financiers are without patriotism and without decency; their sole object is gain."
He established the Bank of France, with himself as president, but refused
to put government money into it.

But it was his shattering ban on borrowing that appalled the French
bankers, as indeed it would most certainly have appalled the seven directors of the twenty-first-century Federal Reserve.

As you may well imagine, G. Edward Griffin's account of the Great
Crash of 1929 is recounted with savage honesty, casting a suspicion
upon the waters that many true insiders in the banking world, and their
preferred clients, had gone to cash earlier that year, and then scooped
up excellent stocks at rock-bottom prices after the market had de-
voured the minnows, thousands of them wiped out in a single day,
October 29.

He wrote his narrative with a cold-blooded certainty, asserting that
a market crash does not mean that great and profitable corporations
suddenly are not worth investing in. It just means that speculators have

panicked and sold, especially those who had bought "on margin" and could not stand any kind of a downturn.

Those who were not "margined" and had bought and sold their securities with their own money had the cash to snap up the subsequent bargains.

"Some of the greatest American fortunes," wrote Edward Griffin, "were made in that fashion."

Another book—John J. Murphy's *Technical Analysis of the Financial Markets*—detailed the modern cycle of finance in which we appear to be trapped. Here's how it happens:

1. The market sells off and business wanes.
2. The Fed injects money by buying bonds, devaluing the dollar.
3. Interest rates fall.
4. Low interest rates inspire Wall Street to start buying stocks on margin.
5. Lower-value dollars cause Saudis et al. to demand higher prices for oil.
6. Gold and other commodities start to rise.
7. Energy prices also rise, and the costs of transporting goods are passed on to you.
8. Suddenly the Fed starts selling off bonds, and the dollar gets stronger, so rates go up.
9. The markets start to sell off because of the huge volume of stocks bought on margin by Wall Street.
10. Commodity prices cool off. But rates rise. And people start getting laid off. The government steps in and issues bonds. The Fed prints the money to buy them and hands the cash to the government.
11. To the never-ending joy of the banks, the borrowing begins anew.

The fateful cycle continues.

I found all of this somewhat unnerving. But it broadened my comprehension of the markets. I began to study the whole syndrome of precious metals. I locked onto the intermarket relationships among stocks, bonds, commodities, foreign currency, and interest rates. They all worked together, and gold was the critical path.

Deep in the heart of the USS *George Washington,* in the year 2000, parked right out there in the middle of the Persian Gulf, I arrived at a progressive conclusion.

It seemed to me the issue for the American investor was to try to avoid these periodic crashes and the subsequent destruction of capital. So far as I could see, nothing really mattered except the preservation of a person's wealth. The government, hand in hand with the Federal Reserve, was doing its level best to reduce that through inflation, without the intervention of self-seeking Wall Street bankers.

Brought up on the accurate assessment of risk, a lifelong member of a United States Armed Forces that placed the evaluation of risk above all else, I could see no merit in any other mind-set for the investor.

I already had read many stock and commodity summaries that to me always seemed too concentrated on the upside, the unknown, the estimates, the hopes, and the guesses. I considered the real brainwork should be concentrated on the downside, what could be lost, and the likelihood of that happening.

In my view the preservation of wealth was paramount. The upside was a fantasy that may or may not evolve. The downside was right there to be examined and quantified. There was history to see, there were warning signs to be located and observed. There were a zillion factors to help an investor get a firm read on what could be lost.

So far as I could see, any damn fool could make some stupid-assed guess about how wonderful it would be if a stock went up 10 percent. However, it would take a master to study a stock and then inform an investor of the odds against losing a pile of money.

Assessing risk was in my blood, as it is with all Naval Aviators. Every last move we make involves the avoidance of piling that thirty-ton strike fighter into the side of a mountain or into the ocean. Risk is our creed and our bible. Every mission we fly, every voyage we make, everything is about possible losses, imminent screwups, what's acceptable, and what isn't.

I arrived at the conclusion that many investors might feel safer with someone like me at the helm than some Wall Street hotshot telling them the chances of a stock doubling in the fourth quarter were "too good to be missed."

All through that long Persian Gulf cruise, and then into the New Year, 2001, I kept at my business studies. When finally I left and returned to my home state, I had broadly mapped out my future. For many reasons, some emotional, some financial, I planned to continue in the military until 2006.

I had been accepted as a commissioned officer in the Ohio Air National Guard, which is, for the uninitiated, one of the largest air forces in the world, with 5,000 airmen and officers and squadrons of F-16 Fighting Falcons. It was outlandishly hard for me to accept that I was no longer in the Navy, but instead a major in the Air Force, attached to the 162nd Fighter Squadron, the Sabers.

In its own way, this was a historic National Guard outfit. The squadron flew with a big cat on the vertical tail, supposedly depicting a saber-toothed tiger, but to me it looked more like a panther. I was now a Saber, stationed up at Springfield, around thirty-eight miles northeast of Maineville. There were eighteen F-16s on the base.

This was a very big and very serious operation. The Ohio Air National Guard has deep roots both in the state and in the nation. It sees itself as a bedrock of the US military, and its emblem betrays its sense of tradition. In addition to a couple of strike fighters, there stands four-square and central on the patch the statue of the *Concord Minute Man of 1775* statue as sculpted by Daniel Chester French. That's the big one cast from Civil War cannon barrels, which stands on its high plinth at the Old North Bridge beside the river at Concord, Massachusetts.

The *Minute Man,* of course, commemorates the first day of the Revolutionary War, 1775, when Major John Buttrick's farmers opened fire on King George III's Regiments of Foot, which faced them across the river.

It's a most unusual emblem for a modern air strike force based in the Midwest, far from the patriotic fervor of the thirteen colonies' struggle against the armies of Great Britain, 235 years ago in New England. But Ohio has a heavily developed sense of history and regards itself as a venerable and time-honored place along with Massachusetts, New York, Pennsylvania, and Virginia.

Ohio is in fact the seventeenth state of the Union, having joined in 1803. It was one of the next four, after the original thirteen, with Vermont, Kentucky, and Tennessee.

My new command would require me to fly the F-16 Fighting Falcon, which I probably could have mastered in about a week, having flown combat *against* it so often at Miramar and Fallon. But, as ever with the US military, I had to go right through the whole qualifying process all over again. None of my previous "quals" counted for anything.

I spent the whole summer of 2001 getting requalified with the 162nd Fighter Squadron, living back in Maineville, in the old town, and working on my financial studies all the hours God made. As for everyone else in the military, 9/11 remains a graphic memory.

I was home when it happened, just watching the morning news when the first jetliner plowed into the north tower. I didn't see that part until the television channel showed the pictures and mentioned they thought there had been an accident.

It did not look much like an accident to me, and then I saw the second Boeing screaming down the Hudson and making its hard left turn toward the south tower. Like most other people I watched in horror as United Airlines Flight 175 plowed into the building, killing everyone on board. I was absolutely stunned, but I was still in the military and they didn't pay me to be stunned.

The correct signal instantly flashed through my mind: *Holy shit! We're at war!* I pulled on my flight suit and charged for the base, demolishing every speed limit as I gunned the automobile toward Springfield. The savage irony weighed down on me: if I'd stayed in the Navy I'd be one of the main men in this upcoming operation. I very well may have led the Navy's F-14 fighter formation to Washington to protect the capital. I'd trained for this all of my life, and now I was off learning to fly F-16s in the middle of Ohio, light-years from the action.

There was a rather startling moment as I sped north with the convertible top down. An F-16 making about 1,000 mph came screaming over my head, causing a massive sonic boom as it broke the sound barrier. It was a major thunderclap, like *b-b-b-booom!*

*Jesus Christ!* I thought. *If he's on our side, that's got to be illegal!* But I had to laugh when the explanation was finally given. One of the F-16 guys, summoned to accompany Air Force One as it headed back to Washington, was late. So the pilot just hit the gas, trying to catch up. He smashed the sound barrier right over the city of Dayton! Which, at his airspeed, was about a minute west of my car. It frightened everyone to death, especially after the Twin Towers disaster only an hour before, but I knew the pilot, and he was just doing his best on a historically shocking morning.

I probably would not have laughed at anything that day if I'd known that my blood brother Moose was actually on Flight 175 out of Boston when it hit the tower. They never even found his remains. I never even found out soon enough to attend his funeral on Cape Cod. I had not seen him for three years, not since the Irish bar in Pensacola. His death did not improve my opinion of the terrorists.

Again and again, I come back to where we started this book. Would any of it had happened if we'd wiped out Saddam's air force the previous year? My own view is a very definite no. If the United States had just shown its teeth, just once, instead of friggin' around with ninety-nine, shut downs, we all think 9/11 probably would not have happened. As things were, bin Laden's killer henchmen were dealing with an opponent they thought was soft, and they've never hesitated to strike when that was their belief.

Militarily there was very little we could do in the Ohio Air National Guard, and while my old boss and mentor, Captain Winnefeld, was out in the Arabian Sea slamming away at the Afghan terrorist camps, I just set about training student pilots for the next five years. In 2002 they promoted me to lieutenant colonel, which was a very high rank in the Guard, and had to be approved by Congress.

For the remainder of my time until 2006, I concentrated on teaching the younger guys dogfighting tactics. I guess I was doing something right, because in 2005 they voted me Instructor of the Year.

My departure from the US Air Force was much more programmed than it had been from the Navy. I'd always known when I would leave, and in my deepest thoughts, I was still Lieutenant Commander Lay (USN) rather than Lieutenant Colonel Lay (USAF).

But at the controls of a fighter aircraft, I guess I was still the guy they all wanted to beat. There was, after all, only one other TOPGUN pilot in Springfield. My last day saw me back in a combat mission with the best guy in the squadron, Major Tony Massa, call sign "Nasty." He gave it everything. But it was like the young Jeff Lay against old Spuds. No chance, kid.

He tried every trick he knew, trying to circle "inside" me. But I ended the dogfight with a long barrier-busting power dive at around 1,000 mph, a hard break to the right, and came up right behind him. And there I re-minded Tony of an old semi-light-hearted lesson I had often repeated: *Missiles are for sissies. It's guns that count.*

I took him out with my trusty 20mm M61 six-barreled Gatling cannon—my final confirmation that the TOPGUN patch I still wore was indeed a badge signifying a standard of excellence rarely achieved in any-one else's fighter squadrons.

We shook hands when we landed, and then I simply told the crew chief I was all done. That was my last hurrah, and I headed off toward that other vicious dogfighting arena, Wall Street, where my TOPGUN patch would be less highly regarded. But I had other weapons.

All through those final five years, I'd been studying finance. I'd even been taking and passing financial exams. I'd actually been killing myself, starting my studies at four a.m. and finishing up at midnight, with a few dogfights in between.

For my new career as a financier, I needed to pass at least two licensing exams, and I have to say, compared to the Navy, they were not difficult. I crushed them in short order. I took one in Chicago, nearly three hundred miles away, and one in Indianapolis, one hundred miles away, and drove to both places, there and back in a day.

By the time I took and removed these hurdles to my new career, I'd been studying finance intensely for several years. In addition, I had a plan I'd put into operation with some success as soon as I felt ready. I was armed with my burgeoning knowledge about the currency markets, the true intentions of the Fed, commodities, and bonds, and I tried to marry everything to my grasp of controls. I honed a new clear objective, to form the bedrock of my future: eliminating mistakes on the critical subject of risk.

Of course I realized some people were a great deal more expert on this subject than I was, and I looked them all up. I found their papers and their projects and, where possible, their books and manuals. Then I located the people, picked up the phone, and called them all. Some may have thought this was a tad ambitious for a rookie bean counter. But I knew better. Or at least I thought I did.

Several dozen phone calls later, I was in touch with some of the key people in the industry. I actually went to see great oracles of the investing world, such as Larry Pesavento in Tucson, Joe DiNapoli in Florida,

Michael Jenkins in New York, and Jordan Kotick in New Jersey and New York. I was consistently impressed by how willing they were to take time to see me and offer advice, which I treasure to this day.

I suppose it was the basic premise of each discussion that amused them: fighter pilot wants to come in to land on the beaches of Wall Street. *How do I get my new wings?*

I started with the revered Larry Pesavento, one of America's best-known trading tutors: "Trade what you see, not what you believe." Right there he had my attention. He would have grabbed the attention of any TOPGUN graduate with that one.

Larry's game was to trade chart patterns, the ratios of proven trade management patterns, which usually enable the investor to make consistent returns on risk capital, regardless of the market. Larry was a forty-five-year veteran trader, a member of the Chicago Mercantile Exchange, and a former director of commodity trading at Drexel Burnham Lambert in Los Angeles. When I met him he'd already written ten books and trained more than 1,000 brokers.

What I loved about Larry's methods were his longtime studies, the fact that he'd seen the same things over and over, his certainty that if something diabolical had happened it was engraved into the charts and it surely would happen again. Because it always did. That's my kind of stuff.

My next stop was another market veteran trader, Joe DiNapoli, renowned throughout the investing world as a dogged, deeply cynical researcher, an internationally recognized lecturer and author. I went to Sarasota several times to see him and to learn more about his most famous creation, the Oscillator Predictor, which for the purpose of this book I'll settle for describing as the study of applying the Fibonacci ratios to the price axis.

Those ratios dated back to a thirteenth-century sage, Leonardo da Pisa, reputed to be the most brilliant Western mathematician of the Middle Ages. Joe swore by this progression of numbers, swore that it was utterly relevant to the trends of the modern stock market. I figured that anything that was still solid after eight hundred years probably was not so far off the mark.

I also visited with Michael Jenkins of New York, mostly because I was fascinated by his first book, *The Secret Science of the Stock Market*. Michael is an advanced mathematician and a financial historian, an expert on the market's highs and a wizard on the lows and their stark reflections of today's markets. In 2001 he was a twenty-eight-year hedge fund trading veteran, and one of the most lucid minds converting cycles into measurable trends.

I spent time too with John J. Murphy, one of the best technical analysts in the country, former director of Merrill Lynch's Futures Division. Every conversation I had with any of them I converted to my own program of dealing with risk.

Naturally I understood I would need credentials if I were to enter the somewhat closed-shop structure of Wall Street. And I searched around for something that was plainly difficult to achieve but worth having if you had the staying power. I spent a long time on this before deciding on the Market Technicians Association, an international group that had been based in the World Trade Center.

Their motto was "Financial professionals managing risk." This was perfect for me, but I quickly realized their program was very tough. Only three hundred people had mastered the exam: the Chartered Market Technicians designation. It's a five-year course, comprising three exams, requiring four hundred hours of study.

The entire course centers on self-study, and throughout this work, I continued seeing my mentors, Pesavento, DiNapoli, Jenkins, Kotick, and Murphy. I managed to pass those exams in one year, which I think is still an all-comers record. I just rammed my TOPGUN hat on my head and got down to it, just as they had taught me.

I applied immediately for full membership and received it, which permitted me to place the letters "CMT" after my name, my first financial credentials. I was surprised how few people knew about that organization, despite its reputation for the brutal marking of prospective candidates. In the five years since I attained that distinction, only seven hundred more people have battled through the exam. It was just a matter of months before I was duly elected a member of the board, and director of the Chartered Market Technician Institute.

At one point they decided to set up their own school to help people pass the examinations, and they chose me to assist in its inauguration. Since then, I have taught four hundred analysts, portfolio managers, and brokers in risk management. I suppose that's what you might expect of a TOPGUN instructor who somehow crammed twenty years' worth of Wall Street study into twenty-four months, as I did.

Of course, during that time, when I was easing myself out of the Ohio Air National Guard, I was earning money on the side, conducting seminars in the Cincinnati area, where I rented space in hotels and taught financial students. This was slightly unusual for someone who had not yet worked on Wall Street, but I had a lot of followers, my seminars were always well attended, and I was even beginning to dispense investment advice to a growing number of wealthy clients.

All through these rather restless months, on a steep learning curve with a ton of knowledge piling into my mind on a weekly basis, I still had Edward Griffin's *The Creature from Jekyll Island* foremost in my thoughts. I was always in search of the big picture, and Griffin was a master at that, seeing through the antics of the American government with a piercing and unremitting gaze.

For me, he shed light on their spending habits down all the years in a way no other book has, before or since. He established in my mind one shining fact: that no organization, in the entire history of the known universe, has ever been as adroit, cunning, or reckless in spending money it did not have as the national government of the United States of America.

In the year I finally left the military, 2006, the national debt required $400 billion a year from the US government just to service the interest payments—that's 17 percent of all federal revenue or $5,000 from every family of four in the land. It does not buy roads or buildings, or pay welfare or medical benefits, or even salaries. It's just there, paying for the colossal expenditures of the past. Say it another way: four hundred thousand million dollars, going nowhere, all paid for out of the American people's taxes.

Add to this the sheer size of the bureaucracy in a US government that is growing annually. They spend one-quarter of all the nation's economy on themselves. More people work for the government than for all the manufacturing companies in the private sector put together. There are more bank regulators than bankers, more farm bureau workers than farmers, more welfare administrators than recipients, more citizens receiving government checks than those paying income tax.

If Edward Griffin was concerned about the government, my own focus was on corporate America, which I had not yet joined but which was borrowing money in volumes to rival the government. In my view, these were sums of cash so vast they could never be paid back by anyone.

There were enormous valuations on corporations at the back end of 2006. Interest rates were very low, and the Fed had no plans to raise them—you bet they didn't. In their place I would have kept everything steady, with a plentiful supply of cheap money, just as they were doing.

And yet, my recent financial history lessons were crowding in on me. This money-making bonanza in the United States surely could not just go on indefinitely. I tried to rationalize it, tried to tell myself that the United States was still the biggest and most powerful economic juggernaut in the world.

But from my new scientific charts, I was seeing a looming catastrophe, like Japan experienced a couple of decades ago. And sometime in the next three or four years, I could see American financial institutions going bust under the gigantic burden of their own debts.

I was not that experienced, but I already knew what not to do, because I could already see the apparition of the subprime mortgage market looming up ahead. I did not yet know enough to take the helm of a ship of finance.

But I saw myself as a similar character to the pragmatic designer of the stricken *Titanic,* the marine architect who was famously berated up there on the foredeck by a truculent first-class passenger who shouted at him, "Sir, this is the *Titanic.* She cannot sink."

"Sir, I hate to tell you," he replied, "she cannot float."

## CHAPTER 11

# Sipping the Wall Street Kool-Aid

There have always been towering heroes in my life. Alongside the immortals, such as Admirals Nimitz, Halsey, and Ricketts, there stands Lieutenant Commander Van Voorhis and my great mentor, Commander Winnefeld. However, it took me approximately seventy-three minutes of Wall Street studies in 2006 to add a brand-new one to that list: Roy Rothschild Neuberger, financier, philanthropist, art collector, and humanitarian.

I found his name in the remnants of Black Tuesday 1929, when the New York stock market caved in. He'd been working on Wall Street as an investment broker for only seven months, and yet he was still standing. He kept going with astounding success, right through all the melancholy years of the Great Depression, protecting his clients, preserving their wealth, answering their pleas not to lose any more of their fortunes.

In 1939, weeks before the onset of WWII, he cofounded his own investment house, Neuberger Berman. Through all the trials, crashes, smashes, and triumphs, it's still there, probably because he kept a weather eye on it to the very end. Neuberger lived until he was 107.

His care and his caution were fabled on Wall Street. He avoided bubbles, spotted potential fraud, and gazed suspiciously at those who had risen too fast. Above all else, he treated his clients' money as if it was his own. This is, I imagine, why the very wealthy loved him, trusted him, and willingly made him a staggeringly rich and fulfilled man.

Neuberger Berman has enjoyed a lofty reputation for generations. It has always invested with its courage high, but has always been razor-sharp with a set of cast-steel brakes at the very hint of trouble.

I studied the history and performance of dozens of investment houses as I prepared to make my entry to Wall Street. But not one of them affected me like the prospectus of the house of Neuberger Berman.

This was the Rolls-Royce of investment houses. I could tell from every paragraph, every set of numbers, that from 1939 all the way to 2006, the word "caution" was its watchword. The managers were experts on all forms of risk, and they steered well clear of anything that could collapse suddenly. They avoided outfits with massive debt like the plague, and in many ways had demonstrated down the years a natural affinity for the philosophies of Warren Buffett.

By the time I finished these studies I was involved with an excellent firm of headhunters trying to place me. They had several offers of interviews from various New York investment houses, but the one that stayed right at the top of my list was Neuberger Berman.

It seemed to me that Roy Neuberger was a prince among money managers. He was from a wealthy New York family and, thanks to an inheritance, went to live in Paris in 1924. He lived the life of a bohemian, visiting the Louvre three times a week for almost five years.

But I thought the key to the man rested in what he read rather than what he saw and loved. He admitted being emotionally stricken when he read Vincent Van Gogh's biography, which detailed how the artist, in pain, poverty, and misery, had committed suicide, having sold but one painting in all of his life.

At that moment Neuberger decided he would devote much of his time toward helping young painters, buying their work when they most needed help. He also decided to return to America and build his fortune on Wall Street—the fortune that would enable him to help those he most admired and, he thought, deserved serious patronage.

His astonishing success enabled him to buy the early works of the modern painters like Jackson Pollock, Ben Shahn, and Edward Hopper. In Paris, he met and befriended the American sculptor and painter

Alexander Calder; Neuberger patronized the modernist Stuart Davis; he bought the earliest works of the most celebrated of African-American painters, Jacob Lawrence; the same for his friend, the Harvard-educated Boston Expressionist Jack Levine.

Neuberger "discovered" and purchased one hundred paintings over time from artist Milton Avery, then donated many of them to various high-profile museums all over the world, which made Avery very famous indeed.

But it was his assistance to the New Mexico painter Peter Hurd that caught my attention. In this lifelong campaign to help artists, Neuberger bought the very first painting he would lend out from Hurd. In 1939, when Hurd was unknown, Neuberger bought a painting of a sun-bronzed young man standing under a Stetson, in a field somewhere on the farming plains of the Midwest. It looked a lot like the field next door to me in Maineville, same haystack in the distance, same standing American farm windmill.

It was titled "Boy from the Plains." And it set Neuberger on the long road to one of the greatest art collections this nation has ever seen. That one picture launched Peter Hurd because the head of Neuberger Berman lent it to his close friend, Nelson Rockefeller, to be part of a grand exhibition of American paintings that would travel the world.

Hurd went on to marry Henriette, the sister of Andrew Wyeth, and established a brilliant career in western painting. He and Neuberger stayed friends for many years, until Hurd died in 1984. They always talked affectionately of that first, now massively valuable picture, "Boy from the Plains."

I won't forget it in a hurry either, because that was my omen, from Roy Neuberger to this other boy from the plains. It was the mystical sign that confirmed, in my mind, that by hook or by crook, I was destined to work for Neuberger Berman. I remember how much I looked forward to it— just the prospect of entering their Wall Street kingdom, because it reputedly contained a fabulous selection of the chairman's art.

I have often tried to analyze precisely why I was so drawn to this corporation. Plainly it was not just the paintings in the office. I think it was because I sensed that Neuberger himself was such a compassionate man, with empathy for his clients, and for the artists who needed cash and sympathy.

True to my belief that a wealth manager will never succeed if he cannot share his clients' anguish, Roy Neuberger was my idea of the perfect investor. Wealthy himself, far beyond avarice, his soul must have pervaded the whole company. And I made that my destination.

From the very start of my campaign, everything went my way. An old friend from the Navy, Eric Gies, a RIO with whom I had served on the flight deck of USS *Nimitz* and later in the Fighting Checkmates, was director of the southeast region of Neuberger, and, I quickly learned, a star on his way up.

Eric knew a lot about me. We'd actually flown together, and for a series of long and arduous interviews, he stuck his neck out for me over and over. I could scarcely believe how thorough they were in selecting their managers. When I received the schedule for the next series of interviews, there were five in one day.

I had the impression this was make-or-break time, and armed with my notebook full of facts about the operation, I was met at JFK airport by a company limo and driven to Manhattan to 605 Third Avenue. I remember I was two hours early, and I swiftly moved a couple of blocks away to the nearest coffee shop for intensive review.

Afterward I walked back up to the Neuberger offices and was escorted to the thirty-second floor. There I was greeted by one of those immaculately turned-out Wall Street women whose achievements are a part of their character. In 2006 they were a twenty-first-century phenom, each of them a major player in financial circles.

Her name was Stephanie Stiefel, and she had a major title and a southwest corner office, floor-to-ceiling glass, with views across the city, right down to the financial district three miles away, where once the Twin Towers had stood. To misquote a legendary Wall Street ad campaign, you only get offices like that the old-fashioned way: you earn them.

It took her about thirty seconds to ask the critical question: "What makes you think you belong here?"

I told her I understood risk, and I understood Wall Street, and although I had been involved with finance for only a very few years, I had a lot of wide experience, and I had not even attempted to come to New York until I was good and ready.

Stiefel proceeded to haul me over the coals, presenting scenario after scenario: "What would you advise and do under the following circumstances?" I stood my ground because I had very little choice. I had my folio and notes in front of me, and we fired back and forth for a significant amount of time.

Then quite suddenly she asked me an unorthodox question in a plainly challenging way: "What would you do if a client came to you with a substantial amount of money, and explained she had a young son, this important amount of money, and that her husband had recently died after a long and courageous battle with cancer?"

Stiefel will never know how that question hit me like an emotional dagger. In a flash I understood there were two ways to answer that: (1) with the cold-blooded sureness of a Wall Street wealth advisor, confident he could help to arrange her life, or (2) with my heart, which for a few seconds seemed to have stopped beating.

I went for (2), not as a careful decision but because I couldn't help it. My rigidly controlled demeanor fell away from me. I gave myself time to think, and I cast my emergency-answering procedures to the back of both my folio and my mind.

I said slowly, "I have survived cancer. Beaten it. And the first thing I want her to know is that if there's anything in this world I can do for her, then please let me know. Because, in a sense, I'd been there. And I knew how hard my own battle was.

"I could not imagine the pain of losing. But I understood the struggle. And I want her to know that money was the very last thing on my mind. Compassion and empathy were the only things that mattered."

Of course I knew that was probably the worst answer anyone could give in an interview like this. To my amazement, I realized that the eyes of my interrogator had welled up, and she was reaching for a box of tissues.

"The woman in the story was me," she said softly. I just stared at this titan of wealth advisory, in this palatial office, moved to tears. Finally she said, "In this business, and I suppose in life, empathy is everything. I have no need to tell you not to forget that. Because I know you never will."

Then she stood up. The interview was over. She shook my hand, smiled, and told me, "You'll do just fine."

We walked in silence to the elevator. There was nothing more to say. We were, after all, both true disciples of the great humanitarian Roy Rothschild Neuberger. I knew, beyond doubt, I was about to be hired.

IN THE ENSUING WEEKS, up to Christmas and beyond, Eric Gies and I vied for a place in the Neuberger archives, testing who would hold the all-time record for being hired with the least time spent on interviews. Eric, who had gone to the University of Florida, had been first in his class training to become a RIO in the US Navy, and he got home in a photo finish. But it was a close-run thing, calculating the short time since Stiefel had driven me over the line.

Once more my prayers had been answered and my dream had come true. I was going to work for Roy Neuberger, who was still alive and contributing at the age of 104. There remained only one tiny blip on my horizon. Actually it was not on the horizon. It was right there in the cockpit, a little warning light that flashed every few minutes, like the one that used to tell me gas was low as I flew slowly in to the carrier over the Gulf of Iran.

This new flickering light had but one dark message: Lehman Brothers. Remember this was the beginning of 2007; the market was awash with cheap money, rolling loans, short-term loans, and God knows what else. It was impossible to go bust in the United States, with billions of dollars continuing to flood in from China.

So far as I could see, the stock market had essentially gone bananas. Financial corporations borrowed big, plunged into investments, and then borrowed more to pay back the original loan. I could not understand why General Motors, staggering under its debt, with a stock that looked to be worth about five cents, did not topple into the Detroit River. But its stock was selling at thirty-two bucks a share.

Lehman Brothers, which I gauged had debts of around $450 billion, was leveraged thirty times its value and was into subprime mortgages up to its garters. So what? Only that Lehman Brothers owned Neuberger Berman, and had for just north of three years. Whatever that meant, I couldn't possibly love it.

I understood that Neuberger was a quasi-independent entity operating as it always had. But I was wary that the mark of Lehman Brothers was upon it. I understood that the only way you get leveraged to the level of Lehman was to have some very rash, very optimistic, and very pushy, hard-driving managers.

In my game, we don't do rash, and we take a long, hard look at anything before we even consider optimistic. We can cope with pushy and hard-driving, but we have mechanisms to slow those guys right down. In my limited experience, there is no such braking system on Wall Street.

Nonetheless, I believed that with the peerless Roy Neuberger himself still in the background, and with people like the sainted Stephanie on the bridge, the exemplary old investment house could still deliver its traditional conservative results, even with the fire-eating hooligans of Lehman rampaging outside the doors.

I prepared for my move to New York or Washington or maybe even Florida, where Eric was. There was a period of Neuberger indoctrination I had to complete before it would be decided where I should be based. I hoped for Washington, which was comfortably close to my alma mater up the road at Annapolis.

At this stage, with the US Navy still so fresh in my mind and always in my dreams, I never liked to stray too far from its environs. Even out of uniform, to me the Navy was still home. I guess it always will be.

It was strange, because although I was gone from the fighter squadrons of US aircraft carriers, none of it was really gone from me. I still lived life the way I had been taught: nothing extravagant, nothing boastful, nothing ostentatious, everything very slightly understated. All executed with an instructor's unspoken sense of duty to others.

Thus, my opening foray into New York was more of a culture bombshell than a shock. For a start I was unused to traveling for business meetings. I'd never done it before, especially for a world-renowned finance house, the founder of which owned an art collection worth something close to the national debt.

I arrived from Maineville with this enormous suitcase, containing three suits, one for each day, socks, ties, and shirts, plus all my exercise clothes and sneakers. This is known colloquially as Ohio Hayseed Come to Town—the Boy from the Plains makes it to the Big Apple.

I quickly felt like a total idiot. The other two going through the process with me were seasoned finance guys, and they arrived with slick, small, wheeled suitcases, with just one suit to be cleaned and pressed overnight by the expensive hotel valet service.

They were both ensconced in one of the most expensive hotels in Manhattan, while I was checked into some $100-a-night flophouse a few blocks south, in a bedroom about two steps up from my lieutenant commander's stateroom in the aircraft carrier, which was, trust me, on the primitive side, but all I had ever known.

I'd never even been in a friggin' hotel like they were in, and they both told me to get the hell out of my cheap digs and get in there with them, as befits a wealth advisor for Neuberger Berman. I don't know why, but I couldn't do it. It wasn't my money. It belonged to the shareholders, and I couldn't spend it like that. What the hell did I know?

Dinner was an absolute eye-opener. Eric Gies was coming as well, and the four of us had a reservation at one of the most expensive and best steak houses in New York: Smith & Wollensky on Third Avenue at Forty-Ninth Street. I glanced down the menu and swiftly realized I could have a share in General Motors for the price of a New York sirloin. Back home you could pick up a two-year-old steer for the cost of those four steaks.

I decided to sit back and let these three sophisticates get on with it; I'd just follow their lead and keep my head well down, get a beer, and try to talk sense. I'd already read a review of this place before we arrived and I'd noticed that *New York Magazine* called it a place for "urban cowboys on expense accounts."

I guess I didn't know much about expense accounts, but I was the rural cowboy among these guys. *Well, dang mah britches,* I'd better shake that dust from the cornfields right off my boots and start my transformation into a New York City boy.

Selecting a steak wasn't much trouble, but the mostly American wine list might as well have been in Greek for me. I stuck to the program and kept my head down while these guys were commenting about Napa Valley vineyards and different years, grapes, and vintages. Eric, my old buddy, whom I'd never even seen taste a glass of wine, was actually sniffing it. Christ knows what that was about. I knew nothing about wine, and engaging my lifetime bullshit gauge, I detected they didn't either.

I had a few glasses and listened while my three new colleagues spoke about the Lehman stock, which had hit an all-time high that very night, and how a senior Lehman manager, George Herbert Walker IV—a cousin of President George W. Bush—had given a brilliant speech.

To say my dinner companions were pleased with themselves and everything life had most deservedly given them would be a mild understatement. But I guess they'd all done something to add to the general jollity of the times, and I did not even ask what the astronomical check came to when it finally arrived. But I saw the tip. Holy shit! That would have paid my monthly mortgage.

Outside the restaurant, they all jumped into cabs to cover the few blocks to their hotel, and I told them I'd rather walk to mine. But I was not about to head back to the old flophouse. I had another call to make a half-dozen city blocks away, to the world headquarters of Lehman Brothers, the 150-year-old investment bank that had shelled out $2.6 billion to buy Neuberger Berman in 2003.

Everyone had told me that Roy Neuberger's firm represented the jewel in the Lehman crown, and I needed to know what this mighty investment house with its huge debt and hotshot managers actually looked like. After all, they'd just paid for dinner, willingly. So I strolled along the cold sidewalks of Manhattan, crossed the great avenues—Lexington, Park, Madison, Fifth, the Avenue of the Americas—and reached Seventh. And there it was: the towering edifice of Lehman Brothers.

The skyscraper was lit by a thousand lights, the fluorescent words "Lehman Brothers" serving as the backdrop to huge moving color pictures of scenes from around the world. The lights of Lehman illuminated the city, all the way to Times Square and probably north to Central Park.

This was global braggadocio, swaggering self-aggrandizement on the grandest scale. They say the Great Wall of China is the only man-made construction on earth that can be seen from space—forget that. You could spot Lehman Brothers from the dark side of Jupiter.

I gazed up more than thirty floors to the top of the tower, and I guessed that the inside was equally impressive. It was a well-known fact that when the purchase of Neuberger was complete, many of the finest paintings from the great collection were brought over to the new parent company. In a corporation where avarice was king, I had no idea whether they were still there or had vanished to multimillion-dollar residences of the big hitters who now ran Bobbie Lehman's bank.

I stood for a while and stared at the building and the long line of black cars that snaked around the corner. Every so often someone came rushing out, jumped into one of them, and took off into the city. The cars moved up, and then someone else came out. At first I thought these were members of the highest management teams on urgent business. But there were so many of them I would not have been shocked if the last guy to jump into the never-ending conga line of black limos was one of the janitors.

I considered the possibility of trying my own luck and jumping into one of them, but decided against it and set off back to the East Side. I dropped in at a cheerful-looking sports bar on the west side of Lexington, had a beer, and watched replays of Steinbrenner's Yankees blast the living daylights out of some team. Then I returned to the hotel and hit the hay.

I'd just borne careful witness to the rate at which the shareholders of Lehman Brothers had their money spent for them. And that put an end to my belief that the days of piracy on the high seas, at least in American waters, were long over. My admirals would not have approved.

The following evening, after hours of indoctrination into the ways of Neuberger Berman, I was required to attend what is known in the trade as a town hall meeting. This was a corporation-wide event—Lehman-wide that is, not just Neuberger—held somewhere that could comfortably handle around six hundred people. We listened to a keynote speech, given by someone who worked within the organization, followed by a question-and-answer session.

This meeting took place in a very upmarket hotel near Grand Central Station, and no expense had been spared. The walls were draped in massive red velvet curtains. There was a huge stage, spotlights, klieg lights, searchlights, and God knows what else. There were luxurious chairs, videos, screens, microphones, drinks, and enough plates of heavy canapés to feed the New York Police Department.

There was also an atmosphere of unmistakable resentment among the traders. You can always detect a cross-section of cynicism, especially in such a gathering, designed as it was to be totally self-congratulatory. Speech after speech made it clear that it was indeed an immense privilege to be involved in an organization like Lehman.

The stock's high value was mentioned many times, plus the plans, the techniques, the trust of the markets, the sheer gratitude every investor should feel as a result of the sensational brilliance of the Lehman investment gurus who nurtured and grew their wealth.

I personally thought what I had always thought: everyone thinks they're a genius in a bull market. But I never heard one single reference to Lehman's $450 billion debt, and I kept hearing phrases like "I don't know what the hell I'm supposed to be doing here . . . Jesus, do they think I haven't got anything better to do than listen to this bullshit? . . . I've been in this ridiculous factory since five this morning . . . I'm too tired for this crap . . . I was trading Japan at four o'clock in the goddamned morning."

For the heavy-hitting traders these gatherings were, apparently, compulsory. It was all part of the Lehman culture, the corporation's cult of self-aggrandizement, preaching to the converted, parading their top people, showing the outside world precisely how great they really were.

I noticed a few members of the media in attendance, eating and drinking earnestly on this stage-managed showboat of an investment bank, which was, as it happened, about a year and a half from total catastrophe.

As we walked out, I'd fallen into conversation with a pack of bond traders, and I asked one of the more volatile members of the group what meetings like this cost. "Don't know about this one," he replied. "But the one we had a couple of weeks ago was around $600,000."

Another guy mentioned, "My desk made that on a couple of trades this morning, so I guess the chiefs figure they can blow it out any way they think fit." Personally I was not at all sure about that, since the corporation paid them all every day, and the shareholders may just have been owed a duty of fiduciary care.

But that, I guess, was Wall Street. Easy come, easy go. But to my somewhat rigid naval officer's mind, that did not make it right. I could not really understand why there was not a department that kept a weather eye on all expenditures. However much power a CEO had, it was still *not his money*.

In the case of Lehman Brothers, my new masters, it was most definitely not their money, though their mammoth debt probably precluded anyone from knowing just who the hell actually owned what, since they owed thirty times their own worth.

So I had to make up my own mind. Was I going to stick to this revered investment bank as it headed to what I considered to be an iceberg, or was I going to share the faith that they had sufficient brilliant people to turn it all around? Or was I going to bail out right now and start my own shop, investing other people's money with the accent on protecting capital, not high risk?

I was drawn to the second option, because the Navy had taught me to be an entrepreneur. But the first option, to stay with the program I'd spent so much time achieving, was tempting, in a self-centered kind of way, because I was electing to jump right on board the Lehman juggernaut and join the "prosperity," with its unbridled borrowing, spending, and then borrowing more.

Perhaps it was because Wall Street had been my Holy Grail for so long. I don't know why, but I decided to stay with it. And from that moment on, I was sipping the Kool-Aid along with all the rest of them, right there in the Lehman People's Temple of Seventh Avenue.

I was actually in a branch office of the main place of worship, at Neuberger Berman on Third Avenue. There, I quickly learned, we had a lot of checks and balances, and our finances were solid. But if Lehman collapsed, it would surely drag us down with it.

So I cast that to the back of my mind and accepted my new masters. The plan was for me to go to Washington, D.C., and begin work as a wealth advisor. By the time I arrived there, I was certain that the heavy hand of Lehman was upon us. Remember, they were ten times the size of Neuberger—and they had a division called the Structured Products Desk, whose sole function was to come up with business investment ideas. And boy, did they ever have ideas.

They bombarded our office with them, amazing examples of mental alacrity. We had to take notice, because they'd been right so many times, creating vehicles for wealth management. At that time, of course, everyone else had been getting it right as well, from the president to the office cat. It was impossible to get it wrong in the boom quarters that were leading irrevocably to 2008.

My own task was to locate high–net worth individuals who needed help with investments and estate planning. It's one thing to create huge wealth, but it's quite another skill to hang on to it and make it grow to benefit the next generation. My problem was to locate such prospective clients and to bring them into the Lehman Brothers fold.

Our parent company had a fairly aggressive though slightly crude method of achieving this goal. It all centered around a mind-set: *We are Lehman Brothers . . . We are the greatest investment bank in the history of the universe . . . Words can barely describe how privileged you are even to be talking to us . . . When you decide to hand over your financial affairs, we will grant you entry to the greatest investment vehicles of our age . . . No one else can even approach what we can do for you . . . So sign here, and there's no need to look too closely at the small print.*

Their goal should not be ignored by any potential investor, because all of these banks aimed to maximize the revenue that could be harvested for them from a client's assets. Every bank had turned itself into a fee machine, with entire departments sitting around thinking up schemes and marketing strategies to convince clients they were superior in every way to everyone else.

Thus, it would be pure folly even to consider looking one yard farther than Lehman's brilliant operators and their amazing insights. All of the above represented a Lehman Brothers strategy. That's what we were told to live by, come hell or high water. Of course, figuratively speaking, the tide had been out for about five years, and the sand was dry and safe.

The dominant factor in my area was trust vehicles—the places we designated as the correct investments for clients looking for tax "efficiency" and the creation of a legacy for themselves and their children. There were a dazzling array of trust vehicles: the GRATs (grantor-retained annuity trusts); the CLTs (charitable lead trusts); the CRTs (charitable remainder trusts); the ILITs (irrevocable life insurance trusts).

Lehman leaned on all of us, urging a hard-disciplined approach, to match the extremely high expectations and undisguised determination to earn back that $2.6 billion the firm had shelled out to buy Neuberger Berman in the first place.

We were to make ten, if not fifteen, appointments per week, to be seen as "doing the job." They called our objective "wallet share"—meaning, of course, the clients' wallets, not our own. They made no secret of the fact that Lehman wanted every last dime we could lay hands on. This was the new heart of the firm, and the pressure was tremendous on Neuberger.

The department heads made certain we understood that everything flowed down to us. We were constantly given new targets, always to raise assets, hard numbers to hit. There was no room to assess whether "uptake" in a section of the market was in a slow period. Revenue was a straightforward sales target. And since Neuberger had such a lofty reputation, Lehman's view was simple: *You guys think you're so good . . . go prove it. Or else.*

My own area was split down the middle in a process called Core/Satellite, the core being regular stocks and bonds managed by

Neuberger, the satellite being the more exotic programs devised by Lehman's Structured Products Desk. I have to say some of these were created out of thin air, by people of such brilliance they often made clients a very good income.

I preferred the core, because there I could see precisely what was going on, and I had honed a special way of looking at stocks and bonds: Initially I was interested only in the downside, because that's quantifiable. The upside's a guess.

Those exotic hedge funds were a personal problem to me, because I could see that very often the firm was taking a client into a one-sided situation—meaning that total concentration was on the profits, steady or erratic, but nevertheless profits. The downside was that they often involved mortgages, possibly subprime, or leveraged buyouts that could go wrong, or the infamous CDSs (credit default swaps), which depended entirely on some huge corporation not going bust.

I could see with laser clarity that if one of them actually went down, it could take about seven financial organizations with it. In other words, if Lehman put a client's money into what looked like a rock-steady situation and it went wrong, Lehman could not possibly pay out the downside. Neither could Merrill Lynch, Bear Stearns, or AIG.

Thus, the Lehman managers and brokers were putting clients into investment vehicles that depended entirely on the survival of Lehman itself. They were bets on the solvency of a probably insolvent bank. My personal view was that this was a spectacularly rotten plan, because Lehman cared only for the profits of selling the products, not the risks. There was no proper, upfront disclosure.

Our parent company was always buying things. They had ceased to build things in the grand old tradition of the firm; rather, they bought corporations, buildings, brokerages, other investment houses. They just swallowed them up, purchasing other operations with borrowed money, on the most enormous scale. As Eliza Doolittle might have mentioned, "It fair took my breath away."

We owned a hedge fund operation called Liberty Capital, right across the Hudson River in Hackensack, New Jersey. One afternoon I was examining their returns the way I examined everything: checking the downside rather than the greedy side. One particular fund relied heavily on real estate and mortgages. Though they were plainly happy with this decision, I was rapidly approaching a stage of advanced neurosis every time I saw the words "collateralized debt obligation."

My reasoning for this was so simple a child could have understood it. These debts, with their healthy regular income stream from people's mortgage payments, were built on a bedrock of people who had barely any money but had been talked into taking the mortgage because the housing market had been going up since the cavemen and would continue to do so: *if you have to sell, there's always a profit.*

But there for all to see, the housing market was showing signs of a serious slowdown. This was not some mystical pool of knowledge to which only I had access; it had been happening for many months, and anyone who read the financial press could scarcely have missed it.

The first inkling arrived in October 2005, fifteen months previously, when David Rosenberg, chief economist for Merrill Lynch, announced that existing home sales had started to collapse, down 36 percent compared with the previous year. It was, he said, the steepest decline in years. In 2005, 43 percent of all first-time buyers had done so without putting down one red cent of their own money.

It didn't look to me as if the car market had been a lot better that year, General Motors having gone in the tank for $8.6 billion. In the late months of 2006, there had been a small but sharp spike in mortgage delinquency. New home prices were off 7 percent. There were also tiny signs that all house prices might drop slightly, which I realized was probably a market blip, but if it wasn't, it might be an atomic bomb.

The Lehman mortgage department was playing things pretty close to their chests, and it was hard to find out precisely how much of our gigantic debt was tied up in thousands of mortgages, issued to guys who didn't have any bread. Whatever else, I did not love it.

Liberty Capital, in my view, was just starting to struggle, and I did mention this to one or two managers, but my fears were abruptly dismissed. This was just a rough spot: *Don't worry about it, Jeff. There's clear sailing ahead.*

Nonetheless, I was really jumpy about anything involving those mortgages, and I was a bit leery about some of our new products that were tempting investors into reasonable income streams with no due regard for the other side of the trade, the counterparty risk that no one dares talk about. *What the hell happens if this goes wrong?*

These exotic products seemed fine in good times, but all I could think of was those shaky mortgages. What if one of the brokerage houses went down? What if these people couldn't pay and they took down a couple of the big American home builders? What if one of those massive credit default swaps found Lehman shouldering all the risk of a gigantic bankruptcy?

One thing I know for sure is that Lehman could not pay, without more massive borrowing. So far as I could tell, we might have been hanging out to dry for $60 billion or so on CDSs. The friggin' corporation was worth only around $18 billion, and that's on the generous side. I really didn't know about all this. But I did know one thing: the TOPGUN risk assessors would have disapproved.

We had our weekly conference calls with the head office, and they talked about all the "new and exciting" products and all the money we could make off our clients by investing in them. But nothing in this world could have persuaded me to expose any one of my own clients to this kind of risk. And I never did.

My own career, now as a wealth advisor, required a very steady start-up process. No mistakes. Same as the old F-14. But I was in a new town, where I'd never lived before, and where I did not know a single soul, except for a few buddies I'd served with. However, the Pentagon would not be first choice for a financier searching for the local billionaires.

This would take time, care, and patience. I realized I needed to connect to the very best people and families. I had a solid knowledge of where they should invest their wealth, and I had solid plans to ensure they would not lose it. I elected to make contact with the top estate-planning attorneys in the city, old and trusted Washington law firms, whose advice had been heeded for generations. I was a fearless cold-caller, because I knew that was the only way for me to make contact.

But I had a well-thought-out story, and to be honest I was surprised how receptive they were. Obviously quite early on in the conversation, I told them my background and almost without exception I sensed an immediate response.

I guess there's something about being called by an ex-front-line fighter pilot in the US Navy. Not because such men are necessarily better than

anyone else, but because of the Navy, the military, especially among educated people, especially in the city where stands the colossus of the US
military, the Pentagon, the largest office building on earth.

In Washington there is a distinct aura about both serving and retired
US naval personnel, men who have been implicitly trusted with the most
expensive military hardware in the world, men whose integrity is a given.
Washington is only thirty miles from Annapolis. The former midshipmen
are all over the place in D.C. Everyone knows the only thing for which
you can be thrown out of the Academy is lying. There's just something
about the culture of dark blue in this city, and in my new career, it did me
no harm whatsoever.

People were receptive right from the start, and many of them were curious about this extraordinary man Roy Neuberger. They were also interested in Lehman Brothers. I was actually surprised how many of them
were seeking opportunities for their clients. Remember, these people were
lawyers, and cautious, and we shared the same mind-set: the preservation
of wealth.

Within a very few weeks, my regular stomping ground was along the
finest streets in the capital, calling on people in the most opulent offices
and discussing investment plans with incredibly smart attorneys. Right
here I was with the TOPGUN fighter pilots of the legal profession, men
and women who really understood their craft.

We talked over ideas for new investments to place into existing trust
vehicles. Unlike some of my more avaricious colleagues at Lehman, they
were riveted by my suggestion that all was not well in the world of derivatives, and if the subprime mortgages ever went drastically wrong, there
would be Armageddon on Wall Street.

I know that some of them moved immediately upon my advice, no
fees, no invoices. But that was the spirit in which I gave it. This was a careful waiting game. And I guessed correctly that these people would open
the gate for Neuberger Berman to forge lasting partnerships with these
powerful and civilized attorneys and their clients.

No one was in a hurry. Those clients were supremely wealthy already,
and no one was chomping at the bit to treble what they already had. The
rules were sparse and simple: *don't lose my fortune, and stay away from
high-risk investments.* I guess we were made for each other.

Meanwhile, back at the factory on Seventh Avenue, Lehman was busy with their ARS Division (Absolute Return Strategies), riding the wave of profits that had not been interrupted for almost five years. During my early months they moved into a new stream of cash flow, urging clients to "pay to play."

This was a devilish little scheme, and so far as I could tell, it was inaugurated when they paid heaven knows how much—I believe hundreds of millions of borrowed dollars—to gain access to a hedge fund that had been closed to investors for some time. This was a classic brainstorm of the Structured Products Desk, and it opened the door to a brilliant new scheme.

They offered clients this rarefied access to a fund that was so successful it was refusing to accept any more shareholders, and Lehman was charging clients a hefty fee to arrange that point of entry. I was not so sure about that, since the firm was already collecting fees on the investment, and right here they were just loading on another fee, because of their own choice of vehicle.

It obviously proved highly profitable. The structured-product guys jumped into this "access" business with both feet. Lehman's storm troopers rushed out and bought "access" to a whole group of previously closed funds. This opened the door to a stampede of Lehman and Neuberger clients rushing into these "best of the best" funds.

But I suspected there was a lot of mortgage and real estate investment in there, and there was huge pressure from the head office to get clients in and then charge the big fees. I never did think much of it and preferred to keep my people in the core side of the business, with their money in stocks and bonds, which I could watch personally and make sure nothing suspect was going on. All that new stuff seemed to me slightly over the top.

You will have gathered that the central management of Lehman Brothers was very big on control. All new products were recommended and fired out to every corner of this vast business all over the world, urging every one of their leading brokers and managers to get in and sell.

These guys were control-freak supremos—if they'd been in the Holy Land a couple of millennium ago, they'd have provided an armed escort, navigator, and lifeguards for Jesus when he walked across the Sea of

Galilee: *yeah, yeah, we know you're the son of God . . . just wanna make sure you're doing this right.*

Their central electronic database was something else. They insisted that everyone worldwide log in the names of every potential client or anyone who might refer us business. All electronic documents had to be filed in the client management system, which was just a warehouse to store details and information—stuff like the potential client's wife's birthday, or his kids' favorite pastimes, whether they had pets or ponies for their daughters.

The volume of detail in there was incredible. And it was all completely useless. I couldn't stand it—reminded me of the KGB. Of course its real purpose was for the bosses on Seventh Avenue to peer into our schedules and check on our activities. It allowed them to sit in their command center and look at all the glorious amounts of money that might be coming into the firm.

Naturally it was grotesquely inefficient. And I found it as offensive as I found the amount of hours it took to navigate this clumsy reporting machine—apparently to inform Dick Fuld of the name, age, and rank of my client's new dog.

I have to say that after all my years in the Navy, where young commanders were entrusted with great responsibilities, this feeling of being watched over the whole time was not much fun. The Navy made you report every last part of your mission, but they essentially let you get on with it. This stuff at Lehman, and indeed Neuberger, was kind of stifling.

But like everyone else, I just pressed on, plying my patient trade among the attorneys who guarded the wealth of this great American capital city. I never slipped into the habit of showering people with gifts and expensive dinners, and I never did get into that wine-sniffing charade. Neither could I get into the mind-set of kissing up to these attorneys, basically trying to bribe them for an introduction to their client.

That was not my way. I wanted to meet these people because I had the correct plan for them, because I knew how to invest and protect their wealth. I did not want to see them because this attorney liked living the high life on Lehman Brothers' ticket. I wanted them to believe I had it right, that I would lose no one's money, and when the time was correct, we would make them a reasonable profit.

I turned out to be pretty good at it too. I had issued a ton of advice to my private clients before I ever came to Neuberger. In the first six months in my new position, I explained to my new friends in the Washington law offices that any major clients considering working with me had to get the hell out of their mortgage and real estate investments, especially residential.

So far as I know, everyone heeded this advice. I never put a client into any of those crazy products involved in the subprime crisis. As I mentioned earlier, any damn fool could see that catastrophe coming. Remember, I was not an investor for clients, I was a wealth advisor. My role was to guide them and their attorneys into the correct trust vehicles in the Neuberger Berman fold.

And there were some very good ones. Roy Neuberger had selected some excellent portfolio managers who had been there for years, top-class experienced men, never those typical short-term investment guys, looking for the main chance, and ever ready with excuses, lightning-fast to blame something. Actually Wall Street might very well be the blame capital of the world: *the market went down because of 9/11 . . . Saddam . . . World-Com . . . Enron . . . oil . . . Middle East . . . war . . . peace . . . the Fed printing money . . . recession . . . depression . . . obsession . . .* whatever.

Never just because things actually went down, as they always have and always will. No, I really liked and admired some of the outstanding people at Neuberger, and in many ways this "little" firm was all I had hoped for. It was the gigantic shadow of Lehman Brothers standing over us all that I found somewhat unnerving. They were probably the most grasping organization I'd ever known. But I guess when you're around $450 billion in the hole that can spur you on a bit. The upshot of this was a highly quantitative but impersonal approach to business.

I cannot tell you the number of graphs, charts, and statistics that were produced, all designed to demonstrate to us that the Lehman way was, in every case, the correct way. In the end I actually considered that the maelstrom of data proved only that no one can control the markets.

Those graphs, charts, and stats evolved because Lehman Brothers, and all of its subsidiaries (us), were under orders to work to one objective: profit, or, as they say, the bottom line. Because this governed the bonus system, and whereas the Christmas bonus for all the top managers was suitably generous, everything paled before the multimillion-dollar harvest that cascaded every year into the personal bank accounts of Lehman Chairman Fuld and his number-two man, Joe Gregory. Not to put too fine a point on it, but they lived like a couple of White rajas.

The rest of us battled away on a far, far lower pay scale, and the knowledge of the Fuld/Gregory annual cash grab inevitably clarified the true objective of this shockingly leveraged organization. The two men whose hands were most firmly on the tiller stood to gain a vast fortune every year, probably, even in real terms, one hundred times more than the victor of the Battle of Midway, Admiral Nimitz, was ever paid in his life.

And that's why Lehman grew into an impersonal and excessively greedy corporation. Its two leaders were prepared to risk the entire ship to reap their personal reward. In my view, during 2007 it all stood a fighting chance of ending in tears, and like most fighter pilots, I knew a lot about those.

But even as the whole house of cards lurched and rumbled toward its ghastly conclusion, I remember with great fondness and admiration a couple of ladies, one inside the firm, one outside, both of whom I counted as corporate friends. One of them was Maria Pappas, a charming woman who was not much short of a mathematical genius, especially on the subject of corporate and government bonds.

What she did not know about fixed income investing was scarcely worth knowing. Maria steered many, many wealthy clients into the correct and safest havens through all the troubles that lurked ahead. The unspoken fact inside the company was that she alone looked after Roy Neuberger's personal fixed-income portfolio. If there's a bigger compliment than that in all of Wall Street, I'd be interested to hear it.

Louise Yamada was another of my all-time favorites. She ran her own operation, and it goes without saying that she was also a financial genius. A tiny woman, barely five feet tall, she offered a smile and a greeting to light up Yankee Stadium. Like me, she had achieved that inordinately difficult Chartered Market Technicians designation, and we each carried that prized "CMT" after our names.

Louise had occupied an exalted position at the former Smith Barney (Citigroup) wealth management empire and had been advising clients for years that should there be an almighty crash—which she plainly feared—the place to be was gold. Many, many investors subsequently awarded her a deified reputation.

When I first heard Louise suggest this, in spring of 2007, the price of gold stood at around $650 an ounce. Since then it has more than doubled, easily withstanding the calamities of 2008, standing tall among the commodities. As I write this in the middle of 2011, gold is selling on the bullion markets for $1,500 an ounce.

It was in that late autumn of 2007, with such obvious dark clouds forming on the horizon, that I began to have the gravest doubts about the Lehman operation. I was absolutely aware of the scale of the company's debt, and I was equally aware of the balance sheets of the other major Wall Street firms, especially Bear Stearns. All around us disaster threatened.

The credit default swaps market had died and seemed poised to take down the biggest insurance corporation in the world, AIG. The demise of these CDS derivatives was also dealing silent hammer blows to Bear Stearns and Lehman. But the real killer was the subprime mortgage market. The international banks and hedge funds that had been buying up those CDO bonds marketed by all the big US investment banks were just beginning to become unnerved.

The huge wave of default mortgages, foreclosures, and bankrupt builders had not yet hit home. But the signs were ominous. It seemed everyone was afraid the roof was about to fall in. And it was growing harder and harder to sell them.

A few months ago, foreign banks and funds would have torn your hand off to get ahold of those rock-solid bonds; they were rated AAA by the agencies, and mortgage-backed, and everyone pays their mortgage, right? Just a few of us understood this might not be the case indefinitely, not in the age of the no-cash-down house purchase.

Slowly the world began to close in on us. There were signs of wariness all over the company, the first one being a dire warning that none of us should use the color printer. Black and white would be fine, and apparently cheaper.

However, my own truly serious warning arrived one November afternoon while I was waiting at LaGuardia airport. An e-mail suddenly arrived from my friend Nick Bhuta at Goldman Sachs, a CMT and former student of mine. I called him back, and he told me there was an online article in a Condé Nast publication called Portfolio.com.

It appeared under the headline "Wall Street Requiem," which quite frankly did not seem all that encouraging given this was the week of the color-printer ban. The tagline read, "The big investment banks, loaded with dangerous amounts of debt, are facing their own version of a sub-prime slump. Can they all survive?"

The story expressed concern about the plight of the heavily leveraged state of Bear Stearns and others like it, including Lehman. It pointed out that Drexel Burnham Lambert had gone south, and Salomon Brothers had survived only on a Warren Buffett bailout. First Boston had "fled into the arms" of Credit Suisse, and Bear Stearns was currently "full of cow-boys" and very much "in the cross-hairs."

Goldman Sachs shares had risen 240 percent, Lehman 200 percent. The rising markets had caused the investment banks to load up on assets and borrowing. But they were "buying high," which the writer considered was not much of a business model. It added that Lehman's leverage was more than thirty times capital, which I already knew.

Thus, if assets dropped 3 percent, Lehman's entire equity would be wiped out. Jesus Christ! I could see the CDOs crashing 50 percent, and the credit default swaps the same.

The writer, Jesse Eisinger, also stated that the most dangerous kind of assets were known in the trade as level-three, which he described as "atomic." It then said Bear Stearns, Lehman, and Goldman were like frat boys at a sports bar, binging on very dangerous stuff. Bear had $18 billion level-three assets on its balance sheet. Lehman had 104 percent of its entire book value in level-three, with Goldman at 141.

There is, said the writer, an end-of-era feel to the whole thing, making it plain he felt the game was almost certainly up.

I'll admit I found the whole thing chilling. In so many ways the article was confirming what I knew but did not much want to face. And from there on, I could feel the operation going south.

We reached Christmas and were told that there would be forced econ-omizing: bonus payments to all staff would be cut. Except apparently for those being paid to Dick Fuld and Joe Gregory, who collected in stock and cash payments one of their biggest-ever year-end rewards: $35 mil-lion and $29 million, respectively.

In the new year the cutbacks bit even more deeply. Aside from the color printer, our corporate credit card bills were being paid later and later. Maybe some ultra-extravagant guys might have felt a bit guilty about their expenses, but I was not among them. I had never fallen into the big expense account hotel syndrome, nor indeed the expensed dinner routine, night after night. My credit card numbers were strict expenditure on the firm's behalf. Those late paybacks, from the company to me, were a major pain in the ass. I was out the money, not them.

In my opinion, the Wall Street banks were in big trouble, being crushed by their own crippling debt. But the one that looked certain to crash was Bear Stearns, and a run started on the eighty-five-year-old investment bank, which had survived 1929. Their stock had crashed from a 2007 high of $170 to $10.

The run was mostly because they held murderous subprime exposure, and by now these bonds could not be sold. No one in their right mind would touch them. The subprime bonanza was over. Mortgage holders were defaulting, and sometimes fleeing, all over the country, especially in California. Bear's bankers were refusing them credit.

This meant that loans could not be repaid, and in mid-March 2008, the partners of the fabled Bear Stearns were preparing, in a matter of days, to file for bankruptcy.

Wall Street literally shuddered. Immediately both the Treasury and the Fed were called in to help deal with the crisis. An enormous bank collapse on Wall Street at this time could have a devastating effect on world markets. The subprime calamity and the onrushing CDS disaster were bad enough without that.

Treasury Secretary Hank Paulson summoned JPMorgan Chase to save the stricken investment house. And the US government, for the first time ever, pumped trillions into such a crisis. They backed Morgan and eventually persuaded their CEO, Jamie Dimon, to buy Bear Stearns for the knockdown price of ten bucks a share. It was March 17, and the St. Patrick's Day rescue entered the annals of Wall Street near-misses.

When I looked at Neuberger's general business operations, nothing was all that bad. It was the Lehman situation that was troubling me. Every possible sign of a corporation in dire trouble was happening. There was the strong inside rumor of a new bond issue, which I considered to be something close to a potential fraud, since the firm had sufficient debt to sink New York, never mind itself. Any damn fool could tell that $450 billion could never be paid back in full.

All over the corporation there were these classic signals: the sudden change in chief financial officer, the shattering resignations of some of the best financiers in the firm, rumors of fights between the leading managers and the men on the thirty-first floor, Fuld and Gregory.

There were some huge losses, and the stock was starting to tank, way down from the all-time highs being applauded that day I first met my big-spending colleagues in New York City. Some of the major investment brains in the city were beginning to question Lehman's public presentation of their annual report. The great David Einhorn—America's most brilliant hedge fund manager and president of Greenlight Capital—was merciless. At one stage he thought the corporation had a $748 billion asset risk over real capital of only $17 billion. He also thought losses were being hidden.

He considered the $4 billion proposed bond issue as some kind of joke, "bond" being merely another word for "debt." As if Lehman didn't have enough.

When a corporation is going down the tubes, there is an innate restlessness. You can feel it everywhere. And it had spread to Neuberger Berman, just in the short months I'd been there. Right now, in that deathly spring of a thousand cuts, I'd had four bosses in a year. This was no place for me. The ship was going down, no doubt in my mind. And there was no merit in going down with it.

And so, on my forty-fourth birthday, May 12, 2008, I tendered my resignation to that fourth boss. I had a few misgivings, a couple of regrets about going, but I still wanted to plow my own furrow and start my own financial business.

I believed I had an advanced method of investing money for clients while avoiding the risks. If I ever found myself in a potential loss-maker, it would always be minor. I'm a Naval Aviator, and I'm never going to just sit there as a stock hurtles into the ground.

I'm going to hit that Martin-Baker GRU-7A ejection seat before the goddamned engine even knows it's on fire. Just the way TOPGUN taught me, same system, same mind-set: *My attainable goal is to become the safest pair of hands on Wall Street. I've set my objective, I've made my plan, I've briefed myself for a thousand hours. And now I'm going to execute.*

## CHAPTER 12

# In the Ancient Land of Blame

Everyone knows why I left the US Navy. And most of them understand why I went for a short, planned five-year commission in the Ohio Air National Guard. But I had to ponder long and hard, even after the fact, to establish precisely why I left the Lehman Brothers–owned Neuberger Berman. Especially since Roy was still alive at the time.

By a process of elimination, I did not bail out for money. I was perfectly adequately rewarded for my work. It was nothing to do with location. I grew to love Washington, with its ties to the Navy, and Norfolk and Annapolis, and the great shorelines of Maryland and Virginia.

I liked almost all the Neuberger people, and I thought they ran a pretty good operation and that we had a fighting chance of surviving what I believed was the oncoming Wall Street Armageddon. It was Lehman that bothered me, and I must admit I thought it might drag us all down with it.

But that wasn't what drove me away. I've always accepted the possibility of going down with the ship. Every naval officer understands that. It was something else, and whenever I examined it, I always returned to the same conclusion.

It was that Wall Street state of mind, the all-encompassing creed of self first. Beyond Neuberger, I never saw anyone put the client's interests before their own. Every new product, every investment idea, every new pop-up plan from the Structured Product Desk was specifically designed to earn more and more fees for Lehman, the ultimate fee machine.

It reminded me of that song from *Les Misérables,* "Master of the House": "Everything has got a little price . . . two percent for looking in the mirror twice . . . three percent for sleeping with the window shut . . ."

> When it comes to fixing prices
> There are lots of tricks he knows,
> How it all increases,
> All them bits and pieces
> Jesus! It's amazing how it grows!

And parked up there on the thirty-first floor were a couple of megalomaniacs demanding *more! more! more!* before going home for Christmas with a grand total of $64 million in their personal rucksacks. All this while David Einhorn was preparing to say straight out that Lehman Brothers was hiding multibillion-dollar losses.

He also wanted to know how the firm could possibly be trying to raise capital with a new bond when they had never even mentioned markdowns in their property portfolio, in a current commercial market that had crashed between 15 and 25 percent. *Raising capital without disclosing losses?* It beat the hell out of David, who mentioned archly that he thought "the whole thing stinks."

And I guess it was the subterfuge that ultimately got to me. The whole strategy of saying one thing to clients and quite another to each other, of saying one thing to the analysts and something different to our own financial officers, of saying one thing to the shareholders and meaning something else entirely different.

Withholding financial information, hiding, obfuscating, operating to a secret agenda, knowingly allowing something to be believed that was indisputably false: like, *Here are the valuations of our multibillion-dollar commercial property empire. And yes, we know the market has crashed, but for our own purposes we don't count that. We just enter the same number we paid out in the first case, instead of reporting billions of lost dollars.*

I was just not accustomed to that; I was not accustomed to anything but the whole, unvarnished, concept of *truth.* And I understand there will be smart, glib, and cunning investment bankers who will call me naive, but if that's so, I served in an organization upon which our nation depends for its safety and freedom, and we're all naive, the whole goddamned lot of us. We might occasionally utter some flowery phrases to confuse our enemy, or to avoid mass panic, but we never, ever lie to each other or to those with whom we work.

In corporate America you never know who the hell's telling the truth and who's not. And in the end, for all the slyness of the banks, the truth caught up. It always does. There's no avoiding it, and that's what they teach every potential naval officer in the first hour on the first day of his enrollment in the United States Naval Academy: *don't even think about lying . . . not here.*

And I return to the point. If lying had not been such an accepted part of the culture, if places like Lehman had somehow come under the ferocious scrutiny of naval admirals, the crash of 2008 would not have happened. How could it have? The abyss of the downside of all those subprime bonds would have been revealed probably two years before.

Certainly the crash of the property market would have been taken into consideration. And the death-defying antics of the stupid stock market would have been revealed, rather than allowing an army of brokers to rush around recommending that this was the time to make money—right here at the top of a market displaying every classic sign of an impending correction. Hell, even I could see that. And I'd only been around for a few months.

Under the rule of the admirals, Lehman never would have been allowed to leverage the firm forty-four times—and then try to sell bonds in their wonderful prosperous company, which carried enough debt to bail out the Dark Continent.

It was all of the above that drove me from the investment banks—a Wall Street world that would be better described as Bandwagon Street: get on board and ride it to hell, until it collapses under its own gigantic debt and has to be bailed out by the US government before it brings down the whole world. With Lehman I was just fraught with worry it would bring down Neuberger.

And when my soul-searching was concluded and I had finally faced precisely who I was, I came up with a few home truths: (1) I was probably the worst liar on earth, (2) I have a conscience about misleading people that keeps me awake at night, (3) I am scared to death of risk, (4) I will do darn near anything to avoid it, (5) I need to prove myself right, (6) I don't need glory or excessive money, just to know that my endless studies and my thoroughness have come through, and (7) that I have kept all those associated with me safe. Just the way they taught me at TOPGUN.

Some may consider me ultracautious, but that's just something I have to live with. I once fired my best client, an investor whose wealth was responsible for half of my income. And I did it because he would not listen to me and kept making extravagant mistakes, losing substantial money in high-risk investments. I could not bear to watch it, and if I'm honest, I really could not bear to be associated with it.

Wall Street contained just too much flying by the seat of your pants for me. As you know by now, I operate only by the hard facts displayed on my instrument panel. I once wrote out a little scenario of some fly-by-night stock broker going on a mission in an F-14 Tomcat:

1. He'd study how to get as high and as fast as possible in the shortest time.
2. He'd skip through the flight manual, just reading enough to start up the aircraft and get the landing gear up on takeoff.
3. He'd arrive in one of the big Lehman black limos right at the aircraft steps and have an assistant fire it up.
4. He'd jump in the jet and charge down the runway on full afterburners without the slightest idea how much gas he had or how long it would last.
5. He'd accelerate to six hundred knots and pull the aircraft upward, loaded with G-forces, all the way to 50,000 feet, where the engines would undoubtedly stall.
6. As the aircraft began to fall, perhaps in an uncontrolled spin, he'd be wondering who the hell screwed this thing up.
7. He'd have no plan of action to kick in the emergency procedure and pull out of this nosedive. God knows where the flight manual is.
8. Suddenly, right before the F-14 crashed into the sea, he would somehow magically replace himself with his client and leave him holding the bag.

9. Sitting in his life raft, he'd survey the wreckage rather proudly, because there was another aircraft, driven by one of his colleagues, smashed into the ocean about a minute earlier. *Not so good as me, right?*

10. And then there would be other brokers, all in their life rafts, all collectively blaming the aircraft manufacturer, or the ground controller, or the weathermen for screwing it up.

Here endeth the parable of the men who were called stockbrokers, from the land of the street called Wall, in the home of the brave called America, in which thou shalt never be caught with thy pants around thine ankles, for fear of having thine testicles cut asunder before the great wrath of the men who are called executive-ites.

Verily I say that you must not linger until the setting sun, but go immediately to seek out the ancient philosophies of the land called Blame, and with those great fantasies, thou must smite thine enemies, which will turn out to be damn nearly everyone, except for thine senior partners, who, on the coming Day of Judgment, will enter the fires of hell for the deadly sin of greed beyond redemption.

All this will come to pass when the shit shall hitteth the fan on the street that is called Wall.

I just needed to clarify the mind-set of so many stockbrokers. All of them pale beside the diligence and level of study practiced by the sharp end of the US military. And one of the purposes of this book was for me to offer a clarification of the world of investment.

It was in fact a matter of clarification that did, I think, drive me out of the Lehman empire. I missed the purity of thought that was always present in the Navy, that absolute certainty of what we were actually doing, supposed to be doing, and how it should be achieved, and why. This whole business of having to tell one story to the client, another to a colleague, and something else to the boss is very wearing and very wrong.

Over that year in Washington, I came up with a list of phrases and trip wires about which every investor should be forewarned. In the end, they are all flaws consistently perpetuated by the investment world. They're bear traps.

*1. Leverage.* This really is the dark side of Wall Street. Excessive leverage kills. It was the red flashing beacon that alerted me to Lehman's possible downfall almost before I'd hung up my coat. Same for Bear Stearns. Everyone, whether they knew it or not, had fallen off the cliff in the fall of 2007, purely because of their borrowing.

The trouble is, Wall Street uses leverage to beat the markets, to borrow and then plunge back into a losing stock on the way down, trying to hide the screw-up. It's reckless and filled with totally unacceptable risk.

*2. Downside risk.* This is the part Wall Street does not wish to tackle or even mention. They'll trim down the graphs that illustrate the potential for losses. They'll even dismiss old data by using longer time periods to assess historical performance, stressing their old-fashioned "buy and hold" attitude.

Most brokers grew up in an age when the market only went up—from 1982 to 2000. And every sell-off since then has always been blamed on some outside force: 9/11, Enron, etc. It has never been their fault. No one has stood up and "taken their grade." Neither have they ever made risk control an absolute priority. Make that your first question: How do you protect me?

*3. Liquidity.* "Lock-ups" happen when your money is trapped in an investment for a predetermined time, sometimes for a year. Even when it's "only" three months, hedge fund bosses and investment bankers can refuse to let people out. And here comes that tired old sermon: *it's a complete privilege to be invested here in the first place.*

Lehman created funds like this, and when they went down, investors could not get their money out. Looking back, they'd only been sold the upside and never even shown the downside. *Never, ever* get into something without an irrevocable escape clause. And if you cannot get one, don't invest. No one flies a strike fighter without an ejection seat. The admirals would not allow it.

*4. Fiduciary behavior.* Brokers keep their clients invested in the biggest income generators for the firm, and for themselves. They are paid from the revenue generated by management fees. Instead of putting the clients in, say, bonds, which provide lower revenue, brokers are obviously motivated to keep them in high-potential stocks, even when the markets are going down. You must demand to know the precise bailout point for any falling stock. Do not leave it to your broker. Your interests are not the same and never will be.

**5. Beware the silken phrases.** Only on Wall Street, after the stock market has fallen 50 percent, could a manger create a phrase like "basis points"— a highly devious method of moving the decimal point, turning 1 percent into "100 basis points," with the objective of making a huge deal out of almost nothing.

If a manager, for example, lost 49 percent when the market crashed 50, he'd say he "outperformed the market by 100 basis points." Have you ever heard a level of pure, southern-fried bullshit greater than that?

It's just a somewhat maddening obsession among Wall Street brokers that they somehow "beat the market," however narrowly. You'll never find one who just stands up and takes his grade: *the friggin' market just went down, and I went down with it, losing the following gigantic amount of your cash.*

If Wall Street could bear to bring itself to say such a thing, they'd probably have a collective thrombosis. In the US Navy, you had better say it, straight out, or you risk court-martial, for deliberately obscuring the truth from senior commanders.

**6. Bad math.** Watch out for phrases like capital asset pricing model (CAPM). It's a theory Wall Street loves to expound to clients. They don't understand it properly. You should not pay attention. And it stems from their way of determining their asset allocation.

To do this they make a plot, which is supposed to organize a mix of stocks and bonds. They'll tell you that with 100 percent bonds you will get 2 percent returns for 2 percent of risk. That's a ratio of 1:1. With 100 percent stocks, you might get 10 percent return for 20 percent risk, 1:2.

Did you ever hear anything that crazy? Ten units of reward for twenty units of risk—a return-risk ratio of one-half. You risk twenty bucks to make ten. If you mix up the stocks and bonds you might get to 6 percent returns for 10 percent risk, but you're still batting less than 1. It's still bad math, and anything less than 1 is totally suspect. However they phrase it, stay away.

**7. *Revealing numbers.*** Everyone reports their numbers differently on Wall Street. Everyone represents themselves in the finest possible light, skating deftly around the bad months when returns were less than acceptable. If a dollar became worth two dollars in ten years, you would almost certainly be told their annual return was 7.2 percent.

But if the manager had turned the same dollar into five dollars in the first six years and then had four awful years, and turned it back into two, that 7.2 percent annual return would be a grotesque distortion, because some clients in the past four years would have lost sixty cents on the dollar. Beware the annualized returns. They can be very tricky. Ten-year returns should be calculated using rolling twelve month periods: 120 results over a decade, which would give investors a fair chance of seeing precisely what the manager's results really were.

The answer lies in the methods of the Navy. Make it standard, make reporting numbers rigidly the same for everyone, as laid down by the admirals. That way there's no bullshit.

**8. *Cheerleaders on the airwaves.*** The markets have dived three hundred points. The news is bleak. There might just as easily be another three hundred–point crash tomorrow. But what do we hear on the slightest upward rally? "We're off the session lows," or "We're 50 percent off the bottom today." Unless it's in free fall, we're always "off the lows." Always something chipper, for obvious reasons.

Nonetheless, it's the same as Moose telling me that old Spuds ripped one hundred cannon bullets straight into us, but during the last attack it was only fifty. Hot damn! We're 50 percent better right there. Let's go long again. It might be only twenty-five tomorrow. We're still dead, still badly beaten. Though no one wants to phrase it quite like that.

**9. *Ignoring risk.*** This is a Wall Street marketing specialty, "overselling the upside," deflecting the possibility that things could go bust, holding on grimly to bad investments. To this day I know people who were buying Lehman stock all the way down, convinced it would come back. The only thing I know that has never been worth zero is gold, and in the past, even that has fallen several hundred dollars in value.

## CONCLUSION

Investors should think like fighter pilots. This is not a game for Wall Street thrill seekers. Do not relish the high drama of a strike fighter that can climb to insane heights. Remember the jet fighter ace is compelled to master every single aspect of that aircraft before he's even allowed to touch it. He has to learn what can go wrong and what to do when it does.

Every one of them is an expert at managing risk. They know when it's getting dangerous, and in split a second they'll wave-off from a landing, cut all potential losses, and fly out into clean air. If your broker had been to TOPGUN, he'd never ride a stock investment into the ground, swearing he'd been right all along. They simply do not think like that. The admirals would not like it.

### ▶ *My Recommendations to the Masters of the Universe*

When I put together a tactical solution for clients, I use all the data. I never throw out anything bad about a particular stock or bond. And I never make excuses for it. It happened. I'm trying to preserve wealth and overcome even the slightest loss. I do not care what the stock market is doing.

I have no desire to tell anyone I "outperformed," despite a down market; those who do are just confirming their performance was not as terrible as the market's, which I consider to be amazingly uninteresting. I'm concerned with absolute return strategies, which can get a proper grip on the downside.

These are highly tactical, based on what could go wrong, rather than right. They have no concern about being better than the stock market, only that they had the risk element buttoned up tight. Built into this strategy is the sure knowledge that this could possibly go wrong. And then you get out, precisely when you told the client you would.

You buy a $100 stock, and if it goes below your maximum allowable loss level—determined well in advance—you are gone, and you take the hit. If the stock continues downward, you might get back in, if you have good reason to believe it's a sound and solid corporation with little debt. But, *you do not RIDE it down, trying to prove you were right all along.*

With an absolute return strategy, you do not "buy and hold," because your concern is always risk. Absolute return strategies represent a higher calling. And if it drops in value, step forward that broker, almost immediately, and *take your grade*. Get out. It's not your money.

For any broker dealing with high–net worth individuals, preservation of wealth is all there is. The upside's just a pleasant bonus; the heart and soul of the investment is the downside. Try to remember, *hope is not a strategy*.

If you make a bad call on a stock, get to your feet and take your grade instantly. Make no excuses for your poor performance. Recognize it, examine it, and *learn* from it. Don't do it again, and try not to fear getting better.

Take in more data, and reexamine the old stuff. In all investments, you will only use the average of upside performance. But always use the *absolute worst* of all downside results.

I feel like I'm teaching a class at the Academy, because these rules I'm laying out are elementary to the US Navy. And they should be to the investment manager who is concerned with preserving wealth.

And if you have not yet mastered that mind-set, remember, they would not even let you into the front gate of the Navy Fighter Weapons School. The admirals *never* squander their assets and will not tolerate anyone who even dreams of doing so.

And now for the four words chiseled deep into the marble tablets of US Navy command, four words that govern every mission we undertake, by land, by sea, and by air. They are the four words by which every naval battle commander lives; by which every Navy SEAL team operates; and by which every Naval Aviator runs his entire existence. There are no exceptions, and they should be hammered into the granite ramparts of Wall Street:

Plan. Brief. Execute. Debrief.

That's the way the SEALs ran their assault on the al-Qaeda stronghold in Abbottabad. That's the way the SEALs run everything. They ran their ground operations in north Baghdad like that every night in 2003. We flew the strike fighters over the Iraqi capital under those rules. Admiral Nimitz fought the Battle of Midway like that.

Those were the four iron words that surrounded the US assault on Tora Bora in Afghanistan. Let me offer this six-point directive to the Masters of the Universe:

*1. Set the objective.*   If it's not clear, and attainable, don't do it. A true military objective should have evolved from a revered and hallowed process passed down through generations. No guesswork. Wall Street does not begin to understand this, which is why they spent years trying to convince people the almost impossible level of returns of the 1990s was normal and certainly would go on forever, if not longer.

We even saw them levering up portfolios they had under management. They actually drove up the stock prices of General Motors, and Lehman, and AIG, piling in with more and more borrowed money, swearing to God it would all come right, before all three of those organizations went spectacularly bankrupt, gasping for government money.

Reason: the objective was never attainable. Not with debts and obligations like they had. The false promises of the brokers never came true. Just remember, millions of investors in their seventies, worldwide, got hurt. But Wall Street marched along, stepping in time to the drumbeat of their own objective, rather than that of the client, and striding toward an unattainable victory.

To my knowledge, the US Navy has never done that. The admirals and their senior commanders have to OK the objective. And should they consider there may be unacceptable losses, the mission is instantly aborted . . . *let's try something else.*

*2. Plan.*   This is initially designed to maximize the odds of achieving the objective, which has already been judged as achievable. Wall Street does not really know how to plan. They think they do, but few of them have grasped even the basic truth that no plan survives first contact with the enemy. And that's when you need to regroup, rethink, maybe sell your investment, protect and preserve wealth, get ready to fight another day.

I am accustomed to taking action the moment we encounter a surprise. We are already prepared for every kind of contingency, for what might go wrong. The trick is to recognize the threat and then move fast, keeping everyone informed. We never just "buy and hold," sitting on our collective ass and hoping for the best. No fighter pilot–turned–investment manager would ever stand by and watch his client lose all his money. That idle hopefulness is not in our DNA. Hope is not, after all, a strategy.

When we planned that mission to take out Saddam Hussein's air force in the summer of 2000, we knew there were serious risks. All we thought about were the risks. Missiles here, MiG-23s all over the place, risks we couldn't even account for. And even after the mission was scrubbed on that first day, we went right back at it, assessed it all again, studied more satellite photographs.

We even updated the plan for the following day, all over again: the distance, the refueling track, the strike route, the airspeed, the altitude, the formations, the drop zones, the target area, the route back out to the coast, the commands, call signs, procedures if someone got hit, tactics if the Iraqis got airborne.

Just imagine if Wall Street put that much work into their investments. For a start, they might get those huge "bubbles" under control, just by downgrading the likelihood of stocks going that high, based on so little data. Certainly people might sleep a little easier at night, if their broker could restrain his tendency to reach for the stars before they'd even refueled the space shuttle.

Most of those Wall Street "plans" would be thrown immediately overboard by the admirals, based on an unacceptable downside, too-high expectations, backed by no historical precedent. They might yet again remind the lightweight investment "planner" that hope is not a strategy.

**3. Brief.** You never have occasion to abandon the brief. That is a Navy rule followed religiously by the SEALs, the battle commanders, and Naval Aviators. I have often asked Wall Street guys how they actually brief themselves before they log in to their trading terminals every day.

Most of them just stare at me half-wittedly. This is because their idea of the brief is to turn on the television and hear what the commentators are saying, or alternately, they may scour their Bloomberg terminals looking for hot tips. I once made the mistake of asking someone how he proposed to sit down and physically calculate the amount of money he might lose on a trade. I thought he was going to order me out of the building for gross impertinence.

Here was a man whose god was hope, whose temple was the Christmas bonus, and whose judgment was dominated by the idols of the upside. Worse yet, like most of Wall Street, he had not yet accepted that investment bankers, by and large, tended to be human beings, and sometimes they were not perfect. In a thousand years he never would have comprehended the Navy checklists, or why we have them. Why we never move without them.

We actually have them for everything. Even for a routine task—for us—like flying strike fighter aircraft off a carrier, we still run our checklists. We still brief. Even I brief, and I've kicked those howling Tomcat strike fighters off those flight decks more than 440 times. I am still treated like a man who must check it all out first. Every single time. The same would apply to Captain Neil Armstrong.

We always talk it over, no matter what, because the number of combat mistakes that have been highlighted, and then prevented, just by the brief cannot even be calculated. No plan, however brilliantly conceived, is foolproof.

Remember that soft cat shot when Chunx and I were nearly killed trying to get off the USS *Abraham Lincoln*? We'd briefed that very scenario less than an hour before. When that catapult flung us forward, when Chunx yelled for the 'burners, I knew in that millisecond what he was saying. I knew what had happened. I didn't know why. But I knew what to do. And I rammed those 'burners on without a question in my mind. If I had not done so, we would have punched a hole in the Pacific Ocean at two hundred mph.

Wall Street is light-years behind us. Just imagine if Lehman had actually briefed itself daily on the things that were going wrong. Maybe certain people would have understood the level of stupidity that was leading them to the precipice of the greatest bankruptcy in history.

Where were the hard-eyed financial "admirals"—the men who should have been there, when departmental heads spoke only to Fuld and Gregory, all of them relishing the prospect of the wealth to come.

Where was the growling "Bull" Halsey demanding to know the range of the Japanese kamikaze: *Are they close enough to hit the carriers? How many US fighters can we launch in the next fifteen minutes? Who's gonna nail Yamamoto's flagship? What if we're late? Where's the nearest US submarine? What if we lose a destroyer? Can we take their first carrier with torpedoes?*

Men like that save lives, and in banking they save people's wealth. Their thoroughness raises the standards, and it all comes out in the brief.

If Lehman had followed the basic management procedures of the US Navy, I'll say again, they probably would have survived.

**4. Execute.** Wall Street kind of knows "how to execute." But really they know little more than just how to place orders, buy things up, and sell them off. The question is, do they really have any way to measure when something is going wrong, when they must do something? Can they tell the difference between a blip and a corporate catastrophe that will lead to the Valley of Death? After a substandard brief, how can they possibly be ready?

Nonetheless, it is normal practice for traders to receive massive amounts of trading authority, and control over people's money. The fall of 2008 suggested, in the Lehman conglomerate and others like it, that they just rushed to execution, every day, without any brief, or even tactical talks, before the morning's trading began.

The events of those wild weeks in September and October, when everyone careened toward the precipice, suggested that many, many somewhat limp left hands had not the slightest idea what the right hand was doing. Some of those sensational collapses, which brought entire departments to their knees, were conducted by people whose activities were run like some sort of secret society.

When the Big Brains were finally let loose in the aftermath, there emerged probably twenty written accounts that illustrate that the investigators were absolutely stunned by what they found. And, of course, that put the CEOs, and their henchmen, into situations that might lightly be described as grotesque.

Either the corporate leaders had to claim they had no idea what was going on, which was essentially the damnation of hell. Or they did not comprehend the numbers, or even the "planning" they had been shown, which was plainly worse. A proper brief before each day began clearly would have solved this. Even on Wall Street, even under the traditional terror the presence of the boss causes, someone might have realized the emperor had no clothes, that the man in command was bewildered.

That is why Wall Street's "execution" was so thoughtless, throughout all the problems that led to September 2008. Departmental heads were striving to get out of their own way, trying to find someone to blame.

Those are the former high-profit heroes who were in charge of the subprime mortgage and real estate bonds, and the guys who had purchased catastrophic brokerage houses, and hedge funds. Plus the men who were grappling with the appalling specter of the credit default swaps coming home to roost.

The leverage men were at their wits' end as the markets dried up. The financial officers were trying to pull the wool over the eyes of the analysts. The public affairs chiefs were trying to baffle the stockholders. The presentation department was trying to spin the silken phrase to confuse the enemy. How could they possibly execute anything, given their own personal interests were surely uppermost in their minds?

None of this could have happened if the admirals had been in charge. They would have demanded daily briefs. No one in the US Navy has the kind of power invested in these Wall Street characters. When great danger threatens, and we know we must sail into harm's way, we all go together. And when we make our plans, we all do it together. Every day. No exceptions.

And when we finally execute, every man is as well versed as he can be; he will be held accountable for his actions; his standard of risk control will be judged, his errors, if any, will be noted. And all criticism will be accepted, because each man knows it will in the end make him better. Without fear, he will stand up and take his grade. Wall Street would be well advised to operate the same system.

I have a vision of a Wall Street trader, having just landed his strike fighter, Bad-Bet 104, clumsily on the deck of the carrier. And here comes the landing signal officer with his clipboard. He's frowning, scribbling, getting ready to issue a cut pass—the harshest grade possible: *too much leverage on start . . . piling on in the middle . . . desperation in close . . . out of ideas at the ramp . . . busted in the wires . . . for a hook slap one-wire . . . nearly killed everyone.*

My vision then blurs, but I can still see the trader in the distance, ducking and diving between the queues of strike fighter aircraft, running with desperation, running blindly for his life, out toward the cliff edge of the bow. He's ignoring the shouts of the yellow-shirts, anything to get away from this tyrant who is about to humiliate him.

*5. Debrief.* If there is one thing that both Wall Street and the entire kingdom of corporate America do not do, it's a thorough debrief. They don't know how. If they did, they would not keep repeating past mistakes. But they're always too busy executing, and anyway, it would be completely foreign to them to subject themselves to the Navy's idea of a debrief.

The debrief is where we conduct the most searching examination of the recent execution of our mission. The forums are structured and organized, and at TOPGUN they made US congressional inquiries look like the annual national membership meeting of the Screen Actors Guild (whatever the hell that looks like—*thespians unite!*).

A US Navy debrief may be the justifiable "reward" for following our proven process. But quite often it's a star chamber of demands: *What went wrong? And why? What went right?*

This last question requires real answers, because we need to know if our triumph was too much down to pure luck, not skill. We need to know what really went right, and whether we really had all bases covered and were not just the recipients of a darned lucky break.

The admirals want that nailed down. They want hard facts and fearless self-criticism, not self-congratulation. Both Wall Street and corporate America need to take that on board and learn how to identify what really went right. Because if it was just luck, it could just as easily have gone wrong.

As for finding out what went wrong, that's the most penetrating inquisition in all the services. Right there we're operating millions and millions of dollars' worth of hardware, the protection of which is paramount. If there's been a mistake, the US Navy will probe ever deeper to find out precisely where we went wrong.

The attitude is hard and unrelenting: *not, okay guys, let's examine this and find a list of reasons that make certain no one takes the rap.* The admirals will insist on answers, and the "request" will be none too polite: *Okay, someone damn well better figure this out, and come up with reasons . . . We want to know WHY . . . and right after that we want a plan to FIX the damn thing. Fast. First time. Don't even think about fucking it up again!*

**6. Capture the lessons learned.** The presentation of a forward-looking solution to a problem is an integral part of the process. We wouldn't even go through the door without a clear pathway to repairing the fault line. All debriefs in the Navy that involve even the slightest screw-up conclude with a section on lessons learned. And those are big words in our dock-yards. Both of them.

The lessons had better be clear and concise. The learning part had better be exemplary. Otherwise, to coin a phrase, there will be an absolute fucking uproar.

For although the Navy is essentially a place of courtesy, one rank to the other, although we don't tolerate backtalk to any commissioned or noncommissioned officer, and although everyone is granted proper respect for what they do and who they are, this is the US military, and it's a place of discipline and command.

Orders are rigidly obeyed. But if the admirals think there's been a screw-up, with even a suggestion of a dereliction of duty, *stand well back.* I'm here to tell you, this will not be pretty.

We have learned the value of the debrief. Wall Street and corporate America most certainly have not. It's that searching, ruthless process of finding out what went awry that matters. I understand this is difficult in corporations, where everyone who matters is trying to duck out of the firing line. Because at that point, the truth becomes evasive, the explanations less likely to emerge.

I can only assure all US corporate boards of directors, if you put three US Navy admirals in there, they'll both frighten the bejesus out of people and at the same time convince them to do the correct thing.

That's the secret of the US military. Discipline and courtesy combined with rules that *cannot* be broken. There's respect for the past, but a steel determination for the future. Above all, there's an unbreakable culture of honesty. No lies. The truth, and only the truth. In that way lies certain redemption, even among those scallywags who damn near bankrupted Wall Street.

### ▶ *The Forward March of Globalization*

*1. Look abroad.* Any investment advisor who is not geared to overseas markets is heading for serious trouble. Globalization is here to stay, and the world has become truly connected. The United States is no longer the only place to invest. Demographics have shifted internationally.

Many countries are beginning to experience the financial boom that America enjoyed after WWII in the 1950s. There is a rising, free-spending middle class in places where once there were only rural communities. Investors are very foolish to look only at the US stock market for their answers.

*2. Be strategic.* Is the United States still top dog? I'm inclined to think not, but do not underestimate Uncle Sam. When the US economy hit the buffers in the fall of 2008, the world almost swooned with fright. However, Wall Street does not advise enough investment in foreign nations, and they are discounting these markets as a kind of anomaly, pointing back to America as still the only place to invest.

Foreign opportunities tend to be grouped into large buckets labeled "emerging markets" or "developing nations." This is as idle as it appears. My own strategy is to take a hard look at individual countries and the advantages they contain.

Every investment manager should assess all the major asset classes on a global scale: bonds, commodities, currencies, and how they dovetail together. Stocks are not just in America, but this apparently elusive truth has mostly escaped Wall Street, which still largely focuses on itself and on the names it knows.

*3. Include commodities.* Whatever anyone says, commodities must be on the rise. The burgeoning middle classes around the world want better food, better living conditions, better goods, and more automobiles and appliances. Washing clothes in the Yangtze River, and the Ganges, is probably an ancient tradition slipping into history. They want a ton of electricity, washing machines, and driers. Now.

Everywhere you look, there's going to be a voracious demand for commodities, especially iron ore (used to make steel), aluminum, and copper—the latter for electronics. World demand for corn, soy, and wheat must increase. Nations with deep resources will export to the highest bidders. Everyone wants commodities, and the only way they're going is up.

**4. *Appreciate energy.*** There is an ample supply of energy in the world. But the nations that have it are in a new and highly competitive game: trying to attract the attention of the oil exploration companies, the big drillers. Bear in mind it's a colossal operation, "sailing" these giant oil rigs from one continent to another, to where the oil is.

They're leaving America's southern shores in the Gulf of Mexico, thanks to the presidential ban on drilling. And when they finally come to their anchorage, wherever that may be, they're going to want a lot of moving. It's too difficult, too expensive, and too time consuming to start over. Once those rigs are on station, they're likely to stay there. I have a dossier on where they're headed, because those countries will have a terrific advantage once the oil begins to flow. The investment opportunities are obvious.

**5. *Anticipate demand.*** The new middle-class world citizens are becoming increasingly mobile as their earning power stretches to air travel. Nations with smallish airlines are increasing the size of their fleets, especially in Southeast Asia and the Middle East. The world will become more mobile than ever.

And with that, there will be heavy competition for the fuel that drives these aircraft. And the countries with the new and larger fleets are already eager for more oil exploration in their own territories, both on- and offshore. I tend to check this data every few days, because we're surely looking at minimal risk and optimistic investments. You cannot slow down the march of that kind of progress.

**6. *Study China.*** More than sixty years ago, America's thirty-third president, Harry S Truman, ordered the creation of the US interstate highway system. Right now the Chinese government is following in his shoes, with the biggest spend on transportation infrastructure since the man from Missouri got busy in 1946.

A recent traffic jam on the old Beijing-Tibet Expressway lasted for nine days! Which more or less confirmed how thoroughly the Asian

Dragon has outgrown its existing transport system. China is to build almost 70,000 kilometers of expressway by 2020, more than 6,000 kilometers in Inner Mongolia alone. Almost 6,000 kilometers will go into Sichuan Province, and 5,000 kilometers into Guangdong.

They're aiming for 300,000 kilometers of new *rural* roads by 2015. And there are huge investment opportunities in Chinese road-paving and cement corporations.

The Chinese New Year represents the largest annual holiday migration of human beings on earth, and the last one saw thousands stranded, sometimes for days, in the stampede out of the cities for rural family homes. This could not be allowed to continue, and Beijing finally decided to take drastic action. As a result, China's old "magic carpets made of steel" are scheduled for a massive increase.

More than $165 billion has been earmarked for massive improvements, not just to roads, but for the railways and airports. Thousands of miles of high-speed-rail links are being built to cope with two hundred–mph trains—from Beijing to Tianjin in the north, and between Shanghai, Hangzhou, Wuhan, and Guangzhou in the south.

Over $100 billion a year is to be spent on the railways alone. The ten-hour journey from Shanghai to Beijing has been slashed to five hours. The arduous thirteen-hour journey from Wuhan to Guangzhou will take a little more than three hours. They're looking at 34,000 kilometers of new track by 2020.

Bear in mind the very canny Chinese government is keenly aware these trains will bring many, many tourists to rural China. It's a big spend that cannot be stopped. And fortunes will be made in construction, the manufacture of steel, and so many commodities. Remember the run on world steel prices leading up to the Beijing Olympics?

In my view, little on Wall Street compares with China's coming infrastructure bonanza. I have already marked out for my clients the international corporations that will benefit not just from the building but from the goods and services that will surely flow along these freeways and railroads in the future.

The Chinese rarely miss an opportunity to make a buck. Or a billion. And I am currently scouring that vast nation for investment opportunities.

I'm following the guidelines taught so rigidly at TOPGUN: thoroughness, methodology, hard study, miss nothing. And I'm doing it for one principal reason: I know the downside is limited, merely because the backing for the project is world-class enormous. Better yet, it's already in place.

The infrastructure of China fits my main criterion: the risk is minimal. I know it seems a million miles away, but Chinese stocks are reliable and very well organized, like the nation. Demand is on the rise, which is why I'm looking at blocks of Chinese corporations directly involved in building the highways and railroads.

It took me awhile, but right now I'm confident. If you plan to look after other people's money you'd better be confident in yourself, confident in your systems, and confident in your discipline. By that I mean always do it honestly, and always admit your errors. I swear to God I have an unseen US Navy admiral watching me sternly, and I hope not disapprovingly. But he, and all the others I have served, have laid down my life's lessons of integrity and regard for others, right from the Academy. And I would find it impossible to ignore them.

That includes tactical decisions that might require a swift and decisive change of course—perhaps a sudden swerve by one of the central banks, or China threatening to go to war with Russia. You simply have to know when to abort the mission, without getting hurt. In the Navy, we are experts at that. We don't hang on grimly and fly into the ocean. We're the samurai of risk control, and this applies to investing just the same as piloting a strike fighter.

Remember, if you're astute, there's no denying when something is going wrong. Discipline has no time for wishful thinking. If you've studied the long, previous history of the markets, you cannot miss the fact that anything can go right up the 'chute very, very quickly. However much you love a stock, however much your analysis suggests it's going to win in the end, when that stock takes a turn south, perhaps against the tide, even against logic, you need to move.

Investment advisors must remember, it's not their money. Any former TOPGUN fighter pilot will reach for that ejection seat handle without emotion, and hit it. That way everyone's safe. But the downside, in both disciplines, is usually unthinkable.

### ➤ *A New Mind-Set for Corporate America*

We have an expression in the US Navy that is used to describe someone or some organization that is basically standing still, not improving or going forward, but equally not getting much worse, and going backward. We call it *baselining*.

And there are various explanations, the first being, obviously, someone who's merely lost interest and thinks they're doing okay anyway. The far more important baseliners are the guys who consider themselves very nearly perfect, and that they can no longer improve because that would be plainly impossible.

In our profession, the latter mind-set is judged to be fatal, because there is no other way to stay out in front except constantly to improve. In our judgment there's no such thing as standing still; unless you're charging forward, you're almost certainly slipping behind. And in our game that's not good, because you might end up dead, facing a more progressive enemy.

The one thing the Navy does know, as I've touched on before, is that no one's perfect, even though we continually strive to be so. And that lifts us ever forward, out in front, way ahead of the world's baseliners.

Both Wall Street and corporate America have baselined. They believe they no longer need to improve, and currently concentrate on marketing, with advertising slogans that demonstrate they are better than the competition.

Now, for a group that managed almost to bankrupt the world's financial system, this would seem an eccentric point of view. Was there not a tiny window that could use some improvement? Maybe. But they have not yet noticed it.

History usually holds the key. And there are a couple of shining examples of times when the US Navy found itself baselining. The first was a few years after WWII when we lost more than 770 aircraft in one year—two a day, or more than fifty accidents per 100,000 flying hours.

I suppose some people thought we couldn't improve much, since we'd just won a gigantic war, and we weren't about to take safety lessons from anyone, especially from guys who worked for *mein Fuhrer,* or that Yamamoto character who managed to lose four Japanese aircraft carriers in one day, facing the wrath of Chester Nimitz and Raymond Spruance.

But the US Navy had plenty more brilliant admirals where those two came from, and the order went out to *fix* that accident rate. By 1961 we were down to twenty accidents per 100,000 flying hours. By 1970 it was down to ten. Today it's less than two.

It was not, however, a smooth graph of improvement. By the 1990s we were feeling mightily proud of ourselves, full of self-congratulation. And, would you believe it, the accident rate started to climb upward once again. With TOPGUN setting the pace, pushing the envelope, making us better, we were flying the aircraft harder, and in turn, they were getting older and more susceptible to mechanical faults. In 1996, with TOPGUN pilots at the pinnacle of combat aviation, we lost thirty-nine aircraft in one year.

And when that statistic turned up, there was a kind of collective gasp. And, as if waking up from a very dark sleep, the Navy made an immediate, aggressive, full-rudder correction into the wind, because this was no minor fluke, it was a definite pattern. We had plainly improved from that terrible rate of crashes at the dawn of the jet age. But the admirals cared not one jot for that. They wanted to know why we had been baselining, standing still, not going forward. Had we become too comfortable? Had we bottomed out? You'd have thought we'd just lost WWII.

But that's the basis of management. We had to get the accident rates under control. We studied the numbers and set our objectives, capturing the obvious lessons, and learning them over again. And all through the process, we used the TOPGUN doctrine, which unfailingly would hold each of us accountable. Plan. Brief. Execute. Debrief. PBED—we call it our "circle of life."

Wall Street and corporate America have each committed those insidious baselining sins that once caused such consternation in the Navy, the difference being Big Business is not trying to *fix* anything. They have not yet identified the problems.

I cannot pretend the admirals were not angry, because they were. And they laid down the law, ranting about the US Navy starting to look like a third-world banana republic! That had a major effect, and everyone hopped to it. They turned the place upside down looking for causes, and in the end they solved their problem by looking much harder at the human element.

To do that, the admirals invented something called DAMCLAS, which turned out to be our own private Seven Pillars of Wisdom. Actually we called them the Seven Critical Skills of High-Performance Organizations.

And all corporations would be advised to embrace them. This is the concept:

D: Decision Making
A: Assertiveness
M: Mission Analysis
C: Communication
L: Leadership
A: Adaptability
S: Situational Awareness

These seven headings represent the corporate skills the US Navy expects of every pilot. During the ruthless baseline study we categorized our successes and our failures, and we refined them down to that formula. Each heading had a clear meaning.

*Decision Making.* Choosing a logical course of action based on a certain level of information. Fighter pilots live or die by the amount, and the quality, of the information they receive. It's our lifeblood, and it's never perfect. Nevertheless, we cannot waste it, because we are always trying to reduce our possibility of error and increase our chances of success. You can't quite decide what to do? You better get out of that cockpit, right now.

*Assertiveness.* Sticking to your guns, in both senses, stating your position. We want fighter pilots with the courage to back their absolute conviction, that something is right or wrong. Assertiveness is mandatory for us; being wrong is never a crime. But warning someone of danger and insisting on a course of action is the only way. It takes a special kind of courage. And if you don't have it, you cannot stay in the program.

*Mission Analysis.* This involves developing our plan of action, coordinating resources. We are always in high mission ready state, both in the air and on the ground. And this takes a certain kind of person. You may be able to fly strike fighter aircraft in the Navy, but you're no good to us if you cannot analyze the mission and execute with precision.

*Communication.* There's nothing more important than this, and no one is better at it than us: transmitting information, one to another via the radio, and receiving it the same way. We utilize methods that will cut through the fog of war—every transmission laser-focused, eliminating all possible doubt about our intentions.

*Leadership.* Taking charge, bringing everyone together, as a team. The letter "I" appears only twice in Naval Aviation: after the "V" and before the "O"—nowhere else. Ever. Because every one of us is expected to be a team leader, at all times. Maybe not in complete command of an entire air wing, but always in command of a strike fighter, and always ready to step in. We all understand we will lead the attack whenever necessary, with conviction, duty and honor.

*Adaptability.* We all understand our initial plan is likely to be shot to pieces, at first contact with the enemy, so our ability to adapt instantly is always paramount. But we know our trade so well. And when things change we are required to remain icy calm in the face of onrushing chaos. We must adapt a new plan, quickly and without reservation. This takes an enormous amount of trust in everyone else. At 1,000 mph, preparing an attack, it's composure such as you have never seen before.

*Situational Awareness.* A second-by-second account of what's happening around us: hundreds of miles, a few miles, or maybe even feet away. Stay focused. We maintain global situational awareness at all times, always knowing who's where, who's doing what, locating the enemy, knowing what resources remain, and the current state of the mission. The objective does not vary: complete the mission, no matter the environment.

We incorporated those seven critical skills immediately. Typical examples: If a pilot paid special attention to the enemy's whereabouts and could re-member the location of the target, even after dodging a hostile MiG com-ing at him from the rear, he was judged to have important situational awareness. If he then made the decision instantly to divert, and go smack that MiG before it swerved once more into his rear vision, that would be judged very sharp mission analysis.

If, however, his wingman had seen it on his radar scope earlier but hesitated to call it, well, that would be judged a screw-up of monumental proportions—a gaping gap in that wingman's assertiveness.

By these new ironclad laws alone, DAMCLAS, the Navy conquered its baselining problems, which emanated when we wrongly thought we were perfect. We went on to lower the safety accident rate to unthinkably low levels. And never again has the service rested on its laurels, not in flying, or in combat. Not since 1996.

DAMCLAS has joined the short list of unbreakable US Navy creeds. I have mentioned several of these during the course of this narrative. But there is one I have avoided because of its rarefied and esoteric overtones, and because I have a sense that it applies only to us; to us whose quest is always so uncompromising.

The words touch my heart, because I believe them. And I have never heard them uttered beyond the ramparts of United States Navy command centers. The key is simplicity, but the meaning is profound, because here is the route to every man's soul. The phrase is: EXCELLENCE IS A CHOICE.

And indeed it is. We are taught that the battlefield belongs to the warrior who accepts those four words without question. Excellence is a choice, and its rejection is also a choice. It's a creed that every graduate of Annapolis accepts—that every man's master is excellence. We believe in perfection, achieving goals that may demand our dying breath. But still we strive. Because we have chosen excellence.

And that's why we live in comparative peace in our homeland, because somewhere on this planet, there is an American fighter pilot, holding the line, living by the creeds of the US Navy.

Just imagine if every Wall Street trader, and every American corporate executive, adopted that approach and judged people that severely, under a system everyone understood. It would certainly be regarded as a triumph of management. And with the deepest regret, but inevitable pride, I am obliged to say that level of leadership can be found only in the US military, where slackness, any slackness, results more often than not in death.

It is not a natural progression to move from fighter pilot to Wall Street financier, though the requirement for first-class mathematicians is identical. But there is one truth that is unyielding: the number-one priority in Naval Aviation is to control risk. There's no need even to mention the level of danger, because that's obvious. At the highest level the entire combat procedure is about controlling the risk. Being prepared. Knowing your subject backward and forward.

You want a risk-aware investment manager? Look no further than a fighter pilot. My dream is to create an investment team that consists entirely of TOPGUN graduates. With them, I'd have the most disciplined group of investors this world has ever seen.

When I sat down to plan this book, I stared at the blank page of my legal pad for about three weeks, during which time I wrote down the number 1. And I placed, left and right, two parentheses: (1). Finally I wrote, "Why the United States Military Should Run Corporate America."

I had believed that, ever since the crisis of 2008.

And I still do.

*Break left! Bandits two-three-zero!*

*Warlock one-one.*

Thanks for listening to me.